35.00

P9-BHS-489

The
Broadcast
Communications
Dictionary

EDITORIAL BOARD

David C. Adams
Vice-chairman of the Board (Ret.)
National Broadcasting Company

David Berlyn
Senior Sales Manager
Broadcasting *Magazine*

Julius Barnathan
President, Broadcast Operations and Engineering
Capital Cities/ABC

Robert Grebe
Senior Vice-president
Television Bureau of Advertising

Professor Loomis C. Irish
Department of Television and Radio
Brooklyn College of the City University of New York

Harold W. Lustig
Chairman of the Board
National Video Center/Recording Studios

Victor Miranda
President
Broadcast Advertising Producers Society of America

Allen Zwerdling
Publisher Emeritus
Back Stage *Publications*

The Broadcast Communications Dictionary

Third Edition, Revised and Expanded

Lincoln Diamant
Editor-in-Chief

GREENWOOD PRESS
New York · Westport, Connecticut · London

Ref
PN
1990.4
D5
1989

LC

Library of Congress Cataloging-in-Publication Data

The Broadcast communications dictionary / Lincoln Diamant, editor-in-
    chief. — 3rd ed., rev. and expanded.
        p.   cm.
    Bibliography: p.
    Includes index.
    ISBN 0–313–26502–X (lib. bdg. : alk. paper)
    1. Broadcasting—Dictionaries. I. Diamant, Lincoln.
PN1990.4.D5   1989
384.54′014—dc19   88–25093

British Library Cataloguing in Publication Data is available.

Copyright © 1989 by Lincoln Diamant

All rights reserved. No portion of this book may be
reproduced, by any process or technique, without the
express written consent of the publisher.

Library of Congress Catalog Card Number: 88–25093
ISBN: 0–313–26502–X

First published in 1989

Greenwood Press, Inc.
88 Post Road West, Westport, Connecticut 06881

Printed in the United States of America

The paper used in this book complies with the
Permanent Paper Standard issued by the National
Information Standards Organization (Z39.48-1984).

10 9 8 7 6 5 4 3 2 1

8-6-90

by LINCOLN DIAMANT, F.R.S.A.

Contents

Introduction

After a decade of update and revision, here is the third edition of *The Broadcast Communications Dictionary*. This unique specialized desk reference, prepared under the direction of an experienced television author, technical authority, and broadcast professional, with the consultation of a distinguished board of editors, provides an indispensable guide to the most frequently used terms in every area of contemporary electronic communications.

The explosive and often confusing growth of international telecommunications since World War II has created a complex language to describe and interpret today's broadcast and narrowcast transmissions, driven by computers and reflected by satellites. This new language is filled with intriguing words that can baffle even the most seasoned practitioner. To meet this problem, *The Broadcast Communications Dictionary* was conceived as a comprehensive and up-to-date professional guide that would also serve as a valuable demystifier for neophytes.

This third revised and greatly enlarged edition triples the number of entries in the original volume, providing both beginning and experienced communications personnel with an invaluable lexicographic tool. Here—cross-referenced to equivalent British terminology—are more than 6,000 of the technical, common, and slang words that make up the language of broadcast communicators in English-speaking countries around the world. Newly included are several hundred terms specifically spawned by the development of today's satellite technology. As audience shares and influence of the once all-powerful networks continue to recede, the accelerating expansion of cable television has also contributed a host of fresh definitions.

All these entries join the thousands of others already in use in areas of radio and television programming and production; network and station operations;

broadcast equipment and engineering; audio and videotape recording; performing talent; agency and client advertising procedures; media usage; research; defense, government, trade, and allied groups.

To note only a few lexicographic sea changes: *video tape* has now crept together and become *videotape; CATV* (community antenna television) is now simply *cable;* as the *VTR* medium of choice, *quad* is out and *helical* is in; enough satellites are now parked between 69° and 139° West longitude to create a brand-new constellation; and as television's commercial and motion picture film production slowly shifts its finishing routines to procedurally simpler videotape, many of the key film completion terms from the first two editions of this dictionary fall into relative disuse.

As each edition of this important reference work strives to stay abreast of such developments, neologisms, and swirling acronyms, one finds compelling reason to cite *The New York Times Book Review:* "A contemporary dictionary maker runs against time. He has to. Unless he gets a move on, he can fall further and further behind, as his dictionary takes longer to record linguistic developments than they take to happen." This is truer today than ever before.

Beyond providing a brief up-to-date bibliography of more detailed technical reference works in individual fields, this dictionary makes no attempt to serve as an exhaustive encyclopedia for any of the many disciplines it covers. Such conciseness is purposeful. Logical, easy to use, simple to understand, this handy work underlines the complex interrelationship of all spheres of contemporary communications activity.

Formal organization is standard; entry words are set in boldface type and listed in strict alphabetical order. Compound terms are alphabetized under the first word of the term. Numerals are alphabetized as if spelled out—*40* following *fifty*. Acronyms are alphabetized. Where the acronym is well known, the entry concludes with the complete term; where the acronym is not obvious, the term is also alphabetized individually. *See:* and *Compare:* offer further detail; each cross reference is *italicized*. Parenthized years—e.g., (1923)—denote invention or initial development.

In short, *The Broadcast Communications Dictionary* is comprehensive, sensible, accurate, and indispensable.

The
Broadcast
Communications
Dictionary

A

A—440 Hz: standard musical instrument tuning reference.

AA—Advertising Association: British trade group exchanging information and establishing general policy and industry standards. Compare: *AAAA, Advertising Council, ANA, IPA, ISBA.*

AAAA—4 A's—American Association of Advertising Agencies: agency group exchanging information and establishing general policy and industry standards. Compare: *AA, Advertising Council, ANA, IPA, ISBA.*

AA (average audience) rating: percentage of *television homes* viewing average minute of *broadcast program.*

A & B rolls: overlapped sections of *negative film* (or *videotape*) wound on separate *reels* to permit *printing* (or *editing*) *dissolves* or other *optical effects.* See: *checkerboarding.* Compare: *A-roll, B-roll.*

A & B winds: *emulsion* location on either side of *16mm single-perf film base.* "A wind" (*emulsion* toward *reel* hub) generally for *contact printing;* "B wind" (*base* toward *reel* hub) for camera *raw stock,* projection *printing, optical* work.

A & E: see: *Arts and Entertainment Cable Network.*

A & R—artists and repertoire: recording company division handling performers and material.

Aaton: *16/35mm* French motion picture *camera.*

A/B: as before.

ABC—American Broadcasting Companies, Inc.: see: *Capital Cities/American Broadcasting Companies, Inc.*

ABC—Audit Bureau of Circulations: joint industry group auditing media circulation claims. Also: Australian Broadcasting Commission.

Abekas: *digital videodisk recorder, still store,* or *dve* unit.

aberration: television *image* distortion, created by *signal interference* or electron *beam* mis*alignment.* Also: Optical *lens* malfunction.

abort: terminate procedure in progress.

above the line: "creative"—distinguished from "technical"—*program production* costs. Compare: *below the line.*

A-box: in Britain, multi-outlet power distribution unit.

abrasion: external *negative/positive film* damage.

ABS—Association of Broadcasting and Allied Staffs: labor union representing British broadcast production personnel.

absorption: retention of transmitted light within a *lens.*

A/B switch: high isolation switch, choosing one of two *input* sources; 1987 *FCC*-mandated *cable subscriber set* modification; permits easy *over-the-air* viewing.

A-B test: direct comparison of *component* quality through *circuit* substitution.

ABU—Asia-Pacific Broadcasting Union: Kuala Lumpur–based Far Eastern government broadcasting group.

A/C—adult contemporary: popular music *radio station* format.

AC—alternating current: electrical power supply reversing direction (polarity) at regularly recurring intervals, i.e., 60 times per second (60 *Hz*) in the U.S. (110 volts), 50 in Britain (220 volts). Compare: *DC.*

AC adapter: step-down *transformer* converting battery-operated equipment to wired power source.

Academy aperture: film *framing* standard established by American Academy of Motion Picture Arts & Sciences. See: *cutoff, reticule, safety.*

Academy leader: (non-projected) *film head* section containing visual *countdown cueing* information in "seconds" (formerly in "feet"), to standards of American Academy of Motion Picture Arts & Sciences. See: *leader.* Compare: *video leader.*

ACC: automatic *contrast* control. Also: Automatic *chrominance* control.

acceleration error: *time base error* created by *recording/playback head* striking *tape* edge.

acceptance: local *affiliate* clearance of *network* program. Compare: *pre-emption.*

access: retrieve specific data. Also: Public availability of *cable* broadcast time.

access channel: *FCC*-mandated *channel* for *cable systems* with more than 3,500 *subscribers;* set aside for public community or individual programming.

access time: time between call for information and its availability.

accordion pleating: see: *buckle.*

account: advertising *sponsor.* See: *client.*

account executive—AE: *agency* or *medium* employee responsible for service liaison with *client.*

account group: *agency* creative and management personnel servicing particular *client.*

accumulation: see: *audience accumulation.*

acetate: transparent plastic sheeting used as artwork surface. Also: Individually *cut* (not *pressed*) *phonograph disk* (actually aluminum, coated with cellulose nitrate). Also: See: *base.*

achromatic: without color.

ACI—area of cable influence: geographic *cable* system coverage.

acoustic: sound not electronically *amplified.* Also: Early non-electronic *disk recording* process.

acoustical noise: *studio* noise as part of *signal.* See: *S/N.*

acoustic coupler: see: *modem.*

acoustic feedback: see: *feedback.*

acoustics: *resonance* qualities of sound *recording studio* or *stage.* See: *dead, live.*

acoustic screen: see: *gobo.*

across the board: *broadcast* material scheduled at same time each weekday. See: *strip.* Compare: *one shot, special.*

ACT—Action for Children's Television: national public interest group promoting upgraded children's *television* programming/advertising.

actinic light: visible or ultraviolet light creating chemical or electrochemical action.

action: rehearsed movement—or director's call for such movement—in front of *camera.* Compare: *cut.*

action line: "consumer assistance" programming.

active: *scanning lines* outside *vertical blanking interval.*

ACTM—all channel tuning meter: *Arbitron* audience survey recording device (1982).

AC transfer: *videotape duplication* by contact between high-*coercivity master* and low-*coercivity slave* in high-frequency *AC* field. See: *bifilar, dynamic.* Compare: *STAM.*

ACTS—American Christian Television System: *satellite/cable* religious programming service; mainly Southern Baptist oriented; via *Galaxy III satellite*. See: *SBRTC*.

ACTT—Association of Cinematograph, Television and Allied Technicians: labor union representing British *film* and *television* trades.

ACTV—advanced compatible television: improved picture *transmission* utilizing existing *NTSC 6 MHz bandwidths*. See: *ACTV-I, II*.

ACTV-I—Advanced Compatible Television: *NBC*-proposed *NTSC*-compatible single *channel* enhanced definition *television* with 410 *horizontal*, 480 *vertical luminance resolution lines;* 1,050 *scan lines* per *frame*, 5:3 *aspect ratio*. See: *HDTV*.

ACTV-II—Advanced Compatible Television: *NBC*-proposed *NTSC*-compatible double channel enhanced definition *television* with 650 *horizontal*, 800 *vertical luminance resolution lines;* 1,050 *scan lines* per *frame*, 5:3 *aspect ratio*. See: *HDTV*.

ACTV-E—Advanced Compatible Television: *HDTV* system similar to *ACTV-I*, with *wide-screen* 16:9 *aspect ratio*.

acutance: optical sharpness.

A/D—analog-to-digital: see: *demodulate*. Compare: *D/A*.

AD—assistant (or associate) director: indispensable "detail man" on set or location—before, during and after *production*. Called *production secretary* in Britain. Compare: *gopher*.

ADAP—automatic digital audio processor: *digital* memory *audio-signal* processing device removing various *frequency spectra*.

adapter: device matching two dissimilar *connectors*.

ADC—analog-to-digital converter: equipment dissecting *analog* television *signals* to *digital transmission* form. Compare: *DAC*.

added scene: non-scripted *production* material.

additive primaries: television's red-orange, green, and blue-violet colors. In varying combinations, they produce all other colors and white. See: *primary colors, RGB, triad*.

address: information location.

addressability: cable system control of specific *subscriber* reception. Also: *Videodisk* sequential programming.

address code—birthmark: *digital videotape retrieval* system, utilizing control *track signals*. See: *time code*.

addy: over-sophistication of *advertising copy*.

ad hoc network: group of *stations* temporarily formed to carry specific program.

ADI—area of dominant (station) influence: County cluster in which most *viewers* watch the "local" *stations*. Middle *ARB (radio)* audience research market classification. Compare: *DMA, metro, TSA.*

adjacencies: periods immediately preceding or following specific *program* or *commercial.*

ad lib—ad libitum: (from Latin *"at pleasure"*) improvise material without rehearsal.

ADO—Ampex Digital Optics: computer-driven *DVE* system for modifying/manipulating *video signal.* Compare: *Harry, Mirage, Paintbox, Quantel.*

advance: number of *frames* between *picture* and *synchronous* sound on *composite film print,* to accommodate projection *pullup* requirements; 20 *frames* in *35mm,* 26 *frames* in *16mm* (21 and 27 in Britain).

Advanced Communications Corporation: planned *DBS satellite* operator; 110° and 119° W, 1991.

Advanced Television Test Center: broadcaster-sponsored facility for *HDTV* research. Compare: *Cable Television Laboratories.*

advertiser: loosely, the *client.*

advertising agency: independent firm commissioned to handle advertising preparation for non-competitive *clients* ("15% commission, 85% confusion."—FRED ALLEN). Compare: *house agency.*

Advertising Council: semi-official U.S. group mounting "public service" compaigns with rotating *agency* assistance. Compare: *AA, AAAA, ANA, IPA, ISBA, NA(RT)B.*

advertising director (manager): corporate executive charged with advertising planning, *agency* contact and supervision. Loosely, "the *client.*"

advisory: internal news service information about upcoming story. Compare: *bulletin.*

aerial—antenna: conductive device radiating or *receiving rf broadcast signals.* See: *dish.* Compare: *balloon, satellite.* Also: **aerial:** *cable* system *transmission* on utility poles.

Aeriola Jr: early (1921) U.S. home *radio receiver.*

Aerosat: *ESA* aeronautical communications *satellite.*

af: *audio frequency.* Compare: *rf.*

AFC: automatic *frequency* control.

affidavit: sworn *station* statement attesting to broadcast of *commercial* as ordered.

affiliate: U.S. *broadcast station* contracted to a *network* for more than 10 hours of *programming* a week. Compare: *O & O's, independent.* Also: *Cable system* transmitting *satellite-networked* programming.

AFI—American Film Institute: creative trade association. Compare: *BFI.*

AFL-CIO—American Federation of Labor–Congress of Industrial Organizations: American labor union parent body. Compare: *Trades Union Congress.*

AFM—American Federation of Musicians: music performers' union.

A format: (1973) *Ampex*-developed *1" helical-scan VTR* system (now replaced by *B* and *C formats*).

AFR(T)S—Armed Forces Radio (Television) Service: U.S. overseas military *broadcasting* organization; operating more than 800 *radio/television* outlets in 56 foreign countries.

AFT—automatic fine tuning: *VCR channel tuning circuitry.*

AFTRA—American Federation of Television & Radio Artists: union covering *radio* and *videotape* performing *talent,* singers and *sound effects* artists. Compare: *SAG.*

AGB—Audits of Great Britain: (U.K. 1962) *television* audience survey service (purchased by Robert Maxwell, 1988) utilizing proprietary *peoplemeters* installed (1987) in sample U.S. homes; individual viewers "log in" electronically. See: *JICRAR, JICTAR.* Compare: *ARB, Nielsen.*

AGC—automatic gain control: audio volume servo circuit preventing *distortion.* Compare: *automatic gain circuit.*

agency: see: *advertising agency.*

agency commission: generally 15 percent of gross *client time* charge *billings,* credited by *broadcast* medium to *agency* placing advertising.

agency of record: *agency* placing *broadcast* advertising prepared for a single corporate advertiser by several of its *agencies.*

agent: broadcast *talent booking* representative, usually sharing small percentage of performance fee.

agreement: in Britain, *contractual* understanding between *producer* and *talent* or trade unions.

AGVA—American Guild of Variety Artists: performers' union. Compare: *AFTRA, SAG.*

AI: artificial intelligence.

AICP—Association of Independent Commercial Producers: trade organization of *film commercial* production facilities. Compare: *VPA.*

aided recall interview: telephone audience survey technique utilizing "clues" to measure recent viewing/listening (usually misses ghetto audiences).

air: loosely, the *broadcast spectrum.*

AIR—All-India Radio: government *radio network.*

air—on air: actual *broadcast.*

air bearing: low-friction bearing "lubricated" by forced air.

airbrush: electronic graphics color transfer (by stylus).

air check: off-the-air *tape, film print* or *storyboard* copy of *commercial* for verification or competitive consideration. Compare: *line check.*

air date: scheduled day of *broadcast.*

airing: program *transmission.*

air play: *broadcast* of musical *recording.*

air quality: produced to technical *broadcast* standards. Compare: *broadcast quality.*

airwaves: loosely, *broadcasting* transmissions.

AITS—Association of Independent Television Stations—INTV: trade organization of licensees without *network* affiliation.

Akai: Japanese electronics firm manufacturing *hand-held television camera.* See: *ENG.*

AKM—apogee kick motor: *satellite thruster.*

Alascom Corporation: *Aurora I satellite* operator.

ALC: automatic *level* control.

"A" lens: see: *anamorphic lens.*

Alexanderson, Ernst: U.S. radio pioneer; inventor of alternator, *video scanning disk.*

algorithm: finite *computer* procedure solving a specific problem.

alias: undesirable jagged edge on *computer*-generated typography. See: *jaggies, stair steps.* Compare: *antialiasing.*

alignment: correct electronic *balance.*

alignment chart: see: *test pattern.*

all: in Britain, full *IBA network.*

all call: *master control circuitry* feeding all terminals simultaneously.

Allen screw: flush-mounted machine screw with (hexagonal) insert head (requiring use of an Allen wrench). Compare: *Phillips screw.*

alligator: temporary *circuit* clip attachment (jaws resembling alligator). Compare: *gator grip.*

all-news: *radio program format.* See also: *CNN.*

allocation—assignment: *FCC* license of specific *frequency* and *power* to a *broadcast station.* See: *call letters, spectrum allocation.*

Ally Pally—Alexandra Palace: London studios for initial *BBC* television *transmissions* (1936–1953).

alphamosaic: digitized *teletext/videotex* dot mosaic-geometric system reproducing letters, punctuation marks, special characters, and designs. Compare: *alphanumeric.*

alphanumeric: information *cable channel,* with type characters transmitting news, weather, stock prices, etc. Compare: *alphamosaic.*

alpha wrap: *videotape* wind configuration around *helical scan drum.* Compare: *omega wrap.*

alternate sponsorship: rotation of *"major"* and *"minor" sponsorships* in a *broadcast program* series; reduces cost of advertising *exposure.*

alternative television: non-establishment television *programming.* See: *public access.*

alternator: in Britain, portable gasoline- or diesel-powered dynamo generating alternating current *(AC).*

AM—amplitude modulation: original *rf transmission* technique—amplitude or power varies; *frequency* remains constant. 15-*kilohertz bandwidth* utilizing 107 *frequencies* from 535 to 1,605 *kHz* (expanded to 1,705, 1988). Subject to atmospheric and local *signal* degradation. 4,900+ *commercial* U.S. *stations* on air, 1988. See: *Class I, medium wave.* Compare: *FM.*

AMARC—Association Mondiale des Artisans de Radio de Type Communautaire: international membership organization of *non-commercial* community-based *radio stations.*

amateur: see *ham.*

Amberola: early (1913) diamond-*stylus* Edison *phonograph.*

ambient (light): general lighting not directed at camera subject. See: *fill light.* Compare: *key, backlight, rimlight.* Also: *Screen* light from source other than *projector.*

ambient (temperature): temperature of gas or liquid around equipment.

Ambisonics: British "360° surround" *audio* system (1975).

AMC—American Movie Channel: *Cablevision satellite/pay cable* feature *film programming* service.

American Academy of Television Arts and Sciences: professional trade association. See: *Emmy.*

American Satellite Co.: *Contel ASC* communications *satellite* operator. See: *Contelsat.*

American Television and Communications Corporation: major (Time Inc.) *cable* systems operator.

American Television & Radio Commercials Festival: annual competition honoring outstanding *broadcast commercials.* See: *Clio.*

ampere—amp: basic unit of electrical current strength; magnitude of current flowing through two long parallel wires separated by one meter in free space, resulting in a force between the wires (due to their magnetic field) of $2 \times 10(7)$ newton for each meter of length. Compare: *ohm, volt, watt.*

Ampex: *audio* and *videotape recorder* manufacturer.

amplifier: device reproducing intensified version of electronic *signal* without drawing power from the *signal.* See: *preamp.* Compare: *receiver, tuner.*

amplitude: vertical vibrations reflecting intensity of *wave.* See: *AM, frequency.* Compare: *wavelength.*

AMSAT IIIC: West German amateur *radio communications satellite.*

AMST—Association of Maximum Service Telecasters: industry group soliciting additional *bandwidth/spectrum* space for terrestrial *transmissions.*

ANA—Association of National Advertisers: 500-member client group (1910) exchanging information and establishing general policy and industry standards. Compare: *AA, AAAA, Advertising Council, IPA, ISBA.*

analog: continously varying *signal voltages.* See: *ADC, DAC.* Compare: *digital.*

analysis projector: *projector* with *film speed* varying from normal to one *frame per second.*

analyze: "break down" *soundtrack* information in preparation for *animation stand* photography. See: *lead sheet.*

anamorphic lens—"A" lens: *camera lens* compressing—and *projector lens* expanding—*film* image; adapts standard width film to widescreen *projection* format with 2:1 to 2.55:1 *aspect ratio.*

anastigmat: *lens* correcting horizontal/vertical plane *aberrations.*

anchor: news program *MC.* Compare: *newscaster.*

ANDY Award: annual recognition for print/*broadcast* creativity by Advertising Club of New York.

anechoic: without reverberation; "dead."

anechoic chamber: "dead" room for acoustical testing.

angel hair: fine *film* shards created by *projector path misalignment.*

Angenieux: French *lens* system; its *zoom* is widely used.

angle of acceptance—angle of view: *lens* coverage.

angle shot: non-head-on *camera* position.

ångström: (from the Swedish physicist) ten-billionth of a meter.

anhysteresis: re*recording* magnetization.

Anik: (from Eskimo *"brother"*) Canadian *Telsat communications satellite*—B at 109° W; C-2 at 107.5° W; D-1 at 104° W; D-2 at 114° W.

animatic: loose term for *limited animation* technique.

animation: any photographic technique utilizing *still* subject material to give illusion of actual motion. See: *persistence of vision*.

animation board—peg board: studded drawing board (or *light box)* accurately aligning sequential animation *cels*.

animation camera—animation stand: motion picture *camera* mounted vertically over flat subject table (bench) for carefully controlled, mainly single-*frame* exposures; movement of both camera and table *computer*-coordinated. See: *stop motion*. Called *rostrum* in Britain.

animation designer: cartoon stylist supplying key drawings—*extremes*—for *animation* sequences. See: *model sheet*. Compare: *in-betweens*.

animator—in-betweener: cartoonist working from master *key* drawings to complete a *cel* sequence.

(Lord) Annan: chair of former parliamentary committee on direction of British *broadcasting*.

announce booth: small soundproof *studio* for isolated voice *recording* on *set* or *stage*.

announcement: euphemism for *commercial*. Also: In Britain, a verbal *slate*.

announcer: program introducer, or *commercial* "pitchman." Compare: *narrator, MC*.

annunciator: loudspeaker.

anode: positively (+) charged *terminal*. Compare: *cathode*.

ANSI—American National Standards Institute: engineering standards organization. See: *ASI*.

answer print: initial *composite* evaluation *film print* from completed *picture* and *track negative*. Called *grading print* in Britain. Compare: *release print*.

ANT—Telecome C4: proprietary German *audio* noise reduction system. See: *S/N*.

antenna—aerial: conductive device radiating or *receiving rf broadcast signals*. See: *directional, dish*. Compare: *balloon, satellite*.

antenna array: several radiating or receiving elements arranged in a system.

antenna farm: *broadcast antenna* grouping to minimize aerial navigation hazard.

Antenne-2—A-2: French public television entertainment/news channel (1963). Compare: *TF-1, FR-3*.

anti-aliasing: low-pass *filtering* removing undesirable jagged edges on *computer*-generated type characters. Compare: *alias*.

anti-G: in Britain, *pantagraph* device suspending *luminaire* over set.

anti-halation: antireflective opaque *film* backing.

Antiope—Acquisition Numerique et Télévisualisation d'Images Organiseés en Pages d'Ecriture: French *teletext* system.

antiskating: device reducing *phonograph pickup* skid tendency.

anti-trafficking: federal legislative action to penalize rapid *station/license* turnover. See: *trafficking*.

AOR—album oriented rock: popular music *radio station* format. Also: (Advertising) *agency of record*.

AP—Associated Press: subscriber news service for *broadcast stations*, newspapers. Compare: *Reuters, UPI*.

APD—avalanche photodiode: *optical fiber* detector. Compare: *PIN diode*.

aperture: opening controlling amount of light (measured in *f-stops*)—or electrons—passing through equipment. See: *Academy aperture*.

aperture mask: color *picture tube* mask registering *RGB beams*.

aperture plate: metal *camera/projector* plate, usually removable.

APL: average *signal* level in repect to *blanking level* during active picture *scanning* time; expressed as percentage of difference between *blanking* and *reference white*.

APO—action print only: balanced print from *optical picture negative* (no soundtrack). Compare: *check print, dirty dupe*.

apogee kick motor—AKM: *satellite thruster*.

apple (full, half): rugged wooden box—or half box—used on *set* to raise apparent height of performers or *props*. Compare: *pancake, riser*.

appropriation: approved *estimated* cost of advertising campaign.

apron: front stage edge protruding beyond proscenium arch.

ARB (American Research Bureau)—Arbitron Ratings Company: *television* audience survey service using written *diaries*/meters distributed to viewers in February, May and October. See: *National ARBitron*. Compare: *NTI*.

arc: camera movement along a curved path. Compare: *truck*. Also: Brilliant electrical discharge resembling daylight *color temperature;* produced by passing *current* between two *carbon electrodes*. Used for illumination or theatrical film projection.

arc gap: distance between *positive/negative* carbon/*xenon* lamp electrodes.

ARD-I,II: West Germany's nine-station "first TV network." Compare: *ZDF*.

ARF—Advertising Research Foundation: trade research organization.

Arianespace: Kourou, French Guiana European Space Agency *satellite*-launching consortium; 28 rockets since 1979.

Armstrong, Major Edwin Howard: U.S. radio inventor: regeneration, with De Forest, 1912; superhetrodyne circuit, 1918; wide band *FM audio,* 1935.

Armstrong Awards: annual recognition for distinguished *FM* programming.

A-roll: master *mixed videotape* sequence used repetitively during *videotape* editing to avoid re-*mixing*. Also: First half of any pair of *film* or *tape* elements for combination. Compare: *B-roll.*

arranger: musician scoring composition for various instruments. Compare: *orchestrator.*

array: multiple *antenna* format.

Arri: (from *Ar*nold and (*Ri*chter) ingenious lightweight ''Arriflex'' *reflex* motion picture camera, in *16mm* and *35mm* versions; initially designed for Wehrmacht.

ARRL—American Radio Relay League: *ham* organization (founded 1915).

art card: cardboard (usually black, 11″ × 14″ and *hot-pressed* in white) with type or designs for *film* or *television camera* photography. See: *title card.* Compare: *balop, telop.*

art department: personnel charged with design responsibility.

art director: design and graphics supervisor for an individual *production.* Compare: *designer.*

artists—artistes: in Britain, *players* and *extras* (the latter called *crowd*).

ARTS—Alpha Repertory Television Service: 1981 ABC/Hearst *cable* cultural programming service. Merged with *Entertainment Channel,* 1984.

Arts & Entertainment Cable Network: Hearst/ABC/RCA *satellite/cable* cultural programming service. Erected from *ARTS* and *Entertainment Channels,* 1984.

Arts Channel: London-based *satellite/cable programming* service.

ASA: see: *ASI.*

ASC—American Society of Cinematographers: cameraperson's trade guild.

ASC—automatic sensitivity control: light-sensing *aperture* control.

ASCAP—American Society of Composers, Authors and Publishers: trade guild protecting musical performance rights. Compare: *BMI, SESAC.*

ascertainment: discarded *FCC* procedure requiring local *broadcast stations* to investigate community programming needs/desires.

ASCII—"askee"—American Standard Code for Information Interchange: common seven-*bit binary* code representing 128 letters, numerals, punctuation, and special controls; transfers data between *computers*.

ASC-I: Contel-American Satellite 6-*transponder Ku-band*/18-*transponder C-band* communications *satellite* at 128° W (1985).

ASFP: Britain's Association of Specialized Film Producers.

ashcan: 1,000-*W* (1*k*) *floodlight*. See: *can*.

ASI: American Standards Institute *film emulsion speed rating*. Compare: *BSI, DIN, ISO*.

ASI—Audience Studies, Inc.: television (in-theater) *audience* research organization.

Asiasat: Hong Kong-based British-Chinese *satellite* operating consortium.

aspect ratio: standardized relationship of film *frame* width to height, normally 4 to 3, or 1.33:1; *widescreen* is usually 2:1; Cinemascope is 2.66:1.

assemble: *edit*-on additional material. Compare: *insert*.

assemble editing: sequential *editing* format for *tape*. Compare: *insert editing*.

assembler: in Britain, *editing* rank between *assistant editor* and *editor*.

assembly: selected *daily footage*, spliced into correct *scene* order. Compare: *rough cut*.

assignment—allocation: *FCC license* of specific *frequency* and *power* to *broadcast station*. See: *call letters*.

assistant cameraman: general aide to *cameraman* or *director of cinematography*, checking camera and *focus*, changing *lenses* and *magazines*, etc. Called *focus puller* in Britain.

assistant (or associate) director—AD: indispensable "detail man" on set or location—before, during and after *production*. Called *production secretary* in Britain. Compare: *gopher*.

assistant editor—editorial assistant: chore-handling aide to *editor*.

associate producer: general assistant to *producer*.

Association of Independent Television Stations—AITS—INTV: trade association representing non-affiliated *stations*.

ASTRA: *Arianespace*-launched Luxembourg (1989) 16-*transponder DBS*.

asynchronous: non-periodic recurrence.

ATA—American Teleport Association: trade organization of *teleport* facility operators.

A.T.&T.—American Telephone & Telegraph Company: communications conglomerate (active in early *radio broadcasting*), *satellite* operator. See: *BOC, Telstar, TAT-7, TAT-8*.

ATC—American Television & Communications Corporation: TIME, Inc., major (between one and five million *subscribers*, 1988) *MSO*.

ATIS—automatic transmitted identification system: coded *satellite uplink signal*.

Atlas Centaur: General Dynamics *satellite*-launching rocket.

atmosphere: in Britain, background sound *level;* ambient noise.

ATR: *audio tape recorder*. Compare: *VCR, VTR*.

ATS—Advanced Television Service: *FCC* trade advisory committee reviewing *HDTV* proposals.

ATS—automatic transmission system: self-monitoring, self-adjusting *transmitting* equipment requiring little or no engineering supervision.

ATSC—Advanced Television Systems Center: trade and *network* engineering group conducting *HDTV* research (1984); funded by *AMST, Big Three, PBS, NAB, INTV*.

ATS-6—Applications Technology Satellite-6: powerful all-purpose *NASA* communications *satellite*, launched in 1974, with 30-foot *antenna* to utilize higher *transmission frequencies*.

attenuate: decrease *signal level*.

attenuation loss: *signal* loss in cable, *attenuator, coupling* or other device when passing electrical *signal;* usually expressed in *decibels*.

attenuator: device decreasing *signal amplitude*. See: *fader, pot, volume control*.

ATV—advanced television: improved *television resolution* systems. Also: One of British *IBA*'s ''*Big Five*'' (the *Central Companies*).

A-2: see: *Antenne-2*.

audible noise: *noise* in the audible portion of sound *spectrum*. See: *S/N*.

audience: *viewers/households* able to hear/view a *broadcast*. See: *broadcast home*.

audience accumulation: research survey count of gross audience buildup through repeated *exposures*. See: *frequency*.

audience composition: research survey classification, replaced by *demographic* statistics.

audience duplication: research survey measurement; people reached by separate versions of same advertising message.

audience flow: research survey count of television *viewers* who (1) remain tuned to same *channel*, (2) switch to another, (3) turn their *receiver* on or off.

audience net unduplicated: research survey count—once—of *broadcast* audiences, even when they receive subsequent *transmissions* of the same *program* series or *commercial.* Compare: *duplication.*

audience potential—sets-in-use: research survey count of home *receivers* actually switched on during specific time period. See: *HUR, HUT, PUT.*

audience profile: *demographic* characteristics of a particular audience.

audience share: research survey percentage of total (local or national) *households* with one or more *television receivers* switched on during specific time period. See: *rating.* Compare: *share.*

audience total: research survey count of all *HUR*'s (or *HUT*'s) tuned to same *program* for at least five minutes.

Audimeter: *Nielsen* audience survey device installed in approximately 2,445 sample households, recording time, set on/of, tuned *channel*—minute by minute during each 15-minute *television* viewing segment. Meter results combined with *diary* for *NTI.* Replaced with *peoplemeter,* 1988. See: *SIA.*

audio: (from Latin *"I hear"*) *recorded* or *broadcast* sound. Compare: *video.* Also: *Storyboard* or *script* "words." Also: Loosely, the sound recordist.

audio frequency: normally audible sound wave (between 15 and 20,000 *Hz*). Standard *audio frequency* ranges are *bass* (0–60 *Hz*), *mid-bass* (60–240 *Hz*), *mid-range* (240–1,000 *Hz*), *mid-treble* (1,000–3,500 *Hz*), *treble* (3,500–10,000 *Hz*).

audio mix: electronic combination of two or more sound elements into single final *track,* usually against *synchronous* picture projection.

audion: electronic *amplifier tube* invented by *De Forest,* 1906.

audio tape: non-*sprocketed* plastic tape in various widths, coated with magnetizable metallic oxides to *record* or *re-record* sound. Available (on cores) up to 7,200 feet. Compare: *videotape.*

audio track: *videotape sound recording* area. Compare: *control track, video track.*

audition: test *talent* prior to selection and hiring. See: *first refusal.* Compare: *book, hold.*

Auntie: *IBA* epithet for the *BBC.*

Auricon: blimped *16mm* hand-held *sound* motion picture *camera.*

Aurora-I: see: *Satcom V.*

Aussat-B: scheduled *GE-AstroSpace* Australian communications *satellite.*

Aussat K-3: *Arianespace*-launched Australian government *broadcasting satellite* (1987).

author: music lyricist.

auto assembly: *videotape* editing from computerized edit decision menu.

auto balance: automatic red/blue *color balance* detection/compensation system.

autochroma: automatic *equilization* of *VTR* color *saturation*.

autocue: in Britain, device rolling up a large *script* in performer's view. When mounted above camera, performer reads (by way of a 45° half-silvered mirror)—while looking directly into *lens*.

auto light range: automatic operating range of television *camera* at specified *output*.

automated services: *alphanumeric* or *frame store cable channels*.

automatic brightness control: *servo* control of *brightness* as function of *ambient* light.

automatic frequency control: *servo* control of oscillator *frequency*.

automatic gain circuit: *vidicon* camera *circuitry* adjusting *target* voltage to *ambient light* conditions. Compare: *AGC*.

automatic iris: camera *lens* device compensating for changes in *brightness levels*.

auto-parallax: system of interchangeable cams matching *viewfinder* angle to different *lenses* of non-*reflex* camera.

auto rewind: device automatically rewinding *tape* after *playback*.

auto stop: device automatically stopping mechanism at completion of mode.

availability—avails: *broadcast* time open for purchase. Also: *Talent* available for specific *booking*.

available light: existing *location* light source.

AVC—automatic volume control: see: *AGC*.

average audience: see: *AA*.

averaging: *noise* reduction *circuitry* extracting repetitive *signal waveforms* from noisy backgrounds.

A-wind: *single-perf 16mm film* with left-facing *sprocket holes*. Compare *B-wind*.

AWRT—American Women in Radio and Television: *broadcast* industry membership organization.

Az-El: *earth station* mounting system. Compare: *polar*.

azimuth—AZ: horizontal *earth station antenna* adjustment. See: *steerable*. Compare: *ELEV*. Also: **azimuth:** Perpendicular relationship of *magnetic head gap* to tape travel direction (should be exactly 90°).

azimuth recording: recording *audio, video, control track* information at dissimilar *videotape* angles; eliminates *guardbands*.

B

Baby: 400-*watt spotlight*.

Baby Bell: see: *BOC*.

baby legs: low camera *tripod*.

baby pup: in Britain, 500-*watt spotlight*.

back: add musical accompaniment.

backdrop: see: *drop*.

Backer Spielvogel Bates: one of seven major (1987 gross *billings* between $3 and $5 billion) worldwide *advertising agencies*.

back focus: distance from *focal plane* to rear of *lens* set at *infinity*. Also: Focus *zoom lens* at *"in"* position.

background—BG: *setting* behind performers. Also: Continuing music or sound source played at low *level*. Also: **background:** atmospheric *signal* noise.

background projector: optical device generating graphic images on *rear projection* screen for live television. See: *vizmo*.

backhaul: terrestrial distribution of *satellite signal*.

backing: in Britain, *set* area seen through doors and windows. Also: *Base* coating improving *film* characteristics.

backing copy: in Britain, first *videotape duplicate* off air *master,* for *protection*.

backlight: illumination striking subject from behind (or back-and-side), increasing background separation. See: *rimlight, triangle*. Compare: *key, fill light*.

back lot: major *studio* area used for *exterior* shooting.

backpack: portable (back-carried) television *recording* or *camera signal transmitting* equipment. Compare: *portapak.*

back porch: 4.77-*microsecond* portion of composite *video signal* lying between trailing edge of *NTSC horizontal sync pulse* and trailing edge of corresponding *blanking pulse.* (Does not include *color burst.*) See: *breezeway.* Compare: *front porch.*

back (screen) projection—BP: in Britain, projection of *still* or *motion picture* as scenic *background.* Normally used for scenes where background is relatively small—e.g., looking through a car or room window. Compare: *reflex projection.*

backspacing: *VTR editing* technique to insure proper equipment speed at moment of *signal transfer.* See: *sync roll.*

backstage: area behind performance area *backgrounds,* etc.

Back Stage: weekly *television commercial* production trade newspaper.

back surface: plane or curved glass mirror concentrating or distributing light waves off protected rear surface. Compare: *front surface.*

backtime: synchronize program material backwards.

back-to-back: consecutive pieces of broadcast material, usually commercials.

backup: new mid-season *television* programming. Also: *Standby* protection. See: *redundant.*

backyard dish: residential *antenna* for multi-*satellite* reception, usually in poorly served *TV/cable* areas. See: *chainsaw.*

baffle: acoustical adjustment panel. See: *gobo.*

Baird, John Logie: British *television* pioneer; demonstrated 240-*line* 25-*fps* mechanical *transmission,* 1936. See: *Phonoscope.*

bait-and-switch: low-priced-item advertising "come-on."

balance: adjustable relationship between two or more elements. Also: Evenly *print film scenes* of varying color, *density,* etc.

balance stripe: extra strip on *magnetic-striped* film (opposite main *stripe*) to provide flat winding.

Balkonur (Cosmodrome): USSR *satellite* launch area 50 mi. SE of Volvograd. Compare: *Cape Canaveral, Kourou, Plesetsk.*

ball: impact-printing (single-character) element. Compare: *daisy wheel, dot matrix, ink jet, thimble.*

balloon antenna: pre-*satellite television signal* distribution technique, utilizing *transponder* balloon tethered at 10,000–15,000 feet; covered ten times the area of normal *television broadcast antenna.* Compare: *antenna, satellite.*

balop(ticon): obsolete *Bausch* & *Lomb television camera chain* device transmitting small (4" × 5") opaque *art cards*. See: *telop*.

banana plug: testing *connector*.

band: sequential location of material on phonograph *disk*. Also: Specific area of *broadcast transmission frequencies*.

banding: *quad videotape* recording/playback head misalignment, creating four horizontal picture bands. Distortion characterized by evenly distributed horizontal variations in color *hue*. See: *velocity compensator*.

bandpass: *circuit* elimination of undesirable *frequencies*.

bandshaping: reduction of *Q* and *I signal bandwidths* to fit allotted color *transmission*.

bandwidth: number of *rf-modulated signal frequencies* contained in designated *channel*. Telephone bandwidth capacity is 3,000 *Hz; AM* radio, 10,000 *Hz; high-fidelity audio tape*, 20,000 *Hz; FM* radio, 200 *KHz;* U.S. television, 6 *MHz; coaxial cable*, 57 *MHz;* optical fibers, multi *GHz*. See: *sideband*.

bandwidth reduction: type of *signal compression* achieved by eliminating *video* redundancies.

bank: equipment or lighting instrument group. See: *strip*.

BAPSA—Broadcasting Advertising Producers Society of America: *advertising agency commercial producers'* group.

BAR—Broadcast Advertisers' Reports: advertising trade organization monitoring *television commercial* activity in 75 markets.

bar: group of notes/rests indicating music composition scheme and meter.

bar breakdown: music sketch underscoring screen events.

bar code: *UBC* optical coded product recognition system. See: *wand*.

bar line: in Britain, horizontal line area moving upward when televising unsynchronized *film screen* projection.

barn doors—flippers: adjustable metal side and/or top shades to narrow *luminaire beam*.

barn door wipe: optical imitation of opening doors.

barney: weatherproof protective *film camera* cover, usually sound-absorbent. Compare: *blimp*.

barracuda: telescopic *luminaire* support braced between floor and ceiling.

barrel: *television* image *sweep* distortion. Also: *Lens* system tube. Also: **barrel—bin:** *editing* receptacle with cloth bag holding un*spliced* lengths of sorted *film* hung from *pin rack*.

barrel marks: *lens* indicia.

bars: see: *bar test pattern, color bars.*

bar sheet: see: *lead sheet.*

barter—trade out: station's fringe air *time,* usually sold through third party, for non-monetary considerations; often a form of free *program syndication* with several syndicator commercials emplaced. Compare: *due bill.*

barter agency: organization exchanging (and reselling) *pre-emptible* air *time* for merchandise or services.

bar test pattern: color—*b/w*—*Q* and *I signal* check.

base: *film substrate* coated with light sensitive *emulsion;* formerly explosive cellulose *nitrate*—since 1952 nonflammable cellulose acetate esters ("safety film")—in thicknesses ranging from 0.0003" to 0.0009". Also: Plastic *audio/videotape substrate* coated with magnetizable metallic oxides; common *bases* are polyester and mylar (replacing acetate). Also: Stage *makeup* foundation.

base light: general light source. See: *ambient light, fill light.* Also: 225 (approx.) *candelas* required for *television studio camera* operation.

BASF: major German electronics manufacturer.

basher: in U.S., 500 *W* circular *floodlight.* In Britain, *camera light.*

BASIC—Beginner's All-purpose Symbolic Instruction Code: popular *computer* language.

basic cable: primary home *signal* service, without *tiering* or packaging.

basic network: minimum group of scattered *affiliates* formerly offered by *network* for national advertising commitment. Compare: *regional.*

bass: standard *audio frequency* range (0–60 *Hz*). Compare: *mid-bass, mid-range, mid-treble, treble.*

bassy: see: *boomy.*

bat blacks—bat down: evenly adjust television *picture* black tones.

bath: *laboratory film developing* tank.

batten: horizontally suspended pipe hanging *luminaires* or scenery.

battery: device storing *DC* electric power. See: *lead acid accumulator, nickel-cadmium.*

battery belt: rechargeable power cells worn by *hand-held* camera operator. See: *power pack.*

battery light: small portable *luminaire* with self-contained power supply.

baud—baud rate: *computer bit*-per-second transmission speed; ranges from 300–1,200.

bay—dock: *studio* storage area for scenic *set* pieces. See: *flat*. Also: **bay:** one of multiple work space areas. Also: **bay:** equipment mounting rack.

bayonet: spring-loaded camera *lens* twist mount (unthreaded).

bazooka: overhead *luminaire* support.

BBC—"Beeb"—British Broadcasting Corporation: (1922) government authority controlling Britain's non-commercial broadcast system; operates *television* Channels I,II,IV. See: *Auntie*. Compare: *FCC, ORTF, RAI*.

BBDO Worldwide: one of seven major (1987 gross billings between $3 and $5 billion) worldwide *advertising agencies*.

BBTV—British Bureau of Television Advertising: television advertising trade development organization. Compare: *TVB*.

BCN: *Bosch Fernseh 1″ videotape* configuration utilizing 190° *omega wrap*.

BCU—big close-up: in Britain, performer's features. Also called *(LCU) large close-up* or *big head*.

beam: unidirectional pinhead electron stream generated by *cathode gun*. Also: Directed light flow from focusable *luminaire*.

beam angle: angle containing 50% of *spotlight* output.

beam lumens: amount of light within *beam angle*.

beam projector—parabolic—sun spot: *spotlight* projecting narrow, almost parallel light *beam*.

beam splitter: *lens* prism system: 1. separating reflected image light into *RGB* components; 2. diverting small amount of reflected image light into camera *viewfinder*. See: *mirror shutter*.

bear trap—gaffer grip—gator grip: heavy-duty spring clamp, often with *luminaire* mount.

Beaulieu: compact French *8/16mm camera*.

beauty shot: product *close-up*. Called *pack shot* in Britain.

beep(s): brief *1,000-Hz tone* signal(s) used for *audio cueing*. Compare: *punch*.

beeper: tone generator placing recurrent audible *signal* on phone line advising speakers they are being recorded.

behind—under: low-level background *audio*.

bel—B: see: *decibel*.

Bell & Howell: *16mm* silent/sound motion picture *camera*.

Bell Lab(oratorie)s: *AT&T* corporate research facility.

bells—"on bells": audible warning (usually followed by continuously flashing red signal lights) before sound is recorded on *set*. Also: **bells:** wire *service bulletin* signal.

below the line: "technical"—as distinguished from "creative"—*program* production costs. Compare: *above the line.*

belt pod: single-leg camera-to-waist-pouch support.

benchwork: see: *animation camera.*

bending: television picture *distortion* caused by improper *videotape/playback head* timing coordination. See: *flagging, hooking.*

best boy: *set* electrician's assistant.

BET—Black Entertainment Television: *satellite/cable* black entertainment programming service (1980). Compare: *National Black Network.*

Beta: *Sony*-developed *omega-wrap* ½" *VCR* format. See: *X1, X2, X3.* Compare: *VHS, 8mm.*

Betamax: *Sony* "home" *videotape recorder/playback* unit with special *cassette.*

Betamovie: *Sony Beta camcorder cassette* format. Compare: *VHS-C.*

bezel: frame masking edge of *television picture tube.*

BFI—British Film Institute: association of cinema buffs. Compare: *AFI.*

B-format: standard *Bosch*-developed (1975) 1" *helical-scan VTR* system. Compare: *C-format.*

BG—background: *setting* behind performers. Also: Continuing music or sound source played at low *level.*

bias: reference electrical *level.* Also: High-frequency *AC* carrier *current* (50–100 *kHz*), combined with *audio signal* in magnetic *recording circuit* to minimize nonlinear *distortion.*

bias light: "wiping" feature of lead oxide television camera *pickup tube*, reducing *lag* or *blooming.* See: *Plumbicon.*

bicycling: physical exchange of *film prints/videotapes* between nonconnected *stations* for staggered *programming.* See: *DB.* Compare: *network feed.*

bidirectional: microphone *response* in back-to-back directions.

bifilar: AC transfer *videotape* duplication from facing master/slave oxide surfaces. Compare: *dynamic duplication.*

big eye: 10,000-*watt floodlight.*

Big Five—Central Companies: in Britain, *Independent Broadcasting Authority's ATV, GRA, LWT, THS, YTV.*

big head: see: *BCU.*

big screen: projected television *picture.* See: *Schlieren lens, Schmidt mirror.*

Big Three: *ABC, CBS, NBC broadcast networks.*

Bildschirmtext: West German *videotex* system (1980). See: *Captain, Prestel, Teletel, Telidon.*

billboard: brief *sponsor* identification near beginning or end of *program*. Compare: *cowcatcher, hitchhike.*

billing: charge to *agency/client* for broadcast advertising *time* purchase. Also: Contractually-agreed *cast credits.*

billyboy: in Britain, heavy *dolly.*

bimbo programming: sex-oriented *television.* See: *T&A.*

bin—barrel: *editing* receptacle with cloth bag holding un*spliced* lengths of sorted *film* hung from *pin rack.*

binary: having only two states (*on* or *off*) or values (*0* or *1*) or charge *(positive* or *negative).*

binaural: two separate sound sources in single *recording,* each intended for a different ear. Compare: *monaural.*

binder: material adhering magnetizable particles to *tape base.*

bin stick: in Britain, sorting *pin rack* above *editing bin* holding ends of sorted un*spliced film* lengths.

Bioscope: early *motion picture projector* (Skladanowsky Brothers, 1895).

bipack—DX: two *negative films* printed as one. Compare: *tripack.*

bird: communications *satellite;* loosely, *transmit* by *satellite.*

birdbath: *satellite* system financial collapse.

bird's nest—buckle: *film camera jam.*

birthmark—address: *digital videotape retrieval* system, utilizing cue track signals.

bit—Binary digIT: single digit in *computer binary* number system (0 or 1), transmitted at up to 6.3 million per second. Compare: *byte.* Also: Brief creative *business.* Also: **bit:** minor role.

bitchbox: small *low-fidelity loudspeaker* used during *audio recording* to simulate average home *receiver* response.

bit rate: speed at which *bits* are generated or transmitted. See: *baud.*

BL: self-*blimped Arri camera.*

black: absence of visible light or distinguishable color. Also: In Britain, call a labor boycott.

black body: theoretical substance radiating and absorbing light with 100% efficiency. See: *color temperature.*

black box: any of several simulated-*broadcast* television audience research techniques. See: *non-air commercial.* Also: Electronic attachment using secret or illegal circuitry.

black burst: 3.58 *MHz subcarrier signal* maintaining *synchronization* during *fade* to black.

Black Entertainment Television: see: *BET*.

black level: darkest part of television picture, transmitted at minimum 30% *voltage* (0.3 *v*).

black light: ultraviolet or *infrared* radiation.

Black Maria: Edison's initial (revolving) *motion picture studio,* West Orange, N.J.

blackout: ban on live local airing of *broadcast* event (usually sports). Also: Sudden switch-off of all lighting. Also: In Britain, labor union boycott.

black reference: see: *reference black*.

black retention: *picture tube* ability to reproduce black image areas.

Black Rock: *Variety's* epithet for *CBS Inc.*'s New York corporate headquarters (located in Saarinen-designed black granite 51W52); matches *Thirty Rock (NBC), Hard Rock (ABC)*.

black velour: non-reflective *background drape*.

black week—dark week: one of four weeks a year in which *Nielsen* does not measure *network* television audiences.

blank(s): clear *animation cel(s)* used to maintain consistent photographic density. Also: Unrecorded *tape* or *disk*.

blanker: *circuit* detecting/suppressing *signal noise*.

blanket area: *1 volt/meter* (1 V/M) *radio signal* reception area.

blanketing: broadcasting a *signal* in excess of 1 V/M, usually close to the *antenna*.

blanket license: 5-year station royalty payment for *ASCAP/BMI* music use.

blanking interval: 10.5-*microsecond* interval during which television receiver *scanning beam* is suppressed by blanking *pulse* while returning to left side of screen to *retrace* next *horizontal scan line*—or to top of picture tube (in 1.3 *milliseconds*) to begin another *field* (the latter move called *vertical interval* in Britain). See: *front porch*.

blanking level: level separating *synchronization* from *picture* information, in *composite* television *signal*.

blanking pulse: see: *blanking interval*.

blast filter: see: *pop filter*.

blasting: performing with excessive *audio level*.

bleachers: movable *studio* audience seats.

bleed: framing out part of television picture. See: *crop*.

bleep—blip—bloop: brief *1,000-cycle tone* signal for *soundtrack cueing*. Also: *Synchronizing tone* at 2-second (3-foot) visual *cue* on *film leader*. Also: *Erase* unwanted *soundtrack* words.

blimp: soundproofed *motion picture camera housing,* eliminating motor noise. Compare: *barney.*

blinge: in Britain, distorted *optical dissolve.*

blip: reflected *CRT radar readout.* Also: *rating* abberration. Also: see: *bleep.*

blistering: excessive heat effect on *film emulsion* surface.

block: sequentially schedule programs with similar audience appeal. Also: Establish camera, *cast* positions, and movement in advance of *production.* Compare: *wing.* Also: Grooved device to *edit* and *splice audio tape.* Also: In Britain, low *set* platform.

blockbuster: (from World War II urban area bomb) heavily promoted major *network program.*

block off—crush out: in Britain, excessively illuminate a surface, causing undesirably white *television picture* area.

block programming: *network* strategy influencing viewer "carry-over."

blonde: *2Kw quartz-iodine lamp.*

bloom: undesirable *television/film* picture *halation,* caused by excessive light saturation; eliminated in *solid-state television cameras.* Called *block off, crush out* in Britain. See: *bias light.*

bloop: see: *bleep.*

blooper: amusing *live* error.

blow: stumble badly in performance.

blower brush: *camera/projector gate* cleaner.

blow up: enlarge optically, usually frame-by-frame from *16mm* to *35mm.* Also: Transcribe smaller formats to 1" or 2" *quad videotape.* Also: **blowup:** *still* photograph enlargement.

blue aging: tendency of blue *picture tube phosphors* to deteriorate faster than red and green.

Bluebird: see: *Entertainment Channel.*

Blue Book: (from its cover) 1946 *FCC* dictum on "Public Service Responsibility of Broadcast Licensees."

bluegrass: commercial music style with Appalachian folk roots. See: *country.* Compare: *folk, western.*

blue gun: device emitting electrons at *picture tube* blue *phosphors.* Compare: *green gun, red gun.*

blue matteing: (earlier) *film* version of *chromakey video* technique. Compare: *rotoscoping, traveling matte.*

Blue Network: early *NBC radio station,* eventually becoming *ABC* Radio. Compare: *Red Network.*

blue pencil: censor air material. Compare: *red pencil.*

blues: American black folk music, originating with spirituals and developing into *jazz, rhythm and blues,* and *rock.*

blurb: news *release.*

BMI—Broadcast Music, Inc.: trade association protecting musical performance rights. Compare: *ASCAP, SESAC.*

BNC: see: *Mitchell.*

board: *control room console.*

board fade: electronic *attenuation* to zero level, from *control room.* Compare: *live fade.*

board on end: in Britain, *clapper board* photographed (upside down) at end rather than start of *take,* for production expediency.

BOC—Bell Operating Company—Baby Bell: one of seven U.S. regional telephone companies, created (1982) by *A.T.&T.* divestiture.

bodywash: dark *makeup.*

Bolex: spring-driven Swiss *8/16mm camera* (1935).

bomb: total failure. In Britain, a rousing success.

bonus spot: additional *commercial time* given advertiser, for promised but undelivered audience.

boob tube: epithet for *television receiver.* Compare: *lube tube.*

book: hire *talent.* See: *first refusal.* Compare: *audition.* Also: Hinged *flat.* Also: *Script* accompanying musical presentation.

boom: cantilevered camera *mount* of varying size and length. Called *jib* in Britain. Compare: *crane, dolly.* Also: Similar rod-like telescopic *mount* for suspended *microphone.*

boom box—ghetto blaster: popular oversized portable *radio/cassette* player.

boom down (up): reposition camera height.

boomerang: *luminaire* holder for interchangeable color *gels.*

boom man: sound technician operating *microphone* boom. Called *boom swinger* or *boom operator* in Britain.

boom shot: high angle shot from cantilevered camera position.

boomy: marked resonance at lower end of *audio frequency* range, accentuating or prolonging low-pitched, "tubby" sounds. See: *bassy, lows.* Compare: *highs.*

bond: safety cord or chain securing suspended *luminaire.*

booster—repeater: low power *transmitter amplifying* inadequate *station signal* on same *channel.* Compare: *translator.*

booth: small soundproof *studio* for isolated voice *recording*, on *set* or *stage*. Also: *Clients'* observation room.

bootleg: illegally reproduce.

bootstrapping—booting up: initial *computer* function.

border: hard or soft line around inserted *television* image. Also: **border—X-ray:** overhead *luminaire* strip.

BORSCHT: *telco* service acronym: *battery*—over*voltage* protection—ringing—supervision—coding—hybrid—testing; *fiber optic* systems poor on *battery* (power), ringing.

Bosch: major German electronics firm manufacturing *hand-held Fernseh television camera.* See: *ENG.*

bottle—bulb: glass envelope of *television picture tube.*

bounce: light source reflecting on subject. Compare: *key.* Also: Rapid changes in *contrast signal level* during *television picture switching.*

boutique: small *advertising agency* emphasizing creative output.

box: four-walled *set.* Also: Loosely, *audio tape cartridge.* Also: **box—gallery:** in Britain, *control room.*

BPME—Broadcast Promotion and Marketing Executives: specialized industry membership group.

brace: *scenery* support strut.

braceweight: slotted cast iron *brace* support.

branch: *video disk* program path divergence.

Bravo: (1980) *Cablevision satellite/pay cable* cultural programming service; includes Rainbow Programming Services.

BRC—Broadcast Rating Council: industry-established watchdog group supervising audience research standards.

break: "time out" in *rehearsal* or production. Also: Move away from. Also: Program section containing *commercials* (see: *pod*) or *station identification* announcements. Also: *Computer* operation interruption.

breakaway: *prop* or *set* built to fall apart during violent on-camera action.

breakdown: analysis of *production* requirements.

breakers: in Britain, main control switches for *set* lights.

breakup: momentary *television picture distortion.*

breezeway: portion of *back porch* between trailing edge of *NTSC horizontal sync pulse* and start of *color burst.* Compare: *front porch.*

BRI—Brand Rating Index: annual national marketing survey covering brand consumption and preference.

bridge: connective *audio* link—sound or music—between two sections of *broadcast*. Also: Connective picture continuity. Also: Two parallel connected *circuits*.

bridge—light bridge: walkway over *grid*. Called *gantry* in Britain.

bridging (amplifier): branch network subdivider.

brightness: see: *luminance*. Also: *Pedestal* control on home television *receiver*.

brightness control: *rheostat* controlling intensity of *picture tube* electron *beam*.

brightness range: relative *luminance* values in *television picture*. Compare: *contrast*.

bring down—hold down: reduce *audio level*.

bring up: raise *audio level*.

British Actors Equity Association: theatre, *film*, and *television artists'* union.

British Board of Film Censors: trade organization issuing certificates of audience acceptability.

British Broadcasting Corporation: see: *BBC*.

broad: box-shaped 2,000 *W floodlight* creating flat, even *set* illumination. See: *half broad*.

broadband: *bandwidths* above 3–4 *kHz*.

broadband distribution: single-system *transmission* of multiple *television*, sound, or data *channels*.

broadcast: see: *broadcasting*.

broadcast band: standard *AM frequencies*.

Broadcast Bureau: *FCC* division administering *broadcast station licensing*, regulation, and operation.

broadcast home: household owning one or more *radio* or *television* broadcast *receivers*.

broadcasting: (from seed-sowing—originally, U.S. Navy fleet instructions via *wireless*, c. 1912) *radio* or *television signals* transmitted for general public listening/viewing. Compare: *cablecasting, narrowcast, closed circuit*.

Broadcasting: weekly industry newsmagazine.

broadcast quality: equipment or *tape* designed or manufactured for over-the-air use. Compare: *air quality*.

B-roll: second half of any pair of *film* or *tape* elements for combination. Compare: *A-roll*.

brolly flash: light source reflected from white umbrella.

broomsticking: see: *flagging*.

BRT: Flemish-language Belgian *television network.*

brute: 10,000 *W, 225 amp fresnel-lensed carbon arc spotlight,* used for poorly lit *locations.* Also called *10K.*

BSB—British Satellite Broadcasting: U.K.-planned *Ku-band DBS* operator (1989).

BSE: experimental Japanese *broadcast satellite.*

BSI: British Standards Institute. Compare: *A(N)SI, DIN, ISO.*

BSS—Broadcast Satellite Service: internationally assigned *frequencies* (12.2 to 12.7 *GHz*) for "true *DBS*" 230-*watt* high-power *satellite* transmission, direct to 2–4 ft. roof *antennas.*

BT—British Telecom: U.K. communications conglomerate.

BTA—best time available; *broadcast* advertising scheduling left to *station's* discretion. See: *ROS.* Also: **BTA—Broadcast Technology Association:** Japanese standard-setting industry organization.

bubble: in Britain, incandescent light *bulb.* Also: (In Britain) overtime.

bubble gum: top-40 pre-teen music *radio station* format.

bubble memory: *computer* storage device; contains more than a quarter-million magnetic domains (or bubbles).

buckle—bird's nest: *film camera jam.*

budget: estimated breakdown of *production* costs.

buff: polish *film* to remove scratches.

buffer: *VTR* (or *computer memory*) area for temporary *signal storage.*

bug: system defect or malfunction.

bug eye—fish eye: extreme *wide-angle lens,* mainly used for comic *close-up* effects. Compare: *telephoto.*

buildup: in Britain, blank opaque *film* (black or white) spliced as spacing between sections of *workprint footage.* Compare: *buzz track.*

bulb: glass or quartz envelope containing *lamp filament* or *fluorescent* material in gaseous element. Also: **bulb—bottle:** glass envelope of *television picture tube.*

bulk eraser—mass eraser—degausser: device demagnetizing all *recorded tape* on a *reel,* without unspooling. Compare: *erase head.*

bulletin: news development interrupting normal *broadcast programming.* Compare: *advisory.*

bull line: heavy-duty *scenery* rope.

bumper: extra *tail program* material. Compare: *cushion, pad.*

bump-in—bump-out: in Britain, instantaneously add or subtract new *optical picture* information to *frame.*

bump up: *dupe* in larger format.

Burke: commercial audience research survey organization.

burlap: coarse natural cloth material for *set drapery*. Called *hessian* in Britain.

burn—burn-in: retention of spurious image by television *pickup tube target* after change of subject. Called *burn-on* in Britain. (Removed by photographing brightly lit white card.) Also: **burn in:** *superimpose* (a title).

burn—burnout: *television camera tube overload,* created by excessive light.

burn-up: in Britain, area of clear *positive film* created by *negative overexposure.*

burst flag: *keying* or *grating signal,* used to form *color burst* from *chrominance subcarrier.*

bus: common (usually uninsulated) central *circuit.* Also: Row of button controls on *video switching console.*

business: minor on-camera action. See: *bit.*

bust shot: performer framed waist-up.

busy: distractingly elaborate.

butterfly: sunlight *diffuser* for *exterior filming.* Compare: *reflector.*

button: strongly accented final note of musical composition. Compare: *sting.*

buttonhook: *dish LNA feed* system. Compare: *Cassegrain, prime focus.*

butt splice—butt weld: nonoverlapping *film* join.

buy: approved scene performance. See: *hold, print, selected take.* Also: *Advertising schedule.*

buyer: see: *time buyer.*

buying service—media service: firm directly purchasing *time* for advertisers.

buyout: one-time *talent* payment for certain minor performance categories, not further compensated by re-use fees. Compare: *residual.*

buzz: low-*frequency audio signal* disturbance, usually generated by *AC* power *circuit.*

buzz track: *SMPTE* test *film* to check *projector sound head alignment.* Also: In Britain, recorded ambient noise used to space *soundtrack.* Compare: *buildup, room tone.*

b/w—black-and-white: monochrome visual material.

B-wind: *single-perf 16mm film* with right-facing *sprocket holes.* Compare: *A-wind.*

B-Y signal: *video* color difference *signal,* obtained by subtracting *luminance signal* from blue *signal.* See: *R-Y signal.* Compare: *Y signal.*

byte: *computer* string of *binary* digits; usually 8 *bits,* expressing an *ASCII* character set.

C

C: celsius; centigrade.

CAB—Cable Television Advertising Bureau: industry trade organization.

CAB—Canadian Association of Broadcasters: standards-setting *broadcast station* organization.

CAB—Cooperative Analysis of Broadcasting: (Crossley) 1930s telephone audience research survey.

cable—cable TV: facility for wire distribution of *television station, satellite,* and *microwave signals,* plus locally originated non-*broadcast* programming—mainly to residential *subscribers;* connected to 48 million U.S. homes (51% penetration, 1988), producing $1.5 billion in advertising revenues. *Bandwidth* (162 *MHz*) can theoretically accommodate 60+ *channels.* Federally regulated under *Cable Communications Policy Act* of 1984. See: *CATV, distant signal, drop line, feeder, head end, trunk.*

cable: electrical conductor(s) in protective sheath. Compare: *coax.*

cablecasting: final program delivery by direct connection—not *over-the-air* reception.

Cable Communications Policy Act: 1984 Federal legislation regulating *cable* industry activities. Affirmed legal home *dish* reception of all *unscrambled satellite signals.*

cable guard: protective molding at base of *television camera dolly.*

Cable Health Network—CHN: 1982 *satellite/cable* health-and-science programming service; merged with *Daytime* (1984) to form *Lifetime Cabletelevision Network.*

Cable Music Channel: *TBS rock* music *satellite/cable* programming service (1984); sold to *MTV* 1984.

cable penetration: proportion of *cabled* homes to area *television households*.

cable ramps: flanking wedges protecting *cable* runs from *set* or *location* traffic.

cable ready: *VCR* equipped for *cable* service connection.

Cable Television Laboratories: *cable* system consortium for *HDTV* research. Compare: *Advanced Television Test Center*.

Cablevision Systems Corporation: major *MSO* (with between one and five million *subscribers*, 1988).

CAD: *computer*-assisted design.

calculator: simple *data processor* performing arithmetic/logic functions. Compare: *computer*.

calibration: *focus* and *aperture* check of mounted *lens*.

calibrations: indication on *animation* art background showing amount of movement between *frame* exposures.

call—call sheet—call board: production timetable for *talent* appearance.

call-in: *talk show format*.

Calliope: *USA Network* children's programming service.

call letters: assigned *broadcast station* identification. In U.S. (with few historic exceptions), "W"-prefixed, east of Mississippi River; "K"-prefixed, west. See: *allocation*.

CAM: *computer*-assisted manufacturing.

camcorder: integrated professional/consumer *videotape camera/cassette recorder*, used mainly with *8mm cassettes;* loosely, "micro video."

cameo: foreground lighting against dark background.

camera—cam.: optical or electronic instrument recording images.

camera card: large card for *television* photography, formerly carrying *titles/ credits*. Compare: *character generator, crawl, cue card*.

camera chain—chain: a *camera*, its *cables, video* controls, *monitor*, and power supply.

camera chart: in Britain, *animator's layout* sheet.

camera cue: in Britain, red light atop *television camera*, indicating if shot is being transmitted.

camera light: *camera*-mounted light for close performer illumination. Called *basher* in Britain. See: *eye light*. Compare: *tally light*.

cameraman: chief camera technician determining visual components of a shot. Called *lighting cameraman* in Britain. Also: *television studio/location camera operator*. Compare: *robotics, blocking*.

camera original: exposed *film* from camera.

camera rehearsal: *dress rehearsal camera* movement and *switching*.

camera report: *camera* operator's *take-by-take* record, with instructions to *film laboratory*. Called *camera sheet, dope sheet, report sheet* in Britain.

camera right, camera left: movement direction (from *camera* point of view). Compare: *stage right, stage left*.

camera tape: see: *gaffer tape*.

camera test: brief *negative* end exposed *in film laboratory development* test. Compare: *cinex, wedge*.

camera trap: niche concealing *camera* in *scenery*.

camera tube: *pickup tube* converting optical images into electrical *signals* by electronic *scanning process*. See: *iconoscope, image isocon, image orthicon, Leddicon, Newvicon, Plumbicon, Saticon, SEC, SIT, Trinicon, vidicon*. Compare: *picture tube*.

cam head: see: *gear head*.

campaign: varied advertising for specific product over specific period of time. Compare: *schedule*.

can: metal container for *film* transportation or storage (''in the can'' = completed). Also: 1,000-*watt floodlight (ashcan)*.

Canale 5: Italian private *television network*.

Canal Plus: Havas-owned French terrestrial *pay television* system (1985).

Cancon: Canadian-generated content of Canadian-distributed programming.

candela (cd): 1936 replacement for *foot candle* (= 1.02 *candelas*) as light source measurement; luminous intensity of 1/600,000 of square meter of black body radiating cavity at the freezing point of platinum (2,042° K).

canned: *prerecorded* laughter/applause *soundtrack*. Also: Completed programming. See: *HFR*.

canoe: section of curved *quad videotape* traveling between *VTR recording/ playback* guides.

Canon Scoopic: *16mm* Japanese *camera*.

Canon 35: 1937 Bar Association rule denying photographic coverage of courtroom proceedings, Extended to cover television 1963; partially removed 1987.

Canovision 8: *8mm camcorder*.

cans: *headphones*.

canting: tilting camera for ''crooked'' shot. See: *dutch*.

CAP: Britain's Code of Advertising Practice. Compare: *NAB Code*.

cap: *lens* cover.

capacitance: storage of electric energy in electric field, measured in *farads*. Compare: *inductance*. Also: See: *CED, VHD*.

capacitor: *capacitance* device replacing obsolete *condenser*. Also: See: *Condenser microphone*.

Cape Canaveral: U.S. *satellite* launch area. Compare: *Kourou, Balkonur, Plesetsk*.

Capital Cities/American Broadcasting Companies, Inc.—Cap Cities/ABC: U.S. conglomerate *broadcasting network (ABC):* 215 primary, 19 secondary *affiliates*. See: *Hard Rock*.

capping: *lens* protection, avoiding *burn*.

capstan: motorized rotating *spindle* to *transport recording tape* at fixed speeds. Compare: *pinch roller*.

capstan servo: *helical VTR head phase* and *tape speed* control system insuring proper sequential reading of *video* information.

Captain: Japanese *videotex* system (1980). Compare: *Bildschirmtext, Prestel, Teletel, Telidon*.

caption: superimposed *subtitle;* usually translated *dialogue*. Compare: *title*.

caption roller: in Britain, roll-up *program credits*.

caption scanner: in Britain, small *b/w television camera* for *superimposing* artwork, *titles,* etc.

capture ratio: ability of *FM receiver* to discriminate between two *signals* at the same *frequency*.

cap up: cover *television camera lens*.

carbon: obsolete *microphone* using diaphragm of carbon granules to vary an electric *signal;* 400 to 4,000 *Hz* capability.

carbons: *DC arc* light (or its *electrodes*).

card: *computer printer circuit* board.

cardioid—unidirectional: single-direction *microphone* with heart-shaped *pickup* sensitivity.

card rate—rate card: *broadcast station*'s standard advertising charges, broken down by time of day, length of message, and frequency of *insertion*.

carnet—tempex: European customs form covering temporary equipment importation.

carpark: in Britain, *program filmed/taped* in studio parking lot.

carpenter: *set* builder.

carriage return: non-printing *computer* character; moves *cursor* to beginning of next line.

carrier: *frequency wave transmitting radio* or *television signals.*

carry—carriage: *transmit* a *broadcast* program.

CARS—cable auxiliary relay service: additional *microwave* coverage for *cabled* system.

cart—cartridge: container holding single *tape* or *film feed reel, threaded* to *take-up reel* in playback/projection system (or run as endless loop). See: *video cartridge.* Compare: *cassette, reel-to-reel.* Also: **cartridge:** *phonograph pickup* device *transducing stylus-groove* patterns into electrical impulses.

cartage: fee for moving large musical instruments between *recording studios.*

(animated) cartoon: children's *television* programming. See: *Saturday morning.*

Cartrivision: obsolete U.S.-manufactured *VCR* system.

cascade: successive electronic-flow components.

Cassandra: nationally syndicated *Nielsen* program *ratings;* advance release barred to press (1988).

Cassegrain: *dish LNA* feed system. Compare: *buttonhook, prime focus.*

cassette: container holding pair of *reels*—one to *feed* (and *rewind*), the other to *take up tape* or *film.* See: *video cassette.* Compare: *cartridge, reel-to-reel.*

cast: select *talent.* See: *audition, book.* Also: Descriptive list of *program talent.* See: *billing, credits.*

cast commercial: *broadcast* advertising message utilizing *program talent.*

casting director: individual handling *talent audition* and selection.

catadioptric: *lens* with mirrors in optical path to shorten *barrel.*

catalog: stored *computer* files.

cathode: *negatively* (−) charged *terminal.* Compare: *anode.*

cathode-ray tube—CRT: large *vacuum tube* containing electron gun generating continuous, focused *beam* of electrons on internal charged or *luminescent screen;* visually displays electronic information. Also: **CRT—** loosely, *(terminal) screen,* plus attendant keyboard.

cattle call: indiscriminate mass *talent audition.*

CATV—community antenna television: (earliest name for *cable television*) *subscriber* reception in difficult geographic areas, by *cable* connection to single high master *antenna.* Compare: *CCTV, MATV.*

catwalk: latticed walkway over *grid.*

CAV—Constant Angular Velocity: *laser video disk* mode; *disks* spin at constant 1,800 rpm, one revolution per *frame;* capable of 54,000 *still frames* (and interactivity). Compare: *CLV.* Also: *Component analog video.*

CB—citizen band: 40-channel *short wave broadcast band* in the 27 *MHz* range for private communication (8–10 miles, subject to *sunspot interference*).

C-band: 4 to 6 *GHz satellite transmission frequency,* subject to *microwave interference.* Requires *FCC* authorization; used by 9-watt quasi-*DBS* systems. Compare: *K-band, Ka-band, Ku-band, S-band.*

C-band direct: low-power *satellite*-to-home-*receiver signal.*

CBC—Canadian Broadcasting Corporation: (Crown corporation) one of five nationwide *networks;* operates English/French language service. Compare: *CRTC.*

CBN—Christian Broadcasting Network—CBN Cable Network: 24-hour religion-oriented *satellite/cable* programming service (1977); uses *Satcom III-R.*

CBS Cable: 1981 *satellite/cable* cultural programming service (abandoned 1982).

CBS Inc.: (formerly Columbia Broadcasting System) U.S. *broadcasting* conglomerate; Loew's Inc. now 25% stockholder. 201 affiliates. Occasionally known as "Cheap But Sexy." See: *Black Rock.*

CBS Records: former *CBS* corporate division; sold to *Sony.*

CBS Technology Center: discontinued corporate research facility. Compare: *Bell Laboratories.*

CC: see: *closed captioning.*

CCD—charge-coupled device: solid state sensor. Also: **Image CCD:** postage-stamp-sized grid with more than 160,000 light-sensitive *diodes*—replaces *vidicon* tube in miniaturized *television cameras.* Compare: *MOS.*

CCETT—Centre Commun d'Études de Télévision et Télécommunications: French government (Rennes) research facility.

CCIR—Comité Consultatif International de la Radiodiffusion: international *transmission* standard-setting organization (1927).

CCIR-601: international *digital videotape recording* standard.

C clamp: spring-loaded clamping device (usually incorporating a *luminaire* mount). In Britain, also called *G clamp.*

CCR: see: *central control room.*

CCTA—Canadian Cable Television Association: cable system trade organization.

CCTV—closed-circuit television: non*broadcast transmission* of *television signal* to *receiver.* Compare: *CATV.*

CCU—camera control unit: *television camera* remote control.

cd: see: *candela.*

CD: see: *compact disk.*

CDL: computerized *videotape editing* system.

CED: (discontinued) *capacitance* groove/*stylus video disk* system *(RCA SelectaVision);* wear and dirt sensitive. Compare: *LaserVision, VHD.*

Ceefax: ("see facts") British *(BBC)* system *digitally* transmitting *alphanumeric* information in *television signal blanking interval* at seven *megabits* per second. See: *Context, Oracle.* Compare: *Antiope, Slice, teletext, Viewdata.*

cel: (from "cellulose") transparent acetate sheet, usually 11″ × 14″ with *"pegged"* alignment holes, on which *animation* artwork is sequentially inked or painted (U.S. technique, developed by Hurd, 1906). See: *blank(s), animation board.*

cel animation: traditional freehand *frame animation*/coloring, photographed from individual *acetate* sheets.

cel flash: *hot spot* caused by uneven *cel* surface.

cell: *computer memory* location for single information unit, usually one *byte.*

cellular system: optimized 900 *MHz computer*-controlled urban relay network (1½ mile spacing) "handing off" mobile radio telephone *transmissions.*

cement: solvent used to pressure-join a *film splice.*

cement splice: see: *overlap.*

centisecond: 1/100 second.

Central Companies: *IBA's "Big Five": ATV, GRA, LWT, THS, YTV.*

central control room—CCR: in Britain, *broadcast* facility control center.

Central Telecommunications: major *MSO.*

centre: in Britain, plastic hub (unflanged) for *reeling* or storing *film.*

Century Cable: major *MSO* (with between one and five million *subscribers,* 1988).

century stand: one-piece, three-legged telescoping metal pipe support for 1,000-*watt spotlight;* each leg at different height to permit close grouping. Compare: *spud, turtle.*

CEPT—Conférence Européen de Postes et Télégraphies: *ECS communications satellite* operator.

ceramic: low-quality *microphone* (or *phonograph pickup*) containing *piezoelectric* element generating a *signal* on deflection by (sound or *stylus*) pressure; fidelity sound reproduction fails around 8,000 *Hz.* Similar to *crystal microphone.*

certificate (of compliance): *cable* system *FCC* approval.

cesium: see: *second.*

C-format: standard *Sony*-developed (1976) *1" VTR helical-scan* format. Compare: *B-format*.

CG: see: *character generator*.

CGI—computer generated imagery: electronic *animation* technique.

CH—critical hours: period in which *broadcast signals* can cause *interference*. See: *daytimer, PSA*. Compare: *clear channel, powerhouse*.

chain—camera chain: a *camera*, its *cables, video* controls, *monitor*, and power supply.

chainbreak: see: station break.

chainsaw: *backyard dish* "creative engineering" tool.

changeover cue: tiny circle giving *film projectionist* visual warning of *reel* conclusion.

changer: equipment playing sequence of disk recordings.

changing bag: simple cloth bag *"darkroom"* with armholes for *film-magazine* location loading (without *fogging* risk).

channel: isolated program *path*. Also: *FCC*-assigned *AM* (15 *KHz* wide), *FM* (200 *KHz* wide), or *TV* (6 *MHz* wide) *broadcast frequency*, distributed geographically to minimize *station interference*. Also: Complete *signal circuit*.

Channel 4: U.K. *television network*.

Channels: monthly industry/consumer magazine.

channel stuffing: technique for *transmitting NTSC* information without increasing *bandwidth*.

chapter: consecutive sequence of *video disk frames*.

character generator—CG: (1964) electronic typewriter creating *television screen* titling in variety of styles. See: *edging*. Compare: *code generator*.

character length: quantity of *bits* in each (letter or number) *byte*.

charge-coupled device: see: *CCD*.

charge hand: in Britain, union foreman.

charger: device restoring power to discharged *batteries*.

chart—resolution chart: standard *camera*-test design. See: *resolution*. Also: **chart:** trade paper list of best-selling records.

chaser: sequentially wired row of *lamps*, giving effect of light movement. Also: Music accompanying performer's exit.

chassis: electronic equipment frame or mounting.

cheat: "non-realistic" *camera* position, used to improve *frame* composition.

checkerboarding: *film editing* technique utilizing *A & B rolls*. Also: Every other day (or week) *program* scheduling.

check print: quick non-*balanced print* from newly completed *optical picture negative,* to check mechanical *printing* errors. Often used for *dubbing.* Called *slash print* in Britain. Compare: *APO, dirty dupe.*

cherry picker: motorized high-angle *camera* position (inside *operator* bucket). Compare: *crane, parallels.*

cherry picking: securing important affiliate from competitive network. Also: Obtaining popular *cable* programming from various sources.

chest shot: performer framed waist-up.

chief engineer: ''in-charge'' *control room* technician. Called *transmission controller* in Britain.

Children's Channel: British *cable network.*

Children's Television Workshop: see: *CTW.*

chimes: see: *G-E-C.*

china girl: identical *leader frame*(s) of an American female face, used as color standard by U.S. *film laboratories.* Compare: *lily.*

china marker: wax-base *film* marking pencil. Called *chinagraph* in Britain.

chinese: combination *pull back/pan.* Also: Horizontal *barndoor* position.

chip: *acetate* filament thrown up by cutting *stylus.* Called *swarf* in Britain. Compare: *fluff.* Also: *Silicon wafer* base for *semiconductor integrated circuit;* about ⅛″ square, contains many *transistors.* See: *LSI, microprocessor, MSI, SSI, VLSI.*

chip chart—chips: standard *b/w* test-swatch chart for *television camera alignment.* Compare: *grid.*

chipmunk distortion: upward *audio pitch* shift when *playback* speed exceeds *recording* speed.

chippy: In Britain, *set carpenter.*

chipset: *DBS receiver decoder circuitry.*

CHN: see: *Cable Health Network.*

choke: inductive device impeding *current* flow.

chopper: *station* helicopter for *SNG*/traffic *broadcasting.*

chord: three or more musical notes played simultaneously.

CHR—contemporary hit radio: popular music *radio station format.*

Christian Broadcasting Network—CBN: 24-hour religious *satellite/cable* programming service.

chroma—intensity: measure of color *hue* and *saturation* (undiluted with white, black, or gray).

chroma control: *television receiver* control regulating color *saturation.*

chroma detector: *b/w circuitry* eliminating *color burst* by sensing absence of *chrominance signal.*

chroma flutter: irregular *quad videotape color* output, mostly caused by *tape* mis*alignment.*

chromakey: *television* (mainly *videotape*) *matteing* technique, usually with vast difference in size relationships; the subject matted is placed against background (usually blue) and the signal is mixed with that particular color channel suppressed. Also called *inlay.* Called *color separation overlay* (CSO) in Britain. Compare: *blue matteing, process shot, roto-scoping.*

chroma noise: *noise* perceived as color degradation. See: *S/N.*

chromatic: pertaining to color television.

chromatic aberration: color *wavelength* dispersion within defective *lens;* creates different focal points as color fringe haloes.

chromaticity: see: *chroma.*

chrominance: color camera *channels* for television's red, green, and blue *(RGB)* signals. Also: *Colorimetric* difference between a color and *reference white* of the same *luminance.*

chromium dioxide—CrO₂: non-compatible *audio tape* coating offering improved *signal-to-noise ratio.* Compare: *cobalt-energized.*

churn: *cable* system *subscriber* turnover.

CHUT—cable households using TV: audience survey estimate of unduplicated *households viewing* television during average quarter-hour time period.

Chyron: proprietary *character generator;* produces up to 1,500 typefaces.

C/I: *satellite carrier*-to-*interference db* ratio (minimum 63:1).

CIA—Central Intelligence Agency: U.S. government agency covertly funding *Radio Free Europe* and *Radio Liberty* following World War II.

CID: charge-injection device.

cinching: improperly tight (and damaging) *film* or *tape* winding.

cinch marks: random vertical black stripes in a *film print,* caused by overtight *negative* winding. Called *stress marks* in Britain.

ciné board: *16mm footage* of actual *storyboard frames,* edited against a *sound-track.*

Cinema Products: *16/35mm motion picture camera.*

Cinemascope—"Scope": *wide-screen film* system, 2.35:1.

cinematographer: supervisor of *motion picture camera* operation. Called *lighting cameraman* in Britain.

cinéma vérité—direct cinema: *documentary film* style imposed upon non-*documentary* material. See: *slice.*

Cinemax: TIME, Inc. *HBO satellite/pay cable* feature *motion picture* programming service.

Cinéorama: 1896 ten-projector 360° *motion picture* presentation.

Cinerama: *wide-screen film* process: 2.59:1.

cinex—synex: fifteen-*frame laboratory* test strips of key *film scenes,* each *frame* printed with slightly different *balances* for final *release print* color selections. Called *pilots, clip roll, four-framer* in Britain. Compare: *camera test, wedge.*

Circarama: 360° screen film process.

circle of confusion: size of *lens*-formed image point.

circuit: interconnected electric current *path.* Also: Chain of motion picture *film* theaters.

circular polarization: improved (right-handed corkscrew) television *signal transmission* pattern; *ghosting* minimized by left-handed polarity shift. Compare: *horizontal polarization.*

circulation: net unduplicated count of *television homes* or individuals actually *viewing* a *network, unaffiliated station,* or *cable* outlet during a week or month.

CISAC—Conférence International de Societé des Auteurs et Compositeurs: worldwide trade association of musical performing rights organizations.

cladding: different density glass layer reducing light loss through *optical fiber* surface.

clam: improperly played musical note.

clambake: poorly produced program.

clamping: establishing fixed reference DC *video level* at start of *scanning line.*

clamping disk—knuckle: adjustable *century stand* head, grooved to accept pipe *booms, flag* stems, etc.

clapper boy—clapper loader: in Britain, *camera* assistant handling *slate* (or *clapper board*). See: *board on end.*

clapstick—clapboard: special hinged *slate* device for picture/sound *synchronization,* inscribed with full production information, "clapped" on *camera* before each *double-system take.* Called *clapper board* or *number board* in Britain.

Clarke Orbit: geostationary *satellite* location, first proposed by Arthur C. Clarke (October 1945 *Wireless World*): "An 'artificial satellite' at the correct distance from the earth would make one revolution every 24 hours; i.e., it would remain stationary above the same spot and would be within optical range of nearly half the earth's surface. Three repeater stations, 120° apart in the correct orbit, could give television and microwave coverage to the entire planet.''

class A,B,C,D: broadcast advertising time period, graded by audience size. Also: **Class A,B,C:** *FCC* 3 *kW* to 100 *kW station* classification.

Class I,II,III,IV: *FCC*-assigned *AM frequency* with 25*kW* to 50 *kW* operating power.

class rate: dollar breakdown of *broadcast time* costs.

classic rock: popular music *radio station format* (Elvis, etc.).

claw: *16mm camera/projector* mechanism, pulling successive *frames* through *film gate* while *shutter* is momentarily closed. Compare: *pins.*

clean entrance (exit): *camera* operation before *action* begins (and after it ends) for *editing* purposes.

clear: *unscrambled television signal.*

clearance: local *station* agreement to carry *network* or *syndicated* program. Also: Copyright use *permission.*

clear channel: powerful (10 *kW* to 50 *kW*) *AM station* dominance over wide geographic area with no competitive *frequency interference; signal* protection reduced to 750 miles by *FCC,* 1980. See: *powerhouse.*

clear filter: *lens* protector.

clear the frame: *rehearsal* request to clear area in front of *camera.*

Clerk-Maxwell, James: Scots physicist; postulated existence of *radio waves* (1867).

click: aberrant *audio signal.*

click track—pulse track: audible music scoring beat (in conductor's *headphones*) generated by *digital* metronome; based on 6 to 36 *fps film speeds* (24 *frame* pulse = one second clicks; 12 *frame* pulse = ½ second clicks; etc.).

client: *agency* or *advertiser* buying *broadcast time.* See: *account, sponsor.*

Clio: annual statuette award for outstanding *commercial* work from *American Television & Radio Commercials Festival.* Compare: *Emmy.*

clip: short section of longer *film* or *tape.* Also: Shear off *signal peaks.* Also: Accidentally omit note, syllable, or word from beginning/end of *audio track.*

clipper: *switcher clipping*-control knob.

clipping: removal of *signal* portion above or below preset level. Also: Illicit *station* practice; substitutes *local* for *network commercial* (for double payment).

clip roll—four-framer—pilot: in Britain, *laboratory film* test strip of *color balance* range, determining final *printing light* selection.

clogging: *tape oxide* buildup on *recording* or *playback head,* causing *distortion,* improper *tracking* or *tape* damage.

closed captioning: *television* picture titling for the hearing impaired; utilizes *vertical blanking interval line* 21 (on specially equipped *receivers*).

closed circuit—CCTV: non-*broadcast transmission* of *television signal* to a *receiver;* often used by *networks* for *affiliate program* previews. Compare: *CATV.*

closed set: private *filming* or *taping* activity.

close-up: see: *CU.*

clothesline—ridgepole: *television* programming technique; scheduling popular *network* shows at 9:00 P.M. throughout week.

cloud wheel: *set* device projecting sky effect on *cyc.*

cluster: group of *commercials/promotional announcements.*

cluster bar: multiple *luminaire mount.*

clutter: excessive transmission of non-*program* materials (*commercials, promos,* etc.), often up to 25% of *prime broadcast time.*

CLV—constant linear velocity: 108,000-frame non-interactive *video disk;* changes rotational speed in play (1,800 *rpm* at center, slowing to 600 rpm at outer edge). Cannot *still-frame.* Compare: *CAV.*

C-mount: 1″ diameter *16mm lens mount.*

CMX: *computer*-driven *hard disk videotape editing* system.

C/N: *satellite carrier*-to-*noise db* ratio.

CNN—Cable News Network: *TBS* 24-hour national (1980) *satellite/cable* news *channel;* carried on *Satcom III-R.*

CNBC—Consumer News and Business Channel: *NBC* financial/business/sports *cable programing* service.

CNN-2—Cable News Network 2—CNN Headline News: news headline *satellite/cable* program service. See: *TBS.* Compare: *Headline News.*

coax—coaxial cable: "hollow" ¾″ television *signal transmission cable* carrying multiple *channels,* offering low power *loss* at high *frequencies,* with *repeater amplification* every ⅓ mile. First installed 1935 between New York and Philadelphia. See: *F.* Compare: *fiber optics, microwave, satellite, triaxial.*

cobalt-energized: compatible *audio tape* coating offering improved *signal-to-noise ratio.* Compare: *chromium dioxide.*

code: *talent* union agreement. Also: rules of practice adopted by *networks/stations.* See: *NAB Code.*

code generator: equipment recording visual identification *signals* onto *videotape*. Compare: *character generator*.

coercivity: amount of magnetic energy (measured in *øersteds,* after discoverer of electromagnetism) required to affect normal *videotape* particle patterns.

cogwheel effect: *microsecond* displacement of alternate *television picture scan lines;* creates staggered vertical image.

coherer: early *wireless wave* detector (Branly, 1891).

Cohu tube: initial *ion*-accelerator device (1921).

coil: wire winding around *conductor;* generates electromagnetic *field*.

coincidental (interview): real-time telephone verification of *television viewing:* "Are you watching?" (Poor at early/late hours; misses homes without phones.) Compare: *diary, peoplemeter*.

cold: without preparation. Also: Bluish or greenish picture tone. See: *cool*.

collimate: optimize *lens* element positioning for maximum light transmission.

color: eye/nervous system sensation arising from spectral composition of radiant energy. Also: Atmosphere or mood.

color balance: proper adjustment of color elements to give subjectively satisfying *film* or *television picture;* usually based on skin tones.

color balanced: *film emulsion* allowing pure light of specified *color temperature* to appear as white in final *print*. Compare: *unbalanced*.

color bars—SMPTE standard test bars—bars: electronically generated rectangular *videotape leader test pattern,* generally containing six colors— yellow, *cyan,* green, *magenta,* red, blue—matching *playback* to original *recording levels* and *phasing*. Usually accompanied by 1,000 *Hz audio level* reference tone. See: *bar test pattern*.

color burst: 3.58 *MHz subcarrier frequency* primary color relationship sample at *back porch* of *scan line;* timed to quarter-millionth second, *synchronizes transmitted* color *signals* to *receiver*. See: *chroma detector*.

color compensating filter: *lens filter* effecting overall *color balance*.

color correction: readjustment of individual color components to match *camera/ lighting* requirements; or, package retouching for that purpose. Also: Readjustment of *videotape color balance*.

color encoder: equipment reconstituting *NTSC* color *signal* from separate *RGB inputs*.

color film analyzer: electro-optical device scanning a color *negative* to establish proper *printing exposures*. See: *Hazeltine*. Compare: *china girl, lily*.

color frame: *luminaire gel*-support.

colorimetry: technical characteristics of any electronic color reproduction apparatus.

coloring: *computerized* graphic *editing* technique adding color to *black-and-white motion pictures.*

color killer: see: *chroma detector.*

color media: any *transparent* material (glass, *gel,* etc.) placed in front of light source to alter color.

color negative: *motion picture film* with spectral complement record of original colors. See: *negative transfer.*

color positive: *motion picture film* with record of original colors.

color response: *output* of *b/w television camera* relative to color subject.

color separation overlay—CSO: in Britain, *television matteing* technique.

color separation—separation positives: individual *b/w* record of each of the three *primary* components of *color negative film,* for *optical* work and future *print (color shift)* protection. See: *prism block, Technicolor, Vidtronics.*

color shift: visibly disturbing *transmitted* color change.

color subcarrier: see: *subcarrier.*

color television: *transmission* of three separated *(primary color) signals,* superimposed at the *receiver* for illusion of full color; 94% U.S. penetration, 1988.

color temperature: (in *degrees Kelvin* [°K], 273.16° lower than centigrade scale) measurement of relative color of light source; temperature to which *black body* must be raised from absolute zero to radiate light of specific color (higher temperature = bluer light; lower temperature = pinker light). Unrelated to *brightness.*

color wheel: early *(CBS) television transmission* technique.

COLTRAM—Committee on Local Television and Radio Audience Measurement: research methodology group.

Columbia Broadcasting System: see: *CBS, Inc.*

Columbia Pictures Television: major entertainment conglomerate.

comb filter: multiple *notch filter* removing specific *signal frequencies.*

combination rate: tie-in *rate* reduction for advertising on two or more *broadcast stations.*

combined: in Britain, "married" *film print* containing picture with *soundtrack.*

Comcast Cable Communications: major *MSO* (with between one and five million *subscribers,* 1988).

comet tail: bright *television picture tube* smear from moving *hot spot* or light source. Eliminated in *solid-state cameras*. Compare: *lag*.

coming up: the *program* following.

command: *computer* instruction specifying particular operation.

commentary over—out-of-vision—OOV: in Britain, performer heard but not seen.

commentator: news analyst. Also: In Britain, neutral *on-* or *off-camera* performer telling *program* story.

commercial: paid *broadcast* advertising message, usually *10, 15, 30* or *60* seconds long. See: *clutter*. Compare: *counter commercial*.

commercial broadcasting: *programming* "underwritten" by *sponsored* advertising.

commercial program: *broadcast* containing paid advertising.

commercial protection—product protection: *broadcast station's* minimum time interval between competing *commercial* messages. See: *separation*.

common carrier: *FCC*-regulated communications system required to lease its *transmission* facilities to any applicant without regard to content. *Broadcast stations* specifically exempt under *Communications Act of 1934*.

Communications Act of 1934: see: *FCC*.

communications satellite: see: *satellite*.

Communications Satellite Corporation: see: *COMSAT*.

Communications Subcommittee: Senate Commerce Committee subcommittee legislating U.S. *broadcast* activities. Compare: *Telecommunications Subcommittee*.

comopt: in Britain, *composite film print* with *optical* (rather than *magnetic*) *soundtrack*.

compact cassette: *Philips*-licensed 1⅞ *ips audio cassette;* numeral after "C" designates two-side length (in minutes). Compare: *Elcaset, Unisette*.

compact disk—CD: pre-*recorded laser*-read 4¾″ single-sided *high fidelity* plastic *phonograph disk* with 1¼ hr. programming time (requires *CD* player). 20 Hz to 20 *kHz frequency* response; theoretical 98 *db dynamic range*. Compare: *45 rpm, 33⅓*.

compander: *noise* reduction device *COM*pressing *audio signal* in *recording*, ex*PAND*ing it in *playback*. See: *S/N*.

comparative renewal: *FCC* procedure permitting competitive challenge during incumbent station license renewal.

compatibility: ability of *b/w television* set to receive *transmitted* color *signals* (or *NTSC* set to receive *HDTV signals*) with minimum picture *distor-*

tion. Compare: *non-compatibility.* Also: **(Cable) compatibility:** *VCR circuitry* accepting *cable* feed.

compatible: *software* operable on different types of *computers.*

compere: in Britain, program host.

component: equipment item.

component color: two-*channel television signal* system separating *chrominance* information from *black-and-white luminance* information. Compare: *composite color.*

composer: musician creating *melodic/harmonic* structure.

composite: "married" *film print* containing picture *soundtrack.* Called *combined* in Britain. Compare: *interlock.* Also: Combined *video signal, vertical* and horizontal *blanking,* and *synchronizing signals* in *television transmission.* Compare: *non-composite.* Also: Different photographs of same *talent* on single *print.* Compare: *head sheet.*

composite color: original *television signal* system *encoding color* and *luminance* information in the same *signal.* See: *Q signal, Y signal.* Compare: *component color.*

composite master: original completed *videotape.*

compressed audio: *video disk audio, digitally recorded* within *picture* information.

compression: *audio recording* technique minimizing excessive *level* variations to prevent *distortion.* Also: Reduction in television *signal gain* at one particular *level. Compare: time compression.*

compulsory license: (established under *Cable Act of 1984)* 2% of cable industry's gross revenues covering use of copyrighted material without further negotiation. See: *Copyright Royalty Tribunal.*

computer: sophisticated electronic device rapidly performing complex programs.

computer animation: abstract or semi-realistic graphic designs created from *computer* keyboard. See: *CGI.*

Computer Inquiry I (1971), **II** (1980: *FCC* proceedings designed to increase competition in *telecommunications* industry.

Comsat—Communications Satellite Corporation: private "public" U.S. *C-band satellite* program (proposed *DBS* service was abandoned, 1984). Serves as U.S. member of *Intelsat,* establishing/maintaining *Comstar/Telstar* international *geosynchronous communications satellites. Comsat earth stations* are *AT&T*-operated.

Comsat General: operating subsidiary of *Comsat.*

Comstar I: (retired) *AT&T-Comsat* 24-*transponder* *C-band* communications *satellite* at 76° W.

Comstar II: *AT&T-Comsat* 24-*transponder* *C-band* communications *satellite* at 76° W (1976).

Comstar III: (retired) *AT&T-Comsat* 24-*transponder* *C-band* communications *satellite* at 87° W.

Comstar IV: *AT&T-Comsat* 24-*transponder* *C-band* communications *satellite* at 127° W (1981).

condenser: obsolete *capacitance* device, replaced by *capacitor*.

condenser lens: *projector/spotlight lens* concentrating light source on projection area.

condenser microphone: (1916) microphone containing miniaturized *amplifier/* power supply, with conductive diaphragm that varies high-voltage *field* to generate *signal;* omnidirectional pickup pattern. Also called *electrostatic, capacitor*.

conductor: any medium transmitting electric *current*. Compare: *dialectric*. Also: Musician rehearsing/leading performers in a composition.

cone: huge reflective *floodlight*—750 to 5,000 watt—illuminating large *set* areas.

Conelrad: (from *con*trol of *e*lectromagnetic *rad*iation) discontinued government *broadcasting* control system for U.S. during *nuclear attack*. *See: EBS*.

confidence head: additional *videotape playback head* to *monitor* actual *recording* progress.

confirmation: *station* acceptance of *broadcast* advertising order.

conform: match *off-line VTR edits* to standard-gauge *videotape;* akin to *film negative* matching.

conkout: equipment failure.

connector: *circuit* linkage. See: *female, male*.

console: *control room switching* desk.

consonance: two or more harmonious-sounding musical notes. Compare: *dissonance*.

Consumer News and Business Channel: see *CNBC*.

contact print: *positive* film printed from *negative* in direct physical contact with identical width *raw stock*. Compare: *reduction print*.

CONTAM—Committee on Nationwide Television Audience Measurement: (1963) trade organization evaluating *AGB, ARB,* and *Nielsen* audience survey methodologies.

contamination: incomplete separation of *color signal paths*.

Contel-American Satellite Corporation: *ASC-I satellite* operator.

Contelsat I: planned *American Satellite 16-Ku-band transponder/24-C-band transponder communications satellite* at 101° W (1993).

Contelsat II: planned *American Satellite 16-Ku-band transponder/24-C-band transponder communications satellite* at 128° W (1993).

Contelsat III: proposed *American Satellite* 16-*Ku-band transponder/24-C-band transponder communications satellite.*

contemporary: "top 40" popular music *radio station format.*

Context: advanced *Ceefax* version.

Continental Cablevision, Inc.: major *MSO* (with between one and five million *subscribers*, 1988). Planned-*DBS satellite* operator, 61.5°, 110°, 148° W, 1995. Compare: *Conus.*

contingency: allowance for unanticipated production expense.

continuity: prepared *script* material. Also: Smooth flow of dramatic events in proper order.

continuity clerk: (formerly *script girl*) clerk recording all *set* action.

continuity discount: special rate allowed *advertiser* purchasing multiple *spot announcements.*

continuity sheets: in Britain, detailed production records kept by *continuity clerk.*

continuous loop: *film/tape* ends spliced together for continuous *projection/ playback.*

continuous printer: film *laboratory* machine printing *optical track negatives.* Compare: *step printer.*

contract: *talent* or union agreement.

contractor: union producer for music recording session. Also: In Britain, commercial *broadcast* group supplying *IBA programming.*

contrast: see: *hard.*

contrast—contrast ratio: highest *luminance* value of *television picture* divided by lowest. See: *video gain.* Compare: *saturation, brightness range.*

contrast range: *camera* ability to distinguish between shades of gray (*television*, 30 to 1; *film*, 100 to 1). See: *gray scale.*

contrasty: lacking middle tones; of poor reproductive quality.

control ring: device raising/lowering *television camera pedestal.*

control room: small room for *production* management, usually higher than performing *studio* and separated by soundproof window and "sound lock." Called *gallery, box* in Britain.

control track: area regulating *videotape playback synchronization;* also used for *retrieval* coding. Compare: *audio track, sprocket, video track.*

Conus (CONtinental US): Hubbard Broadcasting *television* consortium (1986) operating *satellite* distributing news to member *stations.*

convergence: electronically focused three-color *beam* crossover at *aperture mask.*

convergence pattern: *television* test *signal* checking *monitor* picture for camera *scanning linearity, aspect ratio,* and geometric *distortion.*

convergent lens: bi-convex, *planoconvex* or convergent-miniscus *lens,* forming real (positive) images. Compare: *divergent lens.*

conversation: ''phone-in'' *radio station format,* often deliberately insulting. Compare: *talk show.*

conversion filter: *lens* attachment r*ebalancing film (emulsion)* for different light conditions. See: *daylight filter.*

converter: equipment translating *television signal* characteristics—number of *lines,* number of *fields,* and color coding—from one national standard to another for international *transmission.* Also: **(cable) converter:** device converting *cable signals* to home *television receiver channels.*

cookie—cucaloris—cuke: cut-out screen in front of light source; casts random-patterned ''depth'' shadows. Called *gobo* or *ulcer* in Britain.

cool: slightly bluish or greenish *television picture.* Compare: *warm.*

co-op: *broadcast* advertising cost shared by manufacturer and local distributor.

coordinate system: see: *X, Y, Z axes.*

coplanar: *videotape shuttle* mode; avoids *helical scan wrap.*

copy: advertising words.

Copycode: proposed *digital audio recording* anti*duplication* system.

copyist—orchestrator: musician copying scored parts of composition for instrumental performers. Compare: *arranger.*

copy platform: basic creative word (or picture) plan, exploiting reputed product differences.

Copyright Act of 1976: federal legislation updating Copyright Act of 1909 to cover *broadcasting,* electronic *recording,* etc.

Copyright Royalty Tribunal: federal agency assessing and distributing *cable* royalty payments received through compulsory licensing.

cording: visual identification—with string, tape, or plastic tabs—of portions of *film footage.* Called *papering* in Britain.

core: plastic hub (inflanged) for *reeling* or storing *film.* Called *centre* in Britain. Also: *Television commercial* (campaign) main action.

Corgi and Bess: *BBC* epithet for the Queen's annual Christmas *broadcast.*

coring out: eliminating *signal noise* by *digital conversion.*

corporate campaign: advertising directed at selling firm's "image," as distinct from its products.

corrected (print): see: *release print.*

corrective commercial: *FTC*-ordered *broadcast* advertising message, prepared by advertiser to correct original misleading information. Compare: *counter commercial.*

cosmodrome: see: *Balkonur.*

cost management: professional review/control of (advertising agency) *television commercial* production expenditures.

costume house: *wardrobe* rental agency.

costumes: performers' *wardrobe.* Also called *frocks* in Britain.

couch potato: passive heavy *television* viewer.

countdown: one-second indications (from 10 to 2) on *videotape* or *film leader;* permits exact *cueing.*

counter: digital *index* showing amount of *tape* passing *recorder heads.*

counter commercial: unpaid *broadcast* advertising message—usually prepared by public interest group—countering misleading *commercial* information. Compare: *corrective commercial.*

counter-key—modelling: illumination source opposite *key light.*

counter-programming: *broadcast* planning exploiting competitive schedule weaknesses. Compare: *roadblocking.*

country: musical genre with *bluegrass, folk,* and *western* roots.

country and western: popular music *radio station format;* "Nashville sound."

country rock: musical genre with roots in *country* and *rock* music.

county size: *Nielsen* classification (A,B,C,D) of U.S. counties, according to population and metropolitan proximity.

coupler: device to join lengths of *cable* possessing same electrical characteristics. Also: Telephone-to-*audio recorder* connection. See: *modem.*

cove—ground row: *cyc* baseboard (usually concealing *luminaire strip*).

coverage: geographic boundary of broadcast reception; usually designated in terms of counties normally reached by any *level* of signal. Also: Audience survey measurement of *receivers* in use. Also: Scheduled programming.

coverage map: idealized contours of *broadcast station's signal* reception strength. See: *blanket area.*

cover shot—insurance: wide *camera* position, *protection* for *jump cut lip sync close-ups.* Compare: *cutaway.*

cover version: re-recording by established artist of promising hit song by lesser-known performer.

Covidea: ChemBank/*A.T.&T.* home electronic information service. See: *interactive*. Compare: *Trintex*.

cowcatcher: *sponsorship* announcement preceding *program*'s actual start. Compare: *hitchhike, billboard*.

Cox Cable Communications: major *MSO* (with between one and five million *subscribers*, 1988).

CP: *broadcast station* Construction Permit, issued by *FCC*.

CPB—Corporation for Public Broadcasting: government-funded group established under Public Broadcasting Act of 1967 to enhance non-*commercial* television *programming*. See: *PBS, NET, ETV*.

CPM—cost-per-thousand: index of advertising audience effectiveness, expressed in dollars.

CPP—cost-per-point: index of advertising effectiveness, expressed in *rating points*.

cps—cycles-per-second: obsolete unit of *frequency*. See: *hertz*. Also: **characters per second:** *computer printer* speed.

CPU—computer central processing unit: see: *mainframe*.

C-Quam: Motorola *AM stereo* system. Compare: *Kahn sideband*.

crab: *dolly* sideways. Also: In Britain, metal floor brace for camera *tripod*.

crab dolly: hand-propelled *camera* + *operator* mount on which all wheels can be swivelled synchronously for sideways movement. Compare: *spyder*.

cradle head: *camera mount tilting* up or down on cradle-shaped rockers. See: *gear head*.

CRAM—Cumulative Radio Audience Method: obsolete *NBC* investigation of audience survey methodology.

crane: oversized *camera* + crew *boom*, usually mounted on truck. "To *crane*" = move *boom* up (down). Compare: *dolly*.

crank: operate a *motion picture camera* (from days of non-motorized *cameras*). See: *overcrank, undercrank*.

crash: total *computer* malfunction.

crawl: readable text moving horizontally or vertically through *frame;* often *superimposed* over *picture*. Called *creep, roll, caption roller* in Britain. See: *scroll*. Compare: *camera card, draw cards, flip cards (stand)*. Also: apparent motion.

crawl space: area of bottom *frame* used for one-line horizontal *alphanumeric* information.

credit—performance credit: *ASCAP/BMI*-composition usage payment.

credits: opening or closing list of *program* personnel. See: *billing.* Compare: *main title.* Also: Music performance "points," establishing composer *royalties.*

creep: *videotape/capstan* slippage, affecting picture *playback synchronization.* Also: In Britain, roll-up program *credits.*

creeper: performer edging close to *microphone/*camera. Also: Low camera *dolly.*

creepie-peepie: *hand-held television camera.*

crescendo: gradually building musical climax. Compare: *decrescendo.*

crew: loosely, *production* workers other than performing *talent.*

CRI—color reversal intermediate: *single-strand 16mm printing negative* optically compiled from sections of *original camera negative.* Also: **CRI—color rendition index:** numerical evaluation of effects of light source on visual appearance of surface.

crib card: in Britain, *live television cameraman's shot list.*

Crimson: planned *Ku-band satellite* (1990). See: *Satcom K-3.*

Crimson Satellite Associates: (1987) *HBO/GE Americom satellite* partnership.

crispening: *digital* picture information recirculation, for even sharper image.

critical frequency: *frequency* below which (subject to seasonal variations, etc.) *radio signals* are reflected from—instead of passing through—*ionosphere.*

critical path: most effective, time-efficient procedure.

crix: critics.

crop: exclude edges of camera picture by tighter *framing.* See: *bleed.*

cross: performer's move across *set,* usually at right angles to camera.

crosscut: in Britain, rapid picture-to-picture alternation.

cross-fade: one *audio* source rising from another.

crosshatch: *camera/monitor* convergence *test pattern,* composed of vertical/horizontal lines.

crossing the line: changing *camera* position by more than 180°; creates *viewer* confusion *re:* subject direction.

crossover: single-company ownership of inherently competitive media facilities.

crossover network: *circuit* dividing *signal* into its different *frequencies.*

cross-ownership: common control of *broadcasting* facility and daily newspaper in same market; barred by *FCC* 1975 now includes *cable.* Also: Local telephone company control of *cable* operation; barred by *FCC.* Compare: *duopoly.*

cross-plug: *broadcast* advertising mention of *alternate sponsor.*

crosspolarization: doubled utilization of same *satellite transmission frequency,* using special *antenna.*

crosstalk: extraneous electronic leakage or *signal interference;* eliminated by *fiber optics.* Also: Video color "bleeding."

crowd: in Britain, supplementary *on-camera* performers.

crowd noise: low-level background conversation effect. See: *omnies, walla-walla.*

crowfoot: metal floor brace for *film camera tripod.* Called *crab* or *spider* in Britain.

CRT: *cathode-ray vacuum tube* for temporary display of electronic information. Also: see: *Copyright Royalty Tribunal.*

CRTC—Canadian Radio-Television and Telecommunications Commission: regulatory commission established by 1968 Broadcasting Act, controlling both *CBC* and private *broadcasting/programming* requirements, Compare: *BBC, FCC.*

crunch: statistically compute.

crush: electronically intensify *television picture black/white levels.*

crush out—block off: in Britain, excessively illuminate a surface; creates undesirably white *television picture* area.

crystal microphone: (obsolete) see: *ceramic.*

crystal sync: *wireless* system *synchronizing camera* with *audio recorder.*

CS—close shot: in Britain, performers waist-up. Also: **CS:** Japanese *satellite* program.

CSI—compact source iodide: *tungsten-halogen luminaire.*

CSO: *cable* system operator.

C-SPAN—Cable Satellite Public Affairs Network: system-supported 24-hour public affairs *satellite/cable channel* (1979); provides session coverage of U.S. House of Representatives.

C-SPAN II: *system-supported satellite/cable* coverage (1986) of U.S. Senate sessions.

CTAGB-Cable Television Association of Great Britain: British *cable* system operators' membership organization.

CTS/Hermes—Communications Technology Satellite: U.S.-Canadian *DBS* test *satellite* (1976); 40 times more powerful than *Intelsat* series.

CTW—Children's Television Workshop: non-profit *television* production/publishing company. See: *Sesame Street.*

CU—close up: performer's head and shoulders. Called *big close-up (BCU)* or *large close-up (LCU)* in Britain. Compare: *MCU, ECU.*

cue—Q: sight or sound signal to begin (or cease) *action.*

cue card: *off-camera* prompt card in performer's view. See: *idiot card.* Compare: *camera card, deaf aid, prompter.*

cue code: *video disk* code identifying *video fields, picture* stops, *chapter* stops.

cue light: visual signal to control *voice-over narration recording.* Compare: *tally light.*

cue mark: *projectionist's* changeover warning; usually several *frames* of tiny white circle before *film* end. Called *cue dot* in Britain.

cue sheet: editor's breakdown of *screen* events for timed music, effects, etc. Called *dubbing chart* in Britain. Also: *Optical* cameraman's or *animator's layout* sheet. Called *camera chart* in Britain.

cue track: auxiliary *recording* area on *videotape.*

cumulative audience—cume—reach: number of unduplicated broadcast *program* (or *commercial*) *viewers, households,* over specific number of weeks.

Curie point: temperature at which magnetic *tape* loses residual *recorded signal.*

current: electron movement through *conductor;* rate measured in *amperes.*

cursor: *CRT* display marker indicating character-entry position.

cushion: expandable or contractable *program* section. Compare: *bumper, pad.*

cut: call to halt *action.* Also: Instantaneous picture change. Compare: *dissolve.* Also: *Edit* film. Also: Eliminate material. Also: Separate section on phonograph *disk.* Also: Groove an *acetate phonograph recording* with a *stylus.*

cut-and-paste: *CGI circuitry* moving screen material to new location.

cutaway: *film* or *videotape* shot of interviewer (or other material of secondary importance); avoids *jump-cut editing* of interviewee. Called *nod shot* in Britain.

cutback: *editing* return to a previous *scene.*

cut-in: *local station broadcast* material (often alternate *commercial*) inserted in *network feed.* Compare: *tag.*

cut key: in Britain, *intercom* on/off switch.

cutoff: section of *transmitted television picture* information hidden behind home *receiver mask.* See: *Academy aperture, reticule.* Compare: *safety.* Also: In Britain, *high* or *low frequencies* (or both) eliminated from *audio signal.*

cutter: *film editor.* Also: Thin opaque shape obscuring *set luminaire.* See: *finger, flag.* Compare: *dot, gobo, mask.*

cutting copy: in Britain, *editor's* rough combination of *picture/soundtrack.*

cutting ratio: in Britain, relationship of *exposed film stock* to final *edited footage;* averages around 7 to 1.

cutting room: *film editor*'s workshop.

cutting sync—edit sync: *frame-for-frame synchronization* of *work picture* and *soundtrack* with no allowance for *film pullup*. Called *level sync* in Britain. Compare: *printing sync*.

CVC—Compact Video Cassette: obsolete ¼" *VCR cassette* format.

CVN—Cable Value Network: *satellite/cable network* home shopping service.

cyan: greenish-blue subtractive element of color *negative film;* complementary of (and producing) red. See: *magenta, yellow*.

cybernetics: study of man/*computer* interaction.

cyc—cyclorama: large J-profiled *background scenery,* usually white, eliminating visual frame of reference. See: *limbo, no-seam*. Compare: *set, milk sweep*.

cycle: repeated photographed *animation* drawing movement. Also: Period of *broadcast commercial* use—usually 8 or 13 weeks.

cycle time: equipment time required to complete specific function.

Cypher: proprietary *character generator*.

D

DA: *directional antenna.*

D/A—digital-to-analog: see: *modulate.* Compare: *A/D.*

(D.C.)—da capo: musical ''repeat'' instruction.

dailies—rushes: film *positives* processed overnight from previous day's original *negative* photography. See: *one-light.*

daisy wheel: impact-printing (single-character) element. Compare: *ball, dot matrix, ink jet, thimble.*

damp: reduce *level.*

dark: unused facility.

dark current: *photoconductor* current flow in total darkness.

darkroom: lightproof area for *film* loading, unloading and processing. See: *changing bag, fog, safelight.*

dark week—black week: one of four weeks in the year during which *Nielsen* does not measure *network* television audiences.

DAT—digital audio tape: see: *digital.*

data bank—data base: stored *computer* information.

data communication: point-to-point *transmission* of *computer-encoded* information. See: *modem.*

data file: grouped *computer disk* information.

data processing—DP: sequential *computer* information *input,* storage, handling and *output.*

DATE: *PBS digital television system, transmitting* four additional *high-fidelity audio signals.*

date—session: scheduled *audio recording.*

dawn patrol: early-morning *broadcaster.*

day-for-night: underexpose (with *neutral density filter)* film shot in daylight, to obtain nighttime effect. Avoids labor penalty for night work.

daylight: combination of sunlight/skylight (6,500*K*).

daylight filter: *lens conversion filter* permitting use of daylight-*balanced film emulsion* under artificial light conditions.

day part—time: *broadcast* period for *commercial* advertising sale. See: *daytime, drive time, fringe evening time, prime time television day part.*

daytime—housewife time: broadcast *time* sale classification: 10:00 A.M. to 4:00 P.M. See: *time.*

Daytime: 1982 *ABC satellite/cable* homemaker programming service; merged with *Cable Health Network* (1984) to form *Lifetime Cabletelevision Network.*

daytimer: *radio station licensed* for daylight-only operation *(signal* improvement after dark creates *coverage interference).* See: *CH, PSA.* Compare: *clear channel, powerhouse.*

DB—delayed broadcast: local *station transmission* of earlier *network program* by means of *film* or *videotape recording.* See: *bicycling.* Compare: *network feed.*

db: see: *decibel.*

DBS—direct broadcast satellite: high-power (10x) *satellite*-to-small-home-*antenna* service; ½ million viewers in Japan via *NHK,* 1987. Originally styled: "Don't Be Silly"; now, "Do Be Serious." Called DTH in Britain.

dbx: audio *companding noise reduction* system. See: *S/N.*

DC—direct current: electronic power supply flowing constantly in a single direction. Compare: *AC.*

dead: inoperative or failed equipment. Also: Without *acoustical reverberation.* Also: Discarded creative material. Compare: *live.*

dead air: *transmission* without picture or *audio signal.*

dead end: *studio* area of lowest sound reflection. Compare: *live end.*

deadline: last date for receipt of material for *broadcast.*

dead side: low-response side of *microphone.* See: *pickup.*

deaf aid: performer's (usually newsperson's) inconspicuous *cueing earphone.*

dealer spot: *open-end commercial* with added local retail outlet identification. See: *tag*. Compare: *cut-in*.

dealer tie-in: *network commercial* message listing local retail outlets.

debug: correct technical malfunction.

decamired: 100,000, divided by any *K (Kelvin)* value—for a more workable *color temperature* rating. See: *mired*.

decay rate: fade-out rate of electronic *signal* or picture.

decay time: reduction of 60 *db* (1,000 to 1).

decibel—db: (after telephone inventor) logarithmic unit of loudness; human ear can detect 1 *db* changes, from 0 to 130 *decibels,* with physical damage at 180 *db*.

decisecond: 1/10 second.

deck: *audio tape transport* system with *heads* but no *amplifier* or speakers. Also: Portable *VTR*. Also: *Studio floor* level.

decode: *unscramble encrypted signal*.

decoder: *color television receiver circuitry* between *signal* detector and *picture tube electron gun*. Compare: *encoder*.

decrescendo: gradually decreasing *volume*. Compare: *crescendo*.

dedicated channel: permanent link between two or more devices.

de-esser: *audio* sibilance control *filter*.

default: mode automatically supplied by equipment when user does not specify alternate.

defeat: manually override automatic control.

defect noise: *noise* caused by corroded or dirty electronic *terminal*. See: *S/N*.

definition: perceivable detail.

deflection coil: *cathode ray tube yoke* winding; control *scanning beam*.

defocus: deliberate camera-image "softening," usually as transitional effect. Compare: *dissolve*.

De Forest, Lee: inventor of *audion* (electronic *amplifier tube*), 1906.

degauss: (after propounder of mathematical theory of electricity) *erase* previously *recorded tape* by magnetically realigning oxide particles in regular pattern. See: *bulk erase*. Also: Remove stray magnetism from any (metallic) *recording, editing,* or *playback* equipment. See: *Gauss*.

degausser—bulk eraser—mass eraser: device demagnetizing all *recorded tape* on a *reel* without unspooling. Compare: *erase head*.

degaussing pencil: electromagnetic tool for delicate *soundtrack editing*.

degradation: unacceptable *signal distortion*.

degrees Kelvin—°K: measurement of light source *color temperature,* 0 *°K* is − 273.16° C; each *°K* = 1°C.

delay loop: several-second *tape loop* in *hotline studio.*

Del Rey—HD-NSTC: ''compatible'' experimental *ATV/HDTV* system (fits single 6 *MHz channel*). Compare: *Farjouda, MUSE, NBC, NYIT.*

demagnetizer: electromagnetic tool for *degaussing tape recorder heads.*

demo—demonstration: sample execution of projected performance idea.

demodulate: convert *analog signal* to *digital.* Compare: *modulate.* Also: Extract *broadcast signal* from *carrier wave.*

demographics—profile: *broadcast* audience breakdown by varying statistical characteristics: sex, age, family size, education, economic level, etc. See: *audience composition.* Compare: *psychographics.*

demo rate: lower union payment for non-air (demonstration) performance.

dense: *overexposed negative.* Compare: *thin.*

densitometer: *film density* measurement device. Compare: *sensitometer.*

density: degree of opacity; light transmission vs. reflectance. Also: See: *recording density.*

depth of field: distance range (increasing with smaller *lens apertures)* through which scene elements remain sharp. Compare: *depth of focus.*

depth of focus: distance between *lens* and *film* in which sharp *focus* is maintained. Compare: *depth of field.*

deregulation: progressive abandonment of *FCC* rules and procedures governing *broadcast* operations.

designer: *set* technician supervising scenic and *property* construction and installation. Compare: *art director, carpenter.*

deuce: 2,000-*watt floodlight.*

develop: process a *latent* image on *exposed film.*

DGA—Directors Guild of America: *film* and television *directors'* professional group.

dialog(ue): performed conversation.

diaphragm—iris: adjustable *aperture* of overlapping metal leaves; controls amount of light passing through *lens.* See: *stop.* Also: *Microphone* sound-sensing element.

diapositive: see: *transparency.*

diary: *Nielsen* 13-week audience survey methodology (1950); approximately 850-household sample, reporting in writing each 15-minute *television viewing* segment (supplementary household *Recordimeter* verified receiver on/off time). *Diary* results combined with *Audimeter,* for *NTI;* replaced by *peoplemeter,* 1987.

diascope: illuminated *television camera alignment lens* attachment.

Dice—digital intercontinental conversion equipment: British *(IBA)* bidirectional international television picture *field*-rate *digital* converter; makes 6,000,000 calculations per second.

dichroic: selective light *filter* (transmitting certain *wavelengths,* reflecting others) often used to convert *tungsten* or *quartz* light source to daylight *color balance.* See: *macbeth.*

dichroic mirror: *television camera color filter,* selectively separating red, green and blue *(RGB)* light components to their appropriate *camera pick-up tubes.* Compare: *stripe filter.*

Didon: *Antiope* data *transmission* system.

die: *semiconductor circuit* on a *silicon base.*

dielectric: non-conductive *insulating* material.

difference: *stereo audio signal* subtracting right from left *channel* (L-R); sum of left *channel* with inverse of right.

differential gain: *amplitude* change of color *subcarrier* as function of *luminance.*

differential phase: *phase modulation* of color *signal* by *luminance signal.*

diffuser: material used to spread or soften illumination; scatters incident light in all directions. Called *jolly* in Britain.

digital: *distortion*-free *audio tape recording* technology. Replaces *analog voltages* with series of numbers based on powers of two; provides *signal* regeneration without *noise, drift* or *distortion.* See: *A/D, D/A.*

digital counter: *tape recorder* "footage" indicator. Compare: *hour meter.*

digital readout: indicator showing time, or location.

digitizer tablet: color palette for *CGI.*

dilute: reduce color saturation by adding white.

dimmer: device controlling illumination *brightness.*

DIN: Deutsche Industrie Norm *film emulsion speed rating.* Compare: *AS(N)I, BSI, ISO.*

dink: demographic family; double-income-no-kids. Compare: *oink.*

diode: *vacuum tube* ("oscillation valve") invented by Fleming in 1904, based on electronic phenomenon observed by Edison 21 years earlier. Contains *negative filament (cathode)* and *positive plate* elements. Can be used as rectifier. Compare: *pentode, tetrode, triode.* Also: Any two-element device supporting current flow in one direction.

diopter lens: supplemental screw-on optical element shortening *focal length* for *close-up* photography. Compare: *long lens, telephoto*.

diplexer: equipment permitting *transmission* of *television sound* and *picture signals* from same *antenna*.

dipole: *FM antenna*.

Dipstick: in Britain, *AGB* audience research survey.

Direct: planned-*DBS satellite* operator, 1993.

direct cinema—cinéma vérité: *documentary film* style imposed on non-documentary filming. See: *slice*.

directional: *microphone* with narrow "lane" of *pickup sensitivity*. Compare: *non-directional*. Also: Phase-controlled *(antenna)* radiation.

directional coupler—splitter: device dividing *signal input* equally between two or more *outputs*.

director: in-charge person on *set* or in *studio*.

director of cinematography: *film production* title or rank above *"cameraman."*

directory: list of *computer* storage files.

direct positive—reversal: *camera-original film* producing a *positive* image when developed; eliminates intermediate *negative* and *printing* steps.

direct response: *commercial* urging immediate purchase by mail or telephone. Also: shopping *channel*.

dirty dupe: *one-light single-strand* duplication of *work picture*.

disconnects: *cable subscriber* cancellations.

discount: see: *frequency discount*.

discover: reveal by camera move.

Discovery Channel: educational *satellite/cable* programming service (1985); owned by four major *MSOs*.

discrete: *quadruphonic audio broadcast* or *recording/playback* system; utilizes four *audio signals* on one *FM channel*, or four-channel *tapes* or *disks*. Compare: *matrix*.

discrete component: individual *circuit* device.

dish—dishpan: large concave *backyard television antenna* (*focus* design by *Cassegrain*, 1672). See: *DBS*. Compare: *flat plate antenna*.

disk: *grooved audio recording*. Also: *Videotape slow-motion* or *freeze frame* equipment (1965). See: *slow-mo*. Also: Technique for inexpensive mass production of *television recordings*—utilizing *laser* beams, metal *styli*, etc. Also: See: *diskette*.

disk crash: *computer storage* malfunction. See: *crash*.

disk drive: *computer* device *recording/retrieving random access* information from rotating magnetic *disk.*

diskery: *phonograph record* company.

diskette—floppy: flat, flexible micro/mini *computer digital* information *random access storage* medium, with organized hierarchy of tracks, sectors.

disk jockey: *radio* record or *music video* show host.

disk operating system: see: *DOS.*

disk pack: grouped *video disks* storing *recorded* information.

disk recorder: *video recorder* utilizing single magnetizable *disk (slow-mo)* or *disk pack* to store information. Compare: *video disk.*

Disney Channel: Disney/Group W *satellite/pay cable* children's programming service.

(Walt) Disney Company: major entertainment conglomerate.

display: temporary presentation of stored information. See: *CRT, LCD, LED.*

disposable trap: self-deactivating (one-shot) *cable* show *decoder.*

dissector: experimental *television camera pickup tube* (Farnsworth, 1925).

dissolve (lap): fade into new *scene* while fading out of old. Compare: *cut, defocus.*

dissolve control: device fading between two *projector* images.

dissonance: *unharmonious* sound of two or more musical notes. Compare: *consonance.*

distant signal—imported signal: *television programming* taken off air outside *cable* system's coverage area, for local distribution on *cable.* 1972 *FCC* prohibition removed 1980.

distortion: *output signal* modification not present in *input.* See: *degradation, harmonic distortion, intermodulation distortion.*

distribute: route electric *signal* (or *current*).

distribution amplifier: electronic device feeding *television signal* at original *level* to several *monitors* without *loss.*

dither: combine different-colored dots to create a single-color illusion. Also: Soften *DGI* image, often to obtain "film look."

divergent lens: biconcave, *planoconcave* or divergent-miniscus *lens,* forming virtual (negative) images. Compare: *convergent lens.*

dlt.: daylight.

DMA—designated market area: *Nielsen audience* survey research market classification, denoting the county cluster in which most *viewers* watch the local *station.* Compare: *ADI.*

Dobson: in Britain, final *rehearsal* before a complicated performance.

dock—bay: *studio* storage area for scenic *set* pieces.

docking: physical join of related equipment.

docudrama: hybrid fiction/non-fiction *programming.* See: *documentary.*

documentary: non-fiction programming, typically devoted to a single social theme, drawing on actual, unrehearsed events. Compare: *cinéma vérité, direct cinema, slice.*

documentation: *hardware/software* operating instructions.

dog: unsuccessful creative effort.

Dolby—dbx: (after inventor) patented *audio bandpass circuitry* (1965) improving *signal-to-noise ratio* by *encoding frequency response;* (consumer) *Dolby* B *encodes* 80 *Hz* to 9,000 *Hz,* (professional) *Dolby* A also *encodes* below 80 *Hz,* above 9,000 *Hz.*

dolly: wheeled *camera + operator* mount of varying complexity. Compare: *crane.* Also: *"In"* or *"out"* move of such mounted *camera* (altering *parallax*).

dominant area: see: *ADI.*

Dominion: Hubbard Broadcasting-planned *DBS satellite,* 119° W, 1995.

domsat: "domestic" (North American) *satellite transmission.*

D-1: *SMPTE component* ¾" *digital videotape recording format;* international standard (*CCIR,* 1986).

D-I,II,III: three-*channel* PRC (People's Republic of China) 625-*line television transmission* service.

door swing: *screen* image rotation, on front or back axis. See: *dve.* Compare: *page turn.*

dopant: deliberate impurity in *semiconductor* crystalline structure, modifying electrical properties.

dope sheet: in Britain, *camera operator's take-by-take* record, with instructions to *film laboratory.* Also called *camera sheet, report sheet.*

DOS—disk operating system: *computer* system based on *disk* information *storage.*

dot—target: metal disk used as *flag.*

dot matrix: *computer* impact-printing ribbon format, using square or rectangular pin grid. Compare: *ball, daisy wheel, ink jet, thimble.*

double: play more than one part. Also: Star's impersonator for distant or difficult shots.

double band: see: *interlock.*

double broad: box-shaped 4,000 *W fill light.*

double clad: *scenic flat* with designs on both sides.

double 8: obsolete *16mm reversal film* with twice the normal number of *sprocket holes* along both edges; split after *(8mm) exposure* and *development* into two *8mm* strands.

double head: in Britain, separate (but *synchronized*) *work picture* and *magnetic soundtrack*.

double headset: *intercom* with separate *circuit* for each *earphone*.

double perf(oration): *16 mm* silent *film stock* with *sprocket holes* along both edges. Compare: *single perf*.

double print: *printing* each *frame* twice; halves apparent speed of *action*. Called *double frame* in Britain. Compare: *skip frame*.

double re-entry: *television switcher* controlling complicated *optical effects*.

double sprocket: see: *double perf*.

double system: simultaneous *picture* and *sound, recorded* separately in different media (i.e., on *film* and *audio tape)* for later *synchronization*. Compare: *single system*.

double take: identical *film action* from different angles, *edited* (overlapped) incorrectly.

double time: *overtime* hours at twice normal union rate. See: *golden time*. Also: Music performed twice as fast as written. Compare: *half time*.

doughnut: wraparound *recorded commercial* material (usually music), enclosing *live copy*.

down and dirty: inexpensive production.

down converter: equipment altering *satellite microwave frequency* to *VHF* television *signal*.

downgrade: reduce *commercial talent status;* i.e., from *player* to *extra*. Compare: *outgrade*.

downlight: directly overhead *luminaire beam*. Compare: *worklight*.

downlink: *satellite*-to-ground *transmission*. See: *earth station*. Compare: *uplink*.

download: *receive/store computer file*.

downstage: stage area toward audience (or camera). Compare: *upstage*.

downstream: point between *signal* origination and reception. See: *interactive, two-way*. Compare: *upstream*.

down the line: toward a *signal's* destination. Compare: *up the line*.

downtime: equipment malfunction; ''time out.''

DP—director of photography: *cinematographer*. Also: See: *data processing*.

DPCM—differential pulse-code modulation: *digital signal transmission* technique.

drain: *storage battery* power loss.

drape: unpainted hung fabric *background.* See: *velour.* Compare: *drop.*

draw cards: *art cards*—usually *titling* or *credits* stacked in special holder—whipped out of frame horizontally in front of television camera. Compare: *crawl, flip cards (stand).*

dress: prepare *set.* Also: Final *rehearsal* before *broadcast.* Compare: *dry run, run-through.*

dresser: wardrobing assistant.

drift: electronic *circuit's* inherent tendency to alter characteristics with time and temperature changes.

drive pulses: *television blanking* and *sync pulses.*

drive time: *radio time* sale classification—A.M. (6:00 to 10:00) and P.M. (usually 3:00 to 7:00)—when commuting listeners are in automobiles. See: *time.*

drop: *network terminal.* Also: Suspended painted canvas background. Compare: *flat, drape, profile.* Also: Measure of vertical height.

drop-in: inserted *frequency allocation.*

dropline: residential *cable* system connection; can carry 150 *video channels.* See: multitap.

dropout: horizontal *television picture playback* streak, reflecting momentary lack of *video* information; caused by *tape* (oxide) surface irregularities when *recording.* See: *dropout compensator.*

dropout compensator: complex electronic storage device "filling in" *dropout* streak with previous line's picture information.

drop shadow: enhancement of apparent depth and solidity. Also: *Title* lettering with mechanically/electronically introduced screen "shadow" for improved legibility.

drudge: see: *lexicographer.*

drum: flywheel to insure smooth *film* movement past *projector sound head.* Also: Slotted *helical scan record/playback* head assembly. Also: Rotating *slide* holder. Also: Rotating *title/credit* mount.

dry: in Britain, forget one's lines completely.

dry cell: waterless storage *battery.* See: *flashlight battery, nickel-cadmium.* Compare: *wet cell.*

dry run: *rehearsal* without *costumes,* camera *facilities,* etc. Compare: *run-through, dress.* Called *stagger through* in Britain.

DSS—digital scene simulation: *computer*-generated *video animation* technique.

DTH—direct to home: British *DBS.*

D-3: proposed *Panasonic composite* ½° *digital videotape recording* standard.

DTTR—digital television (video)tape recording: see: *D-1, D-2, D-3.*

D-2: *SMPTE composite ¾''*: digital videotape recording format; 8-bit sampling.

dual rate structure: higher *time* rate charged national advertisers vs. lower *time* rate for locals.

dual track: see: *half track.*

dub—dubbing: electromagnetic *duplication* of *audio* or *videotape* masters. Also: Recording *lip-synchronized dialog* against existing *film* picture (and often over existing *sound*) *loops.* (Called *looping* on West Coast.)

dubber: equipment for *recording/playing back magnetic sprocketed film.* Also: One *tape recorder* playing *signal* into another.

dubbing chart: in Britain, written *cue* flow, usually for *audio mixing.*

dubbing theatre: in Britain, a *recording/mixing studio.* Also called *recording theatre.*

dub down: transfer *videotape* to narrower gauge.

dub off: *re-record* portions of existing material.

dub up: transfer *videotape* to larger gauge.

duct: protective *cable* pipe.

due bill: *station's* exchange of *broadcast time* for *advertiser's* actual product or services. Compare: *barter.*

dulling spray: wax-base aerosol spray; reduces reflective surface shine.

dumb terminal: non-processing *receive/send* unit. Compare: *smart terminal.*

dump: *store, display* or *print file(s)* from *computer memory.* Also: Drop a *feed.* Also: Destroy. See: *junk.*

duopoly rule: *FCC* regulation governing common ownership of two or more *broadcast* facilities in single market. Compare: *cross-ownership.*

dupe (duplicate): copy of *film* or *tape recording* (the latter also called *dub*). Compare: *master.*

dupe neg: *b/w duplicate* made by *finegrain* from original *negative material.*

duplexing—multiplexing: accepting two different *signals* for *transmission* in one or both directions on a single *conductor.*

duplication: see: *dupe.* Also: Cumulative research total of *broadcast homes* or individuals exposed more than once to same *transmitted* material. Compare: *audience net unduplicated.*

dutch: angle *camera* position. See: *canting.*

dutchman: canvas strip covering hinge between two *flats.* Also: Condensing *lens* for *planoconvex spotlight.*

dve—digital video effect: *video* image modification/manipulation—door swing, enlargement, page turn, positioning, rotation, shrinking. See: *ADO, Mirage, Quantel.*

DVR—digital video recorder: *videotape recorder* utilizing *digital* (rather than *analog*) *recording* technology. Compare: *VTR*.

DX—bipack: two *negative films* printed as one. Compare: *tripack*. Also: **DX:** *short wave* contact between distant *transmitters*.

dye transfer: *printing* stage of *Technicolor film* process.

Dynalens: vibration-damping liquid *lens* mount.

dynamic: pressure-sensitive *microphone* diaphragm connected to fine wire coil moving in magnetic field; omnidirectional pickup pattern.

dynamic duplication: *AC transfer* system using *videotape master* and several *slaves*. Compare: *bifilar*.

dynamic range: softest-to-loudest sound range reproducible by a piece of equipment without *distortion*.

E

Early Bird (later **Intelsat I**): initial 85-pound commercial *geosynchronous satellite,* capable of relaying 240 telephone *circuits* or one television *channel;* launched April 6, 1965, operational through 1968. Compare: Telstar.

early entry DBS: see: *BSS band.* Compare: *quasi-DBS, true DBS.*

earphone—earpiece: tiny wired speaker worn in ear. Compare: *headphones.*

earth: in Britain, zero *voltage* point in electrical system.

earth station: ground facility receiving *satellite transmission.* See: *pad.*

EBC—European Business Channel: Zurich-based *satellite* programing service.

EBR—electron beam recording: *videotape-to-film transfer* system, utilizing *step printing* of 3 *b/w negatives.*

EBS—Emergency Broadcast System: government disaster warning system, electronically commandeering all U.S. *broadcast stations.* Replaced *Conelrad* in 1960s. Also used for peacetime disasters.

EBU—European Broadcasting Union: multinational *programming* organization.

echo: (leading or lagging) duplicate of primary *signal.*

Echo A: initial (but defective) reflective orbital *satellite* balloon, launched by *NASA* May 13, 1960. See: *Echo I.*

echo chamber: acoustic or electronic device adding about 2 second *reverberation* to *audio signal.*

Echo I: successful 100-ft.-diameter reflective orbital *satellite* balloon, capable of a single transcontinental telephone call, launched by *NASA* August 12, 1960. Followed by **Echo II** (135 ft. diameter). See: *Echo A, Telstar*.

Echostar: planned *DBS satellite* operator, 1993.

Eclair: *16/35mm* French interchangeable-*magazine* camera.

ECS-4: *Arianespace*-launched European consortium *communications satellite*. See: *ESA, Eutelsat*.

ECU—extra close-up—extreme close-up: performer's features. Called *BCU (big close-up)* in Britain. Compare: *CU*.

edge beat—light bearding—twinkle: edge-twinkling during sharp *video* transitions.

edge-fogged: in Britain, *film footage* ruined by inadvertent *exposure* to light.

edge number: multidigit identification number applied by *film* manufacturer to each foot of *negative raw stock;* numbers print through onto *positive work print footage* (for *reprinting* and *negative matching* during film completion). Note: A new and different set of *positive* edge numbers can always be ink printed. Called *key number* in Britain. Compare: *time code*.

edge stripe: *magnetic audio recording stripe* laid on *edited* positive *film print* (or part of *original reversal raw stock*).

edging: *character generator's* electronically produced *"drop shadow."* Also: Undesirable *television picture fringing*.

edit: creatively alter original *recorded* order (and/or length) of *film* or *tape* material.

edit code—time code: *SMPTE* standard *videotape retrieval* system (similar to *motion picture edge number* identification), usually recording an eight-digit *address* (hours, minutes, seconds, *frames)* on *control track*. Compare: *talking clock*.

editing machines: two basic types—"vertical," *film* passing down from *feed reel;* "horizontal," *film* passing left to right from *feed plate*—all with various trade names.

editing ratio—ratio: relationship of *exposed film stock* to final *edited footage;* average around 7 to 1. Called *cutting ratio* in Britain.

edit(ing) sync(hronization)—cutting sync: *frame-for-frame synchronization* of *work picture* and *soundtrack;* no allowance for *film pullup*. Called *level sync* in Britain. Compare: *printing sync*.

edit list: *computer*-generated *hard copy* of *time-coded videotape edit* decisions.

editor: *tape* or *film production house* specialist charged with piecing together a production from varied visual/sound elements.

editorial assistant—assistant editor: chore-handling assistant to *editor*.

edit pulse: see: *frame pulse*.

Editroid: computerized effects *storage* system for *videotape editing* convenience.

EDP—electronic data processing: see: *data processing*.

EDTV—enhanced definition television: less-than-*HDTV* but better than *NTSC transmission* quality.

educational (radio, television): see: *CPB, ETV, non-commercial, NPR. PBS.*

Edwards Air Force Base (Ca.): U.S. *shuttle orbiter* landing site. Compare: *Cape Canaveral*.

E.E.: *(videotape)* electronic *editing*.

EEC—European Economic Community: 12-nation group issuing broadcasting directives with force of law. Compare: *Council of Europe*.

EEO—equal employment opportunity: *FCC* antidiscrimination bureau.

effective reach: number of *viewers*/homes reached by a medium at a scheduled *frequency* level.

effects—EFX: visual designs generated electronically. Also: Extraneous sounds or *audio backgrounds*. Compare: *SFX*.

effects bank—effects switcher: *control room console* providing electronic *opticals*.

efficacy—lumens per watt: number of *lumens* produced by light source for each *watt* of power applied.

efficiency: media cost vs. delivered audience. See: *CPM*.

EFP—electronic field production: location use of portable *videotaping* equipment.

EHF—extremely high frequency: *radio wavelengths* from 30–300 *GHz*.

EIA—Electronics Industries Association: industry trade group.

EIAJ—Electronics Industries Association of Japan: standards-setting Japanese trade group.

Eidophor: obsolete large-screen *television projection* equipment.

eightball: small round *nondirectional microphone*.

8mm: alternative *VCR format* (1984). Compare: *Beta, VHS*. Also: Obsolete *single-perf reversal film stock 8mm* wide; sliced from *16mm*. See: *Super 8*.

eight-track: *audio tape recorder/playback* handling eight separate *signals* on same *tape*.

EIRP—effective isotropic radiated power: *satellite footprint signal* power level; limited by international agreement to 37*dBW*.

EJ—electronic journalism: see: *ENG*.

EL—ELEV—elevation: *satellite antenna* vertical adjustment. See: *steerable*. Compare: *AZ*.

Elcaset: Japanese-licensed ¼″ *audio cassette*. See: *Unisette*. Compare: *compact*.

ELDO—European Launch Development Organization: see: *ESA*.

electret: *microphone* with *signal* generated by permanently charged diaphragm moving in electrical *field;* pickup in any direction, low susceptibility to vibration-induced noise. Compare: *condenser microphone*.

electrician: *set* lighting technician. Called *sparks* in Britain.

electrode: electric source *terminal*.

electrolysis: chemical change obtained by passing electric *current* through *electrolyte*.

electrolyte: *ionized* material (usually liquid or paste) conducting electric *current*.

electromagnet: soft iron core magnetized by electric *current* passed through surrounding *coil*.

electromagnetic radiation: radiant energy in form of invisible waves moving through space or matter.

electromagnetic spectrum: radiant energy range (low to high) of long, *low-frequency radio waves, microwaves,* infrared radiation, visible light, ultraviolet radiation, X-rays, and gamma rays (all traveling at speed of light, 186,000 *mps*).

electron beam recording—EBR: *videotape-to-film* direct *transfer* technique; utilizes *step printing* of three *b/w negatives*. Compare: *EVR*.

electron gun: *cathode-ray tube* device continuously emitting narrow focusable *beam* of electrons. See: *yoke*.

electronic bandspread: two-dial *short wave tuning*.

electronic blackboard: *audio* (telephone line) *transmission* of visual *signals* chalked on special blackboard. Compare: *slow scan*.

electronic editing: *rerecording* original *videotape signals* onto second *videotape* with changes in order and/or length, without physical *splicing*.

Electronic Media: weekly industry newsmagazine.

electronic recording: conversion of *sound waves* into *recorded* electrical impulses. Replaced (1927) *acoustic disk recording*.

electronic slate: non-*broadcast* identifying information, followed by *countdown*, on *videotape commercial/program leader*. Compare: *slate*.

electronic viewfinder: tiny built-in *picture tube* in *television camera*.

electrostatic: *field* produced by stationary electric charge. Compare: *magneto-static*. See: *condenser microphone*.

electrostatic speaker: see: loudspeaker.

elements: *software* components.

elevation: drawing of vertical *set* surfaces.

ELF—extremely low frequency: *radio wavelengths* <300 Hz. Also: U.S. submarine-communications project; utilizes 2,500-mile long 75-*Hz waves* from bedrock *antenna farms* in Wis. and northern Mich. (defeating effect of *EMP*). See: *Projects Pisces, Sanguine, Seafarer, Shelf*. Compare: *Project Tacamo*.

ellipsoidal: *spotlight* with sharp, shutter-shaped *beam*.

embedded command: non-printing word processing character(s), instructing program or *printer*.

embossing: placing screen letters in relief *(dve)*.

EMI—Electro-Musical Industries: U.K. electronics/entertainment conglomerate. Also: Electromagnetic *interference* (eliminated by *fiber optic* systems).

Emitron: 1936 *BBC television camera* system (405-line 25-*fps* electronic *transmission*).

Emmy: annual award for outstanding *television programming* by *American Academy of Television Arts and Sciences*. Compare: *Clio*. See: *image orthicon*.

EMP—Electromagnetic Pulse Project: U.S. Air Force enemy-missile-jamming program (theorized by Christofilos, 1958). Also creates immense surge of radiant energy, simulating nuclear explosion, burning out power/communications *networks, broadcasting stations,* and home *television/radio receivers.*

EMRC—Electronic Media Ratings Council: industry research analysis group.

emulsion: 0.0003 inch think light-sensitive silver halide/gelatin coating placed on triacetate or polyester *film base*. Also: Oxide placed on *tape base*.

en banc: full *FCC* commissioner panel.

encoder: device altering character of electronic *signal,* or superimposing additional information. See: *color encoder*. Compare: *decoder*.

encryption: *television signal scrambling,* for privacy or commercial protection.

end rate: *broadcast station's* least expensive *commercial time* category. See: *class D*. Compare: *prime time*. Also: Final advertising time charge, after station discounts.

end slate: *slate* photographed (upside down) at end, rather than beginning, of *take,* for *production* expediency. Called *board on end* in Britain.

ENG—electronic newsgathering: *television* news *production* with *hand-held camera* and *video cassette recorder*. See: *camcorder*. Compare: *SNG*.

engineering: *broadcast station*'s technical group.

enhanced hand-held: gimballed, gyroscopically balanced camera *mount* strapped to operator's body. See: *Steadicam*.

enhanced underwriting: corporate euphemism for *public television commercialization*.

enhancer—image enhancer: *television signal* processor; creates "crisper" picture.

Entertainment Channel: 1982 (abandoned 1983) *Rockefeller Center Television/RCA* cultural programming service. Merged with *ARTS* (1984), forming *Arts & Entertainment Cable Network*.

EOT: end of *tape*. Compare: *SOT*. Also: End of *transmission*.

EP—extended play: see: *45 rpm*. Also: lengthened *VCR cassette record/playback* time mode. Compare: *LP, SP*.

episcope: see: *opaque projector*.

EQ—frequency equalizer: control device improving *audio* quality, usually by suppressing one of five *frequency* ranges.

equalize: electronically compensate *frequency* and *level* characteristics of *audio* or *video* source.

Equal Time: *Section 315* of *1934 Federal Communications Act* guaranteeing free identical *broadcast time* to competing political candidates when such *time* is made available to a single candidate. See: *FCC*. Compare: *Fairness Doctrine*.

erase—degauss: *wipe* or neutralize previously *recorded* electromagnetic *signal* patterns, prior to re-*recording*.

erase head: small *degaussing* device in *tape path*, removing previously *recorded signals* by magnetically realigning oxide particles in regular pattern. Compare: *record head, bulk erase*.

ERP: effective radiated power.

error rate: ratio of usage to malfunction.

ERT-1,2: Greek government *television networks*.

ERTS—Earth Resources Technology Satellites: *NASA* spacecraft (*Landsat* 1, 1972) carrying two different camera systems for earth imaging.

ESA—European Space Agency: Paris-based 11-government organization (established 1972 from *ELDO, ESRO*) administering joint European *communications satellite* activity. See: *Arianespace, ECS, ESOC, ESTEC, Geos-2, H-Sat, OTS, Sirio, Symphonie*.

esf—expanded sample frame: research survey measurement, including "unlisted" telephone households.

ESG—electronic sports gathering: compare: *ENG, SNG.*

ESOC—European Space Operations Center: Darmstadt, West Germany, *ESA* operations center.

ESPN—Entertainment & Sports Programming Network: *ABC*/RJR 24-hour *satellite/cable* programming service (1979).

ESRO—European Space Research Organization: *ESRO-II* experimental scientific *satellite* (1968). See: *ESA.*

ESS—Electronic Still Store: *CBS frame-store* device.

Essa: Nine U.S. (1966-on) low-orbit weather *satellites.* Compare: *Itos, Tiros.*

establishing shot—est.: initial master scene; identifies *location* and/or *on-camera talent.*

ESTEC—European Space Research and Technology Center: Noordwijk, Netherlands, *ESA* research center.

estimate: assess cost of *production.*

ET—electrical transcription: archaic term for non-*acoustic disk recording.*

ETB: Basque-language Spanish *television network.*

Eternal Word Television Network: *satellite/cable* religious programming service.

ethnic: *radio station format* featuring *programs* of specific interest to one or more racial groups.

ETS: Japanese *satellite* program.

ETU—Electrical Trades Union: British *set electricians'* union.

ETV—educational television: non-commercial/academic *television broadcasting;* redefined as *PBS* under Public Broadcasting Act of 1967. See: *NET.* Compare: *CPB.*

Eureka: massive European electronic research and development program.

European Business Channel: see: *EBC.*

European Conference of Posts and Telegraph: see: *CEPT.*

Eurovision: European *television program* distribution service.

Eutelsat—ECS: European cooperative *satellite* program. See: *ESA.*

ev—electron volt: *photon potential* difference: higher *ev* = higher *frequency,* shorter *wavelength.*

evaluate: determine surface quality of new *videotape raw stock.*

even line field: last half of an *interlaced television picture frame transmission.* Compare: *odd line field.*

event: unit in a programmed sequence.

evergreen: public relations material with no specific release date.

EVR—Electronic Video Recording: obsolete *CBS* system, mass producing *television* programs on special *film*. Compare: *EBR*.

exciter lamp: small *projector* lamp illuminating *photoelectric sound* reading *head* through *optical film soundtrack*.

expander board: peripheral *circuitry* for *computer* control panel.

expansion slots: *computer* slots for additional *circuit* boards.

ex parte: unethical private contact (i.e., *broadcasters* and *FCC*).

Explorer I: initial U.S. orbital *satellite,* launched February 1, 1958. Compare: *Sputnik.*

explosion wipe: sudden *optical effect* bursting outward from center *frame*.

exposure: adjustment of light (radiant energy) falling on film *emulsion;* varied by controlling duration or intensity of light, or by *camera lens aperture*. See: *overexpose, underexpose, rating*. Also: Number of times a *transmission* has been seen on television.

exposure meter—light meter: *photoelectric cell* device in various formats, measuring direct or reflected illumination *intensity* in *candelas*.

exposure rating: manufacturer's designated *film emulsion speed*.

exposure sheet: *cue sheet* for photographing *animation* sequence.

ext.—exterior: outdoor *set* or *location*. See: *lot*. Compare: *int*.

extended play—EP: see: *45 rpm*.

extension tube—extender: device holding *lens* away from camera for *close-up* photography. See: *diopter lens, proxar*.

external key: *television camera signal inlaying matted* image into *background*. See: *chromakey*. Compare: *plate*.

extra: supplementary *on-camera* performer. Called *crowd* in Britain. Compare: *player, stand-in*.

extreme close-up: see: *ECU*.

extremes: important change-of-action drawings in *animation* sequence (called *keys* in Britain); *in-between* material is handled somewhat mechanically.

extrusion: *CGI* transforming *2-D* image into *3-D* image.

eyeball: adjust visually.

eye light: low-level illumination (usually from camera-mounted lamp) producing *specular* reflection from performer's eyes and teeth.

eyeline: direction of performer's gaze.

F

f: mathematical symbol of relationship between *lens aperture* and *focal length*. See: *f-stop, stop.* Compare: *T-stop.*

F: *coaxial connector* symbol. Also: Fahrenheit.

FAA—Film Artists' Association: British extras' union.

faceplate: front of *television picture tube;* also its tricolor coated *phosphor* (dot or stripe) array.

facilities—fax: technical equipment—lights, cameras, *microphones,* etc.—for *rehearsing* or *broadcasting.*

facilities fee: in Britain, payment for use of *location.*

facsimile—fax: *optical/electronic* graphic image *scanning/transmission* (Bain, 1842). See: junkfax, *modem.*

factor: exposure correction figure.

fact sheet—poop sheet: *copy* points for *announcer's ad-lib* use; opposite of prepared *script.*

fade: bring in (or out) slowly. Compare: *pop-on.*

fade-in: come slowly out of black to image. Also: Come slowly out of silence to sound.

fade-out: go slowly from image to black. Also: Go slowly from sound to silence.

fader: sliding control console *rheostat* (slider) raising or lowering *audio* or *video levels.* See: *attenuate.* Compare: *pot.*

fader bar: manual lever for *switcher* transition.

fading: *broadcast signal* variation, caused by time of day, weather, latitude, atmospheric or *sunspot interference*.

fairing: logarithmic speed attenuation (or increase) for smooth stop (or start).

Fairness Doctrine: *FCC*-mandated station requirement (based on frequency "scarcity") to "afford a reasonable opportunity for discussion of conflicting views on issues of public opinion." Upheld by Supreme Court 1969; abandoned by *FCC* 1987. Presidential veto of Congressional legislation, 1987. See: *Red Lion*. Compare: *Equal Time*.

falloff: reduction in luminance from screen center to edges.

Family Shopping Network: *satellite/cable network* home shopping service.

Family Viewing Time: voluntary *network* restriction (endorsed by *FCC*) limiting violent *television* programming during 8:00-9:00 P.M. time period. Ruled illegal by federal court, 1976.

farad: (after 1832 electromagnetic pioneer) unit of *capacitance*.

Faraday, Michael and **Joseph Henry:** electromagnetic theorists, 1831. See: *Poulsen*.

Farjouda: experimental *ATV/HDTV* system. Compare: *Del Rey, MUSE, NBC, NYIT*.

farm: see *antenna farm*.

Farnsworth, Philo: U.S. *television* inventor (image *dissector*, 1927).

fast (slow): *emulsion* more (or less) sensitive to light. Fast emulsions tend to be grainy. Also: Indication of *lens* quality (fast—lower *f-stops*—transmits more light).

fast forward: high-speed transport of *tape* from *feed* to *take-up reel;* rapidly bypasses unneeded material.

fast scan: picture viewing during *videotape shuttle* mode.

fault time: see: *downtime*.

favor: turn *microphone* or *camera* toward particular performer.

fax—facilities: technical equipment—*lights, cameras, microphones*, etc.—for *rehearsing* or *broadcasting*.

fax—facsimile: *optical/electronic* graphic image *scanning/transmission* (Bain, 1842). See: junkfax, *modem*.

FBIS—Foreign Broadcast Information Service: joint U.S./U.K. international *broadcast* intelligence organization.

FCC—Federal Communications Commission: five-member government agency established by Federal Communications Act of 1934, regulating all U.S. *broadcasting* and electronic communications activity. Undertook authority over *cable transmission* in 1950's—(reputed policy: "If it moves, regulate it—if it doesn't move, kick it—when it moves, regulate it").

Compare: *Federal Radio Act, Radio Act.* Also compare: *BBC, CRTC, ORTF, RAI.*

Feathercam: *35mm motion picture camera.*

Federal Radio Act—FRA: Congressional legislation (1927) empowering a five-man Federal Radio Commission to issue three-year *broadcasting station licenses.* Replaced 1934 by the Federal Communications Act. See: *FCC, Radio Act.*

feed: *transmit* a *signal* for *broadcast.*

feedback: *input* return of output *signal* by design (such as striking multi-image effect obtained by pointing *television camera* at its own *monitor*); or default (such as high-pitched acoustic oscillation created by *microphone* picking up its own *speaker,* or by accidental closing of *audio circuit.* Called *howl-round* in Britain.) Also: Electronic performance sampling for correction control.

feeder: *trunk*-dropline *cable* system *connection.*

feedhorn: *earth station satellite LNA signal*-capture device. Compare: *dish.*

feed plate: *editing table* horizontal *film* supply.

feed reel: *film editor/projector* or *tape recorder supply reel.* Compare: *take-up reel.*

feet: (nonmetric) standard *film* length measurement; sixteen *35mm,* forty *16mm* and 72 *Super 8mm frames* per *film foot.*

feevee: *pay television.* Compare: *freevee.*

female: *connector* receptacle. Compare: *male.*

femtosecond: one-quadrillionth second.

Fernseh: see: *Bosch.*

ferrite: metallic compound of high magnetic permeability, used for *video recording heads.*

Fessenden, Reginald Aubrey: U.S. *radio* pioneer; *heterodyne* theory, 1906.

Festival: auxiliary *HBO satellite/cable* programming service; discontinued 1989.

FET: field effect *transistor.*

fiberglass: reinforced plastic; utilized for large, lightweight *scenic props.*

fiber optics—OF—optical fibers: *laser* beam *waveguide* information system (postulated by Kao and Hockham, 1966). Transmits 167 fiber channels of *photons,* at *bandwidths* ranging from 400 *MHz* to 1 *GHz,* over a single 50-micron flexible glass fiber cable with repeater amplification every 1½ miles. Carrying capability of each fiber standardized (1988) at 600 *megabits* per second (8,000 conversations). Unaffected by *EMI.* See: *mini-hub,* RTI. Compare: *coaxial.*

fidelity: capability of playback equipment to fully reproduce original *signal.*

field: one-half a *television picture scanning* cycle; two *interlaced* (alternate *scan line*) fields to each *frame,* or sixty fields per second (fifty in Britain). Also: *Frame* area measurement, in horizontal and vertical steps of 10% each. Also: Depth of acceptable *lens* definition. Also: Area of electromagnetic influence.

field angle: angle containing 90% of *spotlight's* output.

field emmission: *flat-screen* microelectronic technology, based on electron flow in vacuum.

field frequency: number of *transmitted* television *fields* per second; 60 in U.S., 50 in Britain.

field of view: area seen through particular *lens,* expressed in degrees.

field sequential color: color information visually produced by successive *RGB fields.*

15: 15-second *commercial* message. Compare: *minute, 30, split-30, 10.*

15 ips: professional *audio tape recording speed.* Compare: *7½ ips.*

50-Hz system: automatic *projection* advance, triggered by *recorded 50 Hz pulse.*

filament: *conductor* rendered *incandescent* (emitting electrons) by passage of electric *current.*

file: discrete body of information on magnetic *disk.*

fill: optional material if program runs short. Also: *Fill light.* Also: Color selected portion of *CGI* screen.

fill light: nonapparent light source supplying general illumination; reduces shadows or *contrast* created by *key (subject)* lighting. See: *ambient light, base light, triangle.* Compare: *backlight, rimlight.*

film: *sprocket-holed* rolls (usually cellulose acetate) of various widths, coated with light-sensitive *emulsion.*

film base: see: *base.*

film chain: *film projector,* its related television camera, *cables, monitor, video* control and power supply. Also called *teleciné.* Also: **film chain—multiplexer:** *television master control room* device allowing selective *projection* of *film* or *slide* material.

film clip: short *film* section inserted in *live television program* or *commercial.*

film gate: see: *gate.*

film island: *television station's control room* grouping of *film/slide projectors.*

film loop: continuous *film clip* spliced *tail-*to-*head.*

Filmnet/ATN: Dutch *pay-television network.*

Filmo: original Bell & Howell *16mm television* (news) *camera.*

film plane: location of *film* in relation to *lens,* usually indicated by symbol on camera body. Compare: *focal plane.*

film speed: number of *frames* passing through *picture gate* per second. Also: Degree of *emulsion* light sensitivity.

filmstrip: *film* sequence of individual *35mm* or *16mm frames,* shown singly in special *projector,* with or without separate *synchronized soundtrack.* Compare: *slide film.*

filmstrip projector: *frame*-at-a-time *silent/sound projector.*

film transfer: *filmed* copy of *live* or *videotaped television tube* image. See: *EBR, kinescope, Image Transform, Vidtronics.*

film unit: *location crew.*

film videoplayer: (Kodak) device *projecting Super 8mm sound film* through standard television *receiver.*

filter: electric, electronic, optical, or acoustical device rejecting *signals,* vibrations, or radiations of certain *frequencies* while passing others.

filter factor: *exposure* multiplier, compensating for *lens filter* light reduction.

filter mike: *microphone* feeding *circuit* with modified *frequency response; low frequencies* usually eliminated.

filter wheel: *filter* holder, permanently fitted behind *camera lens.*

final: finished presentation of creative material. Compare: *rough.*

Financial News Network: Infotech *satellite/cable* programming service.

finder—viewfinder: special optical system (or screen) showing camera *lens* framing. See: *Academy aperture, reticule, safety.* Also: Adjustable device for that purpose, worn around *cameraman*'s or *director*'s neck. Also: Small *television camera (b/w)* component displaying *camera*'s (or *line*) *picture* to *cameraman.*

fine cut: *film editor*'s final *work print,* ready for approval and *negative matching* without further change. Compare: *rough cut.*

finegrain: special *slow-speed film raw stock* with finer-grained *emulsion* and more transparent *base:* used for quality *duplication* of original *negative* material.

finger: narrow opaque shape to screen *set luminaire.* See: *cutter, flag.* Compare: *dot, gobo, mask.*

fingerprinter: *television* audience survey device measuring *VCR* usage vs. air *viewing.*

fin/syn: *FCC* rules governing joint program financing/*syndication.*

fire shutter: *projector gate* barrier; opens only at *film* operating speed.

fire up: switch on equipment.

first generation: see: *generation*.

first refusal: tentative *hold* on performer services. Called *first call* in Britain. Compare: *book*.

first-run: syndicated programming specifically produced for local market broadcast. Compare: *off-network*.

fishbowl: *studio* observation booth, usually for *advertising agency* and *client* personnel.

fisheye—bugeye: extreme *wide angle lens,* used mainly for *close-up* comic effect. Compare: *telephoto*.

fishing rod—fishpole: long hand-held *microphone boom*.

five—5K: see: *senior*.

525-line: number of horizontal *sweeps* per *frame* in *NTSC* Western Hemisphere and Japanese *television transmission* systems; offers lower *picture resolution* than Britain and Europe's 625, *HDTV's* 1,125 lines.

fixed: immobile, permanently oriented. Compare: *steerable*. Also: specific *satellite/earth station transmission path*.

fixed focus: *lens* holding subjects in *focus* at all distance settings.

fixed position: specified—rather than "open"—*time* period for *commercial,* sold at premium *rate*. Compare: *ROS*.

flag (French flag): on *set,* square shade (usually black cloth) attached to metal support in front of camera to shield *lens* from stray light. Also called *nigger* in overdeveloped countries. See: *cutter, dot, finger, gobo, mask*.

flagging: television *picture distortion* caused by incorrect *videotape-playback head* timing coordination. See: *bending, hooking, time base corrector*.

flagship: major *station* of *broadcast network*. See: *O & O's*. Compare: *affiliate*.

flange: one-sided *film rewind reel*.

flapover: in Britain, optical spin effect.

flapper—swinger: *flat* swung out of path of moving *camera dolly*.

flare: dark "burned-out" area on *television picture tube,* caused by local light oversaturation (usually random reflections). Sometimes used for dramatic effect. Also: Emergency *lighting* torch.

flash: aberrant bright spot caused by unwanted reflection. Also: Very short scene. Also: Accidentally (or deliberately—see: *flash frame*) *overexposed film frame*. Also: *Unprogrammed* news interruption.

flashback: interpolated "earlier" *scene*.

flash frame: *film frame* deliberately *overexposed* by cameraman as visual *editing cue*. Also produced by *pea bulb* in *camera*.

flashlight (torch) battery: traditional zinc shell containing carbon rod in magnesium paste. See: *dry cell*.

flash pan: in Britain, image-blurring *pan* shot, usually used for *transition*. Also called *whip (wizz)* pan.

flat: large framed-canvas or hardboard (semi-permanent, light, moveable, self-supporting) for *set* "walls" or vertical planes. Compare: *drop*. Also: Lacking in *video contrast*. Also: Without *audio equalization*. Also: *Frequency response* of ±3 *db* from 50 to 14,000 *Hz*. Also: *Film projection* at 1.33:1 *aspect ratio*. Also: *Television* imaging technique replacing *CRT scansion* with panel display. See: *flat screen*.

flat plate antenna: small *DBS* home *antenna*. Compare: *dish*.

flat screen: television picture concept utilizing plasma discharge, electroluminescent panels, *light-emitting diodes,* liquid crystals, electrochromic displays, etc., in place of *picture tube*.

flea's navel: see: *integrity*.

Fletcher-Munson effect: tendency of human ear to "hear" less extreme *bass* and *treble frequencies* when *audio levels* are reduced. See: *middle range*.

flicker: cyclical reduction of light intensity. Also: *Viewer* loss of *persistence of vision,* caused by *film projector* running too slow, or *shutter* malfunction.

flicker noise: defect *noise,* caused by imperfect *conductor* contact. See: *S/N*.

flies: *studio* ceiling area for raised *luminaires* and *scenery* storage.

flighting: nonconsecutive calendar periods of *broadcast* advertising. See: *cycle, hiatus*.

flip: change *art card* for *camera*. Also: *Optical* spin effect (called *flapover* in Britain). Also: Rotate *camera lens mount*.

flip cards: large "looseleaf" *art cards* carrying *program titles* or *credits*. See: *flip stand*. Compare: *character generator, crawl, draw cards*.

flipper: *television viewer* constantly switching channels.

flippers—barn doors: adjustable metal side or top shades to narrow *luminaire beam*.

flippy disk: see: *floppy disk*.

flip side: opposite side of *phonograph disk*.

flip stand: stand holding *flip cards* before *television camera* for rapid, almost imperceptible downward "flipping."

FLIR—forward-looking infra-red: thermal video imaging system utilizing large matrix of discrete heat sensors, and very high speed mechanical *scanning* system.

floodlight—flood: *unfocused luminaire* (or *luminaire bank)* illuminating specific area without glare or shadow.

floor: *television set* or *studio* performance area.

floor manager: *director's* representative in charge of *television studio floor* activity, usually connected to *control room* with *headphones;* equivalent to theater stage manager.

floor men: *television production stagehands* or *grip crew.*

floor monitor: *playback monitor* for *cast/crew* reference.

floor plan: layout indication for *properties* and *scenery* for *studio* performance area. Compare: *light plot.*

floor secretary: in Britain, *continuity girl* on *production set.*

flop: reverse double-*sprocketed film* right for left.

floppy—diskette: flexible (1/16″ thick) micro/mini *computer digital* information *random access storage* medium, with organized hierarchy of tracks, sectors.

flow: see: *audience flow.*

flow chart: *video disk* diagram, mapping program events, actions, *branches.*

fluff: performance speech error. Also: *Groove* dust gathered by *stylus.* Compare: *chip.*

fluorescence—luminescence: production of light (and heat) by energy absorption. Compare: *phosphorescence.*

fluorescent: tubular *lamp* emitting light from electrically excited inner *phosphor* coating (Bequerel, 1867). Compare: *incandescent.*

fluorescent filter: *conversion filter;* permits use of *incandescent-* or daylight-*balanced film emulsion* with *fluorescent* (blue/green) illumination.

flutter: rapid change in *audio/video frequency;* caused by *recording/playback speed* variation. See: *chroma flutter, time base corrector.* Compare: *wow.*

flux: amount of light (measured in *lumens*). Also: Rate of energy transfer over a surface.

fly: suspend or store *scenery* over *set* by cable/rope. See: *flies.*

flyaway: ground-to-*satellite* portable *television transmission* system.

flyback: in Britain, *scanning beam* return to left side (or top) of television *picture tube,* during *blanking interval.*

flying spot scanner: video-beam *transfer* technique, directly reading film surface (not projection therefrom).

flyovers: U.S. population between New York and Los Angeles.

FM—frequency modulation: improved *rf transmission* technique—*frequency* varies; *amplitude* or power remains constant. 200-*kilohertz bandwidth* utilizing 100 *frequencies* from 88 to 108 *MHz*. Not subject to atmospheric or local *interference*. 4,000+ *commercial,* 1,300+ *educational* U.S. *stations* on air, 1988. Called *VHF* in Britain. Compare: *AM*.

FMX: proprietary *FM noise-reduction* system.

FNN: see: *Financial News Network.*

focal length: distance index—from optical center of *lens* (at "infinity" setting) to *film emulsion* surface. 50mm *lens* is "normal" (similar to human vision field) for *35mm filming,* 25mm *lens* for *16mm filming.*

focal plane: plane passing at right angle through principal *focus* area of *lens*. Compare: *film plane.*

focal point: spot where *lens* (or reflector) concentrates all distant-source light rays.

focus: place incoming *photon* at point of selected surface corresponding to the point in field of vision from which *photon* was reflected. Also: Bring *luminaire* or *electron beam* to fine point.

focus control: *television picture gun* device for sharpest *beam scanning definition.*

focus group: selective research interview panel.

focus in (out): transitional *editing* device.

focus puller: in Britain, *assistant cameraman*—checking camera and *focus,* changing *lenses, magazines,* etc.

fog: spoil undeveloped *film* by accidental *exposure* to light. See: *changing bag, darkroom.*

fog filter: special *lens filter* affording softened photographic effect.

foldback: in Britain, *prerecorded audio feed* to *studio loudspeaker.*

Foley man: (from Jack Foley) *motion picture sound effects dubber.*

folk: indigenous musical style. See: *country.* Compare: *bluegrass, western.*

follow focus: alter moving-*camera focus* to hold subject in sharpest *definition.*

follow shot: camera move tracking subject in motion.

follow spot: high-power, narrow-beam *spotlight* tracking moving performer.

FOM—film operations manager: in Britain, liaison person between *BBC film* and *production* departments.

font: complete typeface assortment in particular size/style.

foot: end of *film* or *tape reel.* See: *tail.* Compare: *head.*

footage: (non-metric) standard *film* length measurement: sixteen *35mm,* forty *16mm* and seventy-two *Super 8mm frames* per *film foot.* Loosely, *film* itself.

footage counter: direct *readout* indicator showing *raw stock* run through camera—or amount remaining in *magazine*. Also: Illuminated *mixing studio* indicator. Also: *Videotape* digital position index.

foot candle: older illumination standard (replaced by *candela*, 1.02 foot candles) for photography and *projection;* amount of illumination received by surface one foot from lighted "standard candle"; metric equivalent is *lux*.

footlambert: *luminance* measurement equal to reflection of one *lumen*—0.98 *foot candles* of light—covering square foot of surface. Theatrical screen projection requires 10–12 *foot-lamberts*.

footnote: *WARC*-member statement of intent to use *broadcast frequency* for purposes other than stated in international table of *allocations*.

footprint: *satellite coverage* area.

force—push: develop *film emulsion* beyond recommended *exposure rating*, usually half or full *stop*.

foreground: part of *scene* nearest camera. Also: In Britain, call to clear area in front of camera during *rehearsal*.

foreground miniature: in Britain, obsolete technique (often involving painting on glass) preceding development of modern *optical film* or *television matteing*.

format: *radio station programming* concept. Also: *Program* styling. Also: Show *rundown*, in order of appearance. Also: *Projection screen* proportions.

Fortnightly Decision: superceded 1968 Supreme Court ruling allowing *CATV* operators to re-*transmit* on-air television *programming* without copyright restriction.

45 rpm—extended play—EP: popular single-cut jukebox *phonograph record* (1949). Compare: *compact disk, 33⅓*.

Foucault, Jean Bernard Leon: see: *gyroscope*.

four-framer—clip roll—pilot: in Britain, *laboratory film* test strip of *color balance* range, determining final *printing light* selection.

4-H—four-head: in Britain, four-unit *videotape recording/playback* system. See: *quad*.

four-way: in Britain, geared table device to *synchronously edit film/soundtrack*.

Fox Broadcasting: "Fourth TV network."

fractal: dealing with irregular, fragmented shapes, often amenable to *CGI* programming.

frame: single ⅓₀ second (in Britain, ⅕₅) *television tube picture scan* containing *interlaced* information (280,000 *pixels*) of two *fields* (262½ *lines* per *field;* in Britain, 312½ *lines*). Also: Individual *motion picture film* photograph, or the space it occupies; usually projected for ¹⁄₂₄ second (in Britain, ⅕₅). Also: Register *film* in *projector gate;* in Britain, called *rack.* Also: All units included in research sample. Also: One of 54,000 accessible *CAV video disk pictures.*

frame bar: see: *frame line.*

frame buffer: *digital storage* device holding single *video* image for further manipulation.

frame capture—frame grab: single live *video frame* entered in graphics *computer.*

frame conversion: 3/2 *shutter/gate pulldown;* matches 24 *fps sound film* rate to 30 *fps television* systems. See: *30 frames.*

frame cut: extraneous *frames* within *scene* excised without evidence. Compare: *jump cut.*

frame frequency: number of *transmitted* television *frames per second;* 30 in U.S., 25 in Britain.

frame glass—platen: optically clear hinged glass plate holding *cels* flat during *animation* photography.

frame grabber: *digital* storage *circuit* permitting *helical videotape freeze framing* without continuous *head*-to-*tape* contact.

frame line—frame bar: thin horizontal line dividing *35mm frames.*

frame memory: *television receiver circuitry storing* single *frame* for modification or continuous *readout.* See: *freeze frame.*

frame number: address of *videodisk frame*—from 1 to 54,000.

frame pulse: *videotape control track vertical interval frame*-start mark. Also called *edit pulse.*

frame rate conversion: see: *3/2 pulldown.*

framesnatch: *cable* television home control; permits *receiver* to "lock onto" one of 30 completely different frames specially *transmitted* each second, thus allowing *viewing*—for example—of miniaturized 30-page newspaper, one page at a time. Basis of *teletext.*

frames per second—fps: film *speed* through camera or *projector gate.* Compare: *ips.* Also: *Television transmission* standard; 30 frames in U.S., 25 in Britain.

frame store: long- or short-term *digital storage/retrieval* of individual *video* image. See: *ESS, still store.*

frame transfer: *CCD circuitry* transferring full *video fields* to *chip storage.*

frame up: adjust *camera* position for better composition. Also: Properly *register film* in *projector gate*.

framing: subject area included by *camera lens*.

France Régions 3: French *public television channel*.

franchise: contractual agreement between *cable* operator and a government authority; essentially, municipally awarded license to operate a *cable* system. Municipal fees limited (under *Cable Communications Policy Act* of 1984) to 5% of gross system receipts.

franchise area: in Britain, *IBA*-company coverage area.

Franklin: *(payola)* $100 bill.

FRC—Federal Radio Commission: government agency set up under *Federal Radio Act* of 1927 to control U.S. *radio broadcasting;* replaced in 1934 by *FCC*.

freebie: something of value exchanged for media publicity. See: *junket, plugola*.

free-lancer: self-employed individual.

free perspective: illusion of realistic dimension on studio *set*.

freevee: over-the-air *television*. Compare: *feevee*.

freeze: agree on final *format*. Also: Forget one's lines. Called *dry* in Britain.

freeze frame—stop action: individual *film negative frame*, reprinted as continuous *positive* in middle of normal motion footage. Also: Identical effect achieved by *videotape disk recorder* or storage.

Freeze Order: *FCC* September 30, 1948, halt in *television station construction permits*, presumably to promulgate improved *transmission* standards; vacated 1952.

French brace: swing-away permanently attached hinged *scenery* support.

French flag: see: *flag*.

French shoot: in Britain, seven continuous hours of production (from noon on) with no *break*.

French side: see: *Radio Canada*.

frequency: rate at which electronic impulse/ sound/ light wave passes given point in specific time period (see: *amplitude, hertz, cps);* loosely, broadcast transmission *wave-length*. Also: Average times audience is exposed to *program* series or same *commercial* over specific number of weeks. See: *audience accumulation, impressions*. Compare: *reach*.

frequency discount—quantity discount: lower *station rate* for advertisers scheduling *commercials* over 13-week *cycle* or multiples thereof—or at agreed minimum number of times each week. See: *rateholder*.

frequency equalizer—EQ: control device improving *audio* quality, usually by suppressing one of five *frequency* ranges.

frequency response: relative *signal amplitude*-to-*frequency* over specific *frequency range*.

frequency reuse: two-signal *transmission* technique using different *antenna polarization* (right hand/left hand or horizontal/vertical).

fresnel: planoconvex *lens* thinned down in "stepped" form. Also: *Spotlight* with such *lens*.

Frezzolini: improved *16mm* Auricon *camera* (1969).

friction head: rotating camera *mount*, mechanically snubbed for smooth *panning* motion. See: *pan head*. Compare: *gear head*.

frilling: edge-loosening of *film emulsion* from *base*.

fringe area: outer limit of broadcast *signal* reception.

fringe evening time: *broadcast* periods preceding/following *prime time*. Early (5:00-7:00 P.M.); Late (11:00 P.M.-1:00 A.M.). See: *time*.

fringing: multiple image mis-*registration*.

frocks: in Britain, performers' *wardrobe*.

from the top: *rehearsal* from very beginning of performance.

front focus: *focus zoom lens* at "in" position.

front loading: *VCR* equipment with *cassette/disk* insertion from front. Compare: *top loading*.

front porch: 1.59 *microsecond* interval between beginning of *television blanking retrace interval* and *synchronizing signal* that follows. Compare: *back porch, breezeway*.

front (axial) projection: scenic *background* effect, achieved by low-intensity *projection* of *location slides* or *film* along the taking-*lens* axis (by 45° half-silvered mirror) directly on performers and on huge *Scotchlite* screen behind them. Called *reflex projection* in Britain. Compare: *background projector, rear screen projection, vizmo*.

front surface: plane or curved glass mirror concentrating or distributing light waves from exposed surface, preventing double image. Compare: *back surface*.

FRP: see: *SFP*.

fr/sec: see: *fps*.

FR-3: French government *television network*. Compare: *A2, TF1*.

frying pan: round *set* screen softening light source.

FS—full shot: performers and entire *background*. Compare: *LS, MS*.

FSS band: 20–40 *watt* "early entry" medium-power *satellite transmission* system (11.7–12.2 *GHz*) to 4–6 ft. rooftop/*backyard antennas*.

f-stop: *aperture setting* indicating theoretical amount of light passing through *lens;* determined by dividing *focal length* by effective *diaphragm* diameter. Adjacent *f-stop* numbers double (or halve) amount of transmitted light. See: *f, stop.* Compare: *T-stop.*

FTC—Federal Trade Commission: government agency eliminating "false and misleading" advertising. Compare: *FCC.*

FTM—flat tension mask: flat-faced *CRT* design.

F-2: *ionospheric* layer creating heavy 10–40 *MHz radio wave* reflection when subjected to *sunspot ionization.*

fuff: in Britain, plastic snow flakes.

Fukiniki (Takahiko) Hole: *NTSC spectrum* "open" area, developed by *Hitachi* scientist for *ADTV* use.

full coat: *35mm sprocket-holed film,* completely coated one side with metallic *oxide* for multiple-track *magnetic recording.* Called *full stripe* in Britain. (When used for single-track recording, U.S. practice is to record down edge; Britain uses 200 mil center path.)

full-duplex: *computer* data wire *transmission* in two directions at same time. Compare: *half-duplex.*

fuller's earth: mineral powder simulating *set* "dust."

full net: all-*affiliate network hookup.* Called *all* in Britain.

full network station: *affiliate* carrying at least 85% of *network prime time programming.*

full track: *recording* on all the available *audio tape surface.* Compare: *half track.*

funnel—snoot: cone or tubelike attachment pinpointing *spotlight beam.*

funny paper effect: electronic offset of *chrominance* and *luminance signals* in a television picture.

fuse: temperature limiter *disconnecting overloaded* equipment *circuits.*

fusible link: protective *fuse* element.

FV: see: *Family Viewing Time.*

FX: extraneous effects. Compare: *SFX.*

FYI—for your information: routing notation.

G

GaAs-FET—gallium-arsenide field-effect transistor: high-grade *LNA* amplifier.

GAC: in Britian, General Advisory Councils providing both *BBC* and *IBA* with public input.

gaffer: chief *set* electrician. See: *sparks*.

gaffer grip—gator grip—bear trap: heavy-duty spring clamp, often with *luminaire* mount.

gaffer tape: strong, extremely adhesive aluminized-surface pressure-sensitive tape for temporary *set* or *location* rigging.

gain: *signal volume*. Also: *Audio amplification level,* usually expressed in *decibels*. Also: *Video contrast level*. See: *black level, reference white*. Also: Ability of *projection screen* to reflect light.

Galavision: *SIN pay television* service.

Galaxy C: planned *Hughes 24-transponder Ku-band communications satellite* at 101° W.

Galaxy D: planned *Hughes 24-transponder Ku-band communications satellite* at 89° W.

Galaxy I: *Hughes 24-transponder C-band communications satellite* at 134° W (1983); utilized by *HBO*.

Galaxy II: *Hughes 24-transponder C-band communications satellite* at 74° W (1983).

Galaxy III: *Hughes 24-transponder C-band communications satellite* at 93.5° W (1984).

Galaxy V: planned *Hughes 24-transponder C-band communications satellite* at 101° W (1944).

Galaxy I-R: planned *Hughes 24-transponder C-band communications satellite* at 134° W (1993).

Galaxy II-R: planned *Hughes 24-transponder C-band communications satellite* at 72° W (1993).

gallery—box: in Britain, small room for *production* management, usually higher than performing *studio* and separated by soundproof window and "sound lock."

game: see: *video game.*

game show: television giveaway *program,* with host and elaborate questioning and scoring *props.*

gamma: *contrast* characteristics of developed *film.* Also: *Television camera input/output contrast* ratio.

gang: two or more switches on single control.

gantry: in Britain, peripheral walkway affording access to *runners.*

gap: microscopic space ($\frac{1}{10,000}$–$\frac{1}{20,000}$ inch) between two poles of magnetic *recording, playback* or *erase* head.

garbage: unwanted or meaningless data. Also: *RF* spillover *interference* on adjacent *frequencies.*

gas: pressurize a camera *boom* tank.

gash: in Britain, worthless *film.*

gate: *(picture gate) camera* or *projector* opening in which each *frame* is held momentarily for *exposure* or *projection; (sound gate) projector* mechanism "reading" *optical soundtrack.* Also: Electronic *circuit* with several *inputs* and one *output;* no *output* until *input signal* meets specified parameters.

gator grip—gaffer grip—bear trap: heavy-duty spring clamp, often with *luminaire* mount.

Gauss, Carl Friedrich: electromagnetic theorist, 1832. See: *degausser.*

gauss: unit of magnetic *induction.*

gauze: light *diffuser.* See: *spun, butterfly.*

GCE—ground communication equipment: see: *earth station.*

G clamp: (British) see: *C clamp.*

GE—General Electric Corporation: U.S. electronics/appliance manufacturing conglomerate; owner of *NBC, RCA.*

GE Americom: (formerly *RCA Americom*) *communications satellite* operator. See: *Satcom.*

gear head: hand-operated camera *mount;* gear wheels control *pan/tilt* movement. See: *cradle head.* Compare: *friction head.*

G-E-C: traditional three-note *NBC radio/tv* chime *logo;* originally derived from initials of erstwhile (now current) owner, General *E*lectric *C*ompany.

gel(atin): translucent celluloid-like *filter* altering color characteristics of a light source. See: *color media.* Called *jelly* in Britain.

Gemini: obsolete *videotape/16mm film* simultaneous *recording* system, developed as an *editing* technique. Compare: *video assist.*

General Dynamics: *Atlas satellite* rocket construction corporation.

General Instrument: see: *VC-II.*

generating element: *microphone transducer.*

generation: duplication stage; "first *generation*" is original, "second" is duplicate, "third" is duplicate of "second," etc. Each *generation* theoretically represents a quality loss. Also: Developmental leap.

generator: portable gasoline- or diesel-powered dynamo generating alternating current *(AC).* Called *alternator* in Britain.

generator truck: conveyance for above entry.

generic: in Britain, *on-air* promotional material for *television* series.

genlock: device synchronizing *television signal* sources.

GEO(synchronous): any (formerly non-retrievable; see: *shuttle orbiter*) *communications satellite* in geosynchronous orbit, 22,240 miles high, moving at earth's rotational speed—thus "standing still" in relation to fixed position on earth surface (theorized by *Clarke,* 1945). Compare: *LEO.*

geodesic: shortest distance between two surface points.

geometry errors: *videotape velocity* and *time base* dimensional shifts.

Geostar: U.S. government maritime location *satellite.*

Geos-2: experimental *ESRO satellite.*

get out: in Britain, time required to *strike set.*

Gev: one billion electron-*volts.* Compare: *Mev.*

ghetto blaster—boom box: popular oversized portable *radio/cassette* player.

ghost: offset secondary *picture tube* image, caused by reflected (earlier or later) *television transmission signal.* See: *multipath.*

ghoster: in Britain, *overtime* production beyond 1:00 A.M.

Gibson Girl: obsolete *audio tape splicer* design. Compare: *splicing block.*

gigahertz—GHz: one billion *hertz.*

gigawatt—GW: one billion *watts;* one million *kw.*

gigo—garbage in, garbage out: inability to obtain good output from bad input.

gimmick: trick or device. See: *schtick.*

giraffe: in Britain, small *microphone boom.*

glass bead: shiny *projection screen* surface for bright viewing over narrow viewing angle. Compare: *lenticular, matte.*

glass shot: obsolete technique—painting on glass—preceding development of modern optical *film* and *videotape matteing.* Also: Package, etc., affixed to *limbo* sheet of glass.

glitch: undesirable electronic *noise* or *interference,* causing system error or failure; appears in *television picture* as ascending horizontal bar.

Global: Canadian regional (Ontario) *television network.*

Global Positioning System: see: *GPS.*

global search: word processing program identifying each occurrence of a character, word, or phrase.

"global village": Marshall McLuhan's original concept of a *television*-shrunk world.

glossy: shiny-finish photographic print.

GM—general manager: local *station* executive supervising overall *broadcasting* operations.

GMT—Greenwich Mean Time: mean solar time along *Greenwich,* England, meridian.

gnat: in Britain, a tiny amount.

gobo: sound-absorbing material or screen. Also: Opaque shade to screen a *set* light. See: *finger, flag, cutter, dot, mask.* Also: In Britain, a *cookie.*

Godslot: (now discontinued) statutory British Sunday evening religious hour. Formally called *closed period.*

golden time: Sunday, holiday, or other special *overtime,* compensated under union agreements at more than normal $1\frac{1}{2} \times overtime$ rate.

goose: increase slightly.

gooseneck: bendable *microphone* stand.

gopher: *production* assistant who "goes for" coffee, etc.

Gospel Music Network: *satellite/cable* religious programming service.

Gostelradio: Soviet *television network.*

go to black: fade from *image* to blank screen.

gozinta: ("goes into") *input.*

gozowta: ("goes out of") *output.*

GPS—Global Positioning System: world navigation system transmitting (1989) from 13 *Navstar satellites* inclined 43° to Equator. Compare: *loran*.

GRA—Granada: one of British *IBA*'s *"Big Five"* (the *Central Companies*).

grad: in Britain, partial *neutral density filter*.

Grade A: 90 percent satisfactory *television signal coverage* in 70 percent of *receiving* locations. Compare: *Grade B*.

Grade B: 90 percent satisfactory *television signal coverage* in 50 percent of *receiving* locations. Compare: *Grade A*.

grading: in Britain, subjective alteration of *printing light intensities* and *color filters* to achieve *balanced film positive* from *unbalanced negative* material.

grading print: in Britain, initial *married* evaluation *film print* from completed *picture* and *track negative*. Compare: *double head, show print*.

grain: molecular *film emulsion* structure.

Grammy: (from *gramophone*) annual U.S. recording industry award.

gramophone: in Britain, *audio disk* player.

grandfathering: permitted use of pre-existing procedures (or materials) following imposition of restrictions.

Grant: *(payola)* $50 bill.

graphics tablet: flat-surfaced *digitizing* device; images created by moving *stylus* over tablet, translating shapes into *computer* input.

graticule: electronically generated screen pattern of intersecting lines, positioning live images, titling, etc. Called *grating* in Britain. Compare: *chip chart*.

gray scale: ten-step intensity scale evaluating *shading* of *black-and-white* television picture. [Note: Nos. 1 (high, pure white) and 10 (low, pure black) cannot be adequately reproduced by a television *picture tube*.] See: *contrast range*.

grazing: continuous *viewer television program* sampling (facilitated by remote *channel*-switching devices).

Great Wall: Chinese satellite launching/operating group.

green book: CCIR rule book.

green gun: device emitting electrons at picture tube green phosphors. Compare: blue gun, red gun.

green print: newly developed positive film on which emulsion has not hardened (affects focus).

green room: performers' lounge.

greensmen: studio *crew* members handling *set* foliage.

96   GREENWICH TIME

Greenwich time: 24-hour Greenwich Observatory time (without local adjustment). See: *GMT, military time.*

grid: see: *graticule.*

grid(iron): metal girders or pipe latticework suspending *luminaires,* etc. over *set.* Called *runners* in Britain. See: *catwalk.* Also: **grid:** *television camera alignment* chart. Called *grating* in Britain. Compare: *chip chart.* Also: Wire mesh *vacuum tube* element.

grille cloth: *loudspeaker* covering.

grip: *set* worker charged with lifting, carrying or pushing.

groove: see: *microgroove.*

gross impressions: total number of *impressions* made by an advertising schedule.

gross rating points—GRP: total number of *rating points* delivered by an advertising *schedule,* prepared without regard to viewer *duplication.* Compare: *net rating points.*

Groucho: in Britain, performer's *floor mark.*

ground: zero *voltage* point in electrical system. Called *earth* in Britain.

ground glass: translucent glass screen on which *viewfinder* image is *focused.*

ground row—cove: *cyc* baseboard (usually concealing *luminaire strip*).

groundwave: primary portion of *A.M. broadcast signal,* following ground contour. Compare: *sky wave.*

group delay: common *filter*-caused delay of some *frequencies* and not others.

Group W: Westinghouse *broadcasting/cable network;* sold 1985 to broadcasting consortium.

GStar-I: *GTE Spacenet 16-transponder Ku-band communications satellite* at 103° W (1985).

GStar-II: *GTE Spacenet 16 transponder Ku-band communications satellite* at 105° W (1986).

GStar-III: *GTE Spacenet 16 transponder Ku-band communications satellite* Arianespace-launched (1988) into useless orbit.

GStar-IV: *GTE Spacenet 24-transponder Ku-band communications satellite* at 103° W (*GStar-I* replacement, 1985).

G/T—gain-to-noise temperature: *earth station* reception capability, expressed as *db* ratio.

GTE—General Telephone & Electronics Corporation: U.S. electronics industry conglomerate.

GTE Spacenet: *communications satellite* operator. See: *GStar, Spacenet.*

Guandong: largest Chinese *television station.*

guard band(s): protective space between similarly angled *recording tracks*. See: *azimuth recording*.

guide track—playback: prerecorded music or speech cueing *MOS* action.

guillotine splicer: *editing* device using continuous roll of pressure-sensitive tape applied across *film,* punch-perforated and knife-trimmed on both sides.

gulp: group of *bytes*.

gun: *television cathode-ray tube* source, continuously emitting narrow *focusable beam* of electrons.

gyroscope: single-axis stabilizing flywheel (Foucault, 1852). See: *Steadicam*.

H

HAAT: height of *transmitting antenna* above average terrain.

hacker: *computer* enthusiast.

half apple: rugged low wooden box used on *set* to raise apparent height of performers or *props*. See: *apple*.

half broad: box-shaped 1,000-*watt floodlight*. See: *broad*.

half-duplex: *computer* data wire *transmission* in one direction at a time. Compare: *full-duplex*.

half-inch. see: *½″*.

half time: music performed half as fast as written. Compare: *double time*.

half track: reversible *audio recording tape* with *signal* on top 40% only. Compare: *full track*. Also: Combination of *optical* and *magnetic soundtracks* on *single film print*.

halide: binary compound containing a halogen—bromine, chlorine, fluorine, iodine. See: *CSI, HMI, tungsten-halogen*.

halo—halation: dark television *picture tube* area ringing *overloaded* bright area. Also: *Print flare* caused by excessive light bouncing back through *emulsion* from *film base*.

ham: amateur *short wave radio* operator.

hammock: unpopular *network* program position between two popular programs. Compare: *ridgepole*.

hand-held: without camera *tripod* or *dolly*— or *microphone* support. See: *enhanced hand-held*.

hand model: extra performer using hands (only) in *frame*.

handoff: cellular telephone *transmitter signal* transfer.

handout: publicity *release* provided by subject.

hand props: small personal *properties*.

handshake: conformance *signal* between two *computers*.

hands on: equipment under human control.

happy talk: inconsequential news *programming* or commentary. See: *infotainment*.

hard: high *contrast*.

hard copy: conversion of *CRT* information/screen image to *printout*/photograph. Compare: *soft copy*.

hard disk: permanently installed rigid *computer disk* system.

harden: sharpen *focus*. Compare: *soften*.

hard rock: brash, loud *rock 'n' roll;* popular music *radio station format*.

Hard Rock: *Variety's* epithet for New York corporate headquarters of *Cap(ital) Cities/ABC;* matches *Thirty Rock (NBC), Black Rock (CBS)*.

hardware: *computer* equipment. Also: *Broadcast* equipment. Compare: *software*.

hard wire: permanent electrical *connection*.

harmonic distortion: addition of spurious *frequencies* as integer multiples of *input signal*.

harmonics: multiples of original *frequency*— 60 *Hz,* 120 *Hz,* 180 *Hz,* 240 *Hz* . . . to limits of audibility.

harmony: musical relationship between *melody* and accompaniment.

harness: grouped and tied wires or *cables*.

HARP—high-gain avalanche rushing amorphous photoconductor: improved-sensitivity (10x) *camera tube target*.

Harry: proprietary *digital video recorder,* storing up to 84 seconds of *real-time video* in a *random access hard disk* with single *frame memory*. See: *Paintbox*. Compare: *ADO*.

haze filter: *lens filter* removing some ultraviolet and blue light and reducing effect of atmospheric haze.

Hazeltine: electro-optical *negative color film* analyzer determining proper *printing exposure*.

HBO—Home Box Office: TIME, Inc., *satellite/pay cable* feature *motion picture* programming service (first to use *satellite transmission,* 1975).

HDTV—high definition television: Japanese-developed 1,125-*line*/60 *Hz MUSE transmission/reception* system requiring 30 *MHz* bandwidth; offers greatly improved *picture* quality with 5:3 *aspect ratio*. Would obsolete existing *receivers*. Called *Hi-Vision* in Japan. Proposed European version, 1,225-*line*/50 *Hz*.

head: small electromagnetic *transducer recording/reading/erasing magnetic tape* or *disk* information. Also: Beginning of *reel* of *tape/film*. Compare: *tail*. Also: *Picture* or *sound gate* on *film editing* machine; *sound gate* on *film projector*. Also: *Camera mount* on *tripod, dolly*, or *boom*.

head alignment: magnetic *head* adjustment for maximized *recording/playback* characteristics. See: *bias*.

head demagnetization: removal of *recording/playback head* residual magnetism.

head end: *cable* system equipment *receiving* original *broadcast/satellite/micro-wave television signal for further transmission*.

header: in Britain, short opening sequence in advance of *television program main title*.

headlife: nominal *video recording head* overhaul-to-overhaul period.

Headline News: *TBS satellite/cable* news summary *programming*.

headphones: tiny wired *speakers* worn over each ear. Compare: *earphone, headset*.

headroom: space between top of framed object and top of *frame*.

headset: *intercom* or *PL* station; consists of headband-mounted earpiece-and-mouthpiece. Compare: *headphones*.

headsheet: *talent* photograph. Compare: *composite*.

head shot: *framing* performer's head and shoulders.

heads out: *film* (or *tape) reel* ready for *projection* (or *playback*). Compare: *tails out*.

headwheel: rotating magnets of *quad videotape record/playback* assembly.

heat filter: *condenser lens* stage; filters *IR waves* to reduce *film projection* temperature.

heaviside layer: (after British physicist who discovered it, 1902) *ionosphere*, 25 to 250 miles high, "bouncing" *radio* waves (up to 30 *MHz)* back to earth for wider *signal coverage*. Compare: *troposphere*. See: skywave.

hectohertz: 100 *hertz*.

height: vertical size of *television picture*. Compare: *width*.

helical scan (slant track): *videotape* with one or two *recording heads* "writing" information in long parallel slants across tape "wrapped" as a helix (1965, as replacement for *quad*). Uniquely offers *still picture*, but is somewhat susceptible to stretch and slippage. Originally used in miniaturized *videotape recording* systems, now standard *1" VTR (A, B, C formats)*.

helios noise: five-minute all-wave *interference* when *satellite* passes between sun and *tracking earth station*.

helmer: *film/television director*.

Henry, Joseph, and Michael Faraday: magnetic playback theorists, 1831. See: *Poulsen*.

henry: (after the electromagnetic pioneer) unit of *inductance*.

Henson, Jim: television *Muppet* (*M*arionette-p*UPPET*) creator.

Heritage Communications: major *MSO* (with between one and five million *subscribers, 1988*).

Heritage Ministries: see: *PTL*.

Hermes: see: *CTS/Hermes*.

hertz—Hz: (after discoverer of *electromagnetic* or *radio waves*) frequency unit equal to one *cycle per second*. Male voice range, 500–800 *Hz;* female, 1,000–2,000 *Hz;* "*Hi-fi,*" 20–20,000 *Hz;* human audibility range, usually 50–15,000 *Hz*.

hessian: in Britain, coarse *set drape* material.

HFR—hold for release: pending *air* material.

hiatus: planned interruption of *commercial broadcast schedule,* usually to extend advertising budget. See: *cycle, flighting*.

HID—high-intensity discharge: mercury, *metal halide* and high-pressure sodium *lamps*.

hidden camera: impromptu *television* interview technique.

hi-fi—high-fidelity: sonic reproduction characterized by uniform *frequency response* (less than 3 *db* deviation from 20 to 20,000 *Hz*), low *distortion* (less than 0.5%) and low extraneous *noise* (at least 50 *db* below *signal*).

high band: improved *videotape recording* technique utilizing 7.1 to 10 *megahertz band* for improved *signal-to-noise ratio;* or, equipment for such *recording*. Compare: *low band*.

high con(trast): special *film* used in *optical printing* to drop *emulsion* background from *titling mattes*, etc.

high definition television: see: *HDTV.*

high end: top of the audible *frequency spectrum*. Compare: *low end*.

high-energy: tape requiring strong magnetic recording field strength (improving *signal-to-noise ratio*).

high fidelity: accurate reproduction of original; absence of *distortion*. See: *hi-fi*.

high hat—top hat: *tripod* extension for high *camera* angles; also used alone for low *camera* angles. Also: **high hat:** pedal-operated cymbals in drum set.

high gain—high level: *signal level* of one *volt* or more. Compare: *low gain*.

high impedance—high Z: 50,000 *ohms* or more. See: *impedance*.

high key: bright illumination emphasizing upper *gray scale;* produces few or no dark areas. Compare: *low key*.

highlight: maximum *brightness* of a positive *image*.

high resolution: *video* images with *scan lines* or *pixels* exceeding *NTSC* standards.

highs—high frequencies: sound *frequencies* around 15,000 *hertz*. Compare: *lows, middle range*.

high-speed duplication: *re-recording* one or more copies from *tape master* at a speed many times faster than original *recording*.

high-speed photography: special *film cameras* offering *exposure* rates from 25 to 30,000,000 *frames per second*. Called *fast motion* in Britain.

highway: *channel path* or *circuit*.

high Z: see: *Z*.

hire: in Britain, equipment rental.

hiss: aberrant *high-frequency* (''white'') noise, audible during *tape playback*.

hit: undesirable brief, distinctive *audio* noise. Also: Sudden *effect*.

Hitachi: major Japanese electronics manufacturer.

hitchhike: *sponsor announcement* following *program's* actual end. Compare: *cowcatcher, billboard*.

hit the mark: move to predetermined *set* point. Compare: *miss the mark*.

Hi-Vision: *HDTV* in Japan.

HMI—hydrargyrum medium iodide: *tungsten-halogen* light source.

Ho Chi Minh Trail: in Britain, unorthodox path around *production* difficulty.

hold: any *cel* in multi-layered *animation* photography not changed from *frame* to *frame*. Also: Repetitive *printing* of single *live-action frame*. Also: Successful *tape* performance held for review before final selection. See: *buy*. Also: Tentative performer *booking*. Compare: *audition*.

hold down—bring down: reduce *audio level*.

holding fee: scheduled payment to *commercial* talent between reuse *cycles*.

hole: see: *Fukinuki Hole*.

hologram—holography: *laser*-produced ''three-dimensional'' image. See: *wavefront reconstruction*.

holy factor: *high-key* illumination for color photography.

Home Box Office: see: *HBO*.

home brew: amateur-built electronic equipment.

Home Office: British department regulating U.K. *broadcast* activity. Compare: *FCC*.

Home Premiere Television: *MSO pay-per-view cable programming* service. Merged into *Viewer's Choice* 1988.

homes: basic audience survey count of U.S. *households* owning one or more *television receivers;* 88.7 million, 1988.

homes passed: actual/potential *subscribers* on *cable* system *paths;* 71-½ million in U.S., 1988.

home video: see: *HV*.

hook: catchy musical (or advertising *copy*) phrase.

hooking: television picture *distortion;* caused by incorrect *videotape/playback head* timing coordination. See: *bending, flagging*.

hookup: *circuit* connection. Also: Loosely, multi-*station program* interconnection. Also: First and last interchangeable *cels* of two *animation cycles*.

Hooper(ating): *radio* audience telephone survey service. Sold to *A. C. Neilsen* in 1950s.

horizontal: *television scan line signal,* requiring 0.4 *nanosecond* stability.

horizontal blanking: *signal* suppression during horizontal *retrace*.

horizontal polarization: original television *signal transmission* pattern—along horizontal plane—subject to *ghosting*. Compare: *circular polarization*.

horizontal resolution: camera ability (expressed in "lines") to detect *intensity* changes along single *scan line*. See: *pixel*. Compare: *vertical resolution*.

horizontal saturation: heavy *broadcast* advertising *schedule* in same *time* period for several consecutive days. Compare: *roadblocking, vertical saturation*.

horn: *microwave signal*-capture device. Also: Colloquially, *loudspeaker*.

horse: in Britain, *film editing feed reel* stand.

hot: *audio track* recorded at fullest possible *level* without *distortion*. Also: Extremely bright *image*. Also: Energized equipment or *circuit*. See: *live*. Compare: *dead*.

hotline: audience *call-in* program.

hot press: *title card* imprinting technique utilizing highly reflective colored foil in place of ink.

hot spot: excessive reflection from part of illuminated object.

hour meter: digital counter measuring equipment's elapsed operating time (for maintenance scheduling).

house agency: *agency* function partially or fully controlled by advertising *client*.

housecleaning: sweeping personnel replacement.

housedrop: see: *drop line*.

(TV) household: one of 90.4 million (1988) U.S. homes (98%) with *television receivers*. Compare: *radio home*.

housewife: in audience surveys, any female head of household aged 16+.

housewife time—daytime: *broadcast time* sale classification: 10:00 A.M.-4:00 P.M. See: *time*.

housing: protective equipment shell.

H-rate: *scan* time for one complete horizontal *line* with *trace* and *retrace*.

H(heavy)-Sat: *ESA communications satellite,* 1983. See: *ECS, OTS, Sirio, Symphonie*.

HSN—Home Shopping Network: *satellite/cable network* home shopping service.

hub: keyed center of *film/tape reel*. Also: **hub:** *cable* system *downstream* service area.

hue: distinctive color *wavelength* (black, gray, and white have no *hue)*. See: *chroma, intensity*. Compare: *saturation*.

Hughes Communications: *communications satellite* operator (owned by General Motors); planned *DBS satellite* at 101° W, 1995. See: *Galaxy*.

hum: pure *low-frequency tone* adulterating *audio signal;* induced by *AC* power line. See: *hum bar, S/N*.

hum bar: horizontal *video bar* moving vertically at rate relative to difference between power line *frequency* and *vertical* rate of *video* system. See: *S/N*.

hunting: equipment failure to maintain correct *speed*.

HUR—homes using radio: audience survey count of *broadcast homes* listening to *radio* during average quarter-hour *time* period. See: *audience potential*.

HUT—homes using TV: audience survey count of *broadcast homes* viewing television during given *time* period. See: *audience potential*.

HV—home video: *VCR cassette/video disk* programming.

hybrid (satellite): utilizing *C-band* and *Ku-band transponders*.

Hyperfocal: distance between *lens* at *infinity* setting and nearest object in acceptable *focus*.

hypo—sodium thiosulfate: photo-developing fixative. Also: **hypo:** promotion technique distorting normal audience survey levels during station rating periods. See: *rating book*.

Hz: see: *hertz*.

I

IATSE—International Alliance of Theatrical Stage Employees and Moving Picture Machine Operators of the United States and Canada: *set* workers'/*projectionists'* union.

IBA—Independent Broadcasting Authority: organization (until 1972, ITA—Independent Television Authority) established under 1964 Television Act to supervise Britain's *commercial broadcasting;* consists of fifteen *program contractors* (see: *Big Five*) supplying regional *transmitters.* See: *ICTA.* Also: **IBA:** Israel Broadcasting Authority.

IBEW—International Brotherhood of Electrical Workers: *broadcast* technicians' union.

IBM: communications equipment manufacturer and *satellite* operator. See: *SBS.*

IC—integrated circuit: encapsulated *semiconductor chip* affixed to tiny *dielectric* base, performing control function. See: *microprocessor, silicon wafer.*

iconoscope: (coined by inventor Zworykin—from Russian "holy image") early *television camera pickup tube* (1923).

ICTA—Independent Television Companies Association: Britain's 15-*IBA*-member trade association. Compare: *NAB.*

ID—station identification: formerly *10-second commercial* announcement with *audio* limited to 8 seconds or less, allowing for shared *station identification;* now any *10-second spot.*

ident board: see: *number board.*

idiot card: off-camera *cue card* in performer's view. Compare: *deaf aid, prompter.*

IEEE—Institute of Electrical and Electronic Engineers: standards-setting professional engineering group. Compare: *SMPTE*.

if—intermediate frequency: standard (41-47 *MHz*) frequency for *television signal path* within *receiver*. Compare: *rf*.

IFRB—International Frequency Registration Board: world *frequency* use control group.

Ikegami: Japanese electronics firm manufacturing *hand-held television cameras*. See: *ENG*.

ILR—independent local radio: in Britain, small neighborhood *radio* service contractors.

image: *film* or *television picture*.

image dissector: see: *dissector*.

image enhancer: *television signal* processor creating "crisper" picture by "filling in" missing *luminance* detail without increasing actual resolution.

image intensifier: electronic *lens* adapter improving low light *levels* by using *fiber optics* to break up *image* into series of *amplified* points.

image isocon: sensitive *camera pickup tube* designed for low light *levels*. Compare: *SEC, SIT*.

image orthicon—I.O.: older sensitive (15–20:1 *contrast range*) *television camera pickup tube* (1945). Origin for *"Emmy* (immy) Award" epithet (Henry R. Lubcke, 1948). Compare: *Leddicon, Newvicon, Plumbicon, Saticon, vidicon*.

image pickup tube: see: *camera tube*.

image retention—lag: two (or more) *frame* "ghosting" behind fast-moving *television camera* subjects; caused by insufficient illumination (accentuated in low *field*-per-second *television* systems). Eliminated by *solid-state cameras*. See: *bias light*. Compare: *comet tail*.

Image Transform: proprietary computerized high-quality *video tape-to-film transfer* system.

imbibition: final *dye transfer* stage of *Technicolor printing* process.

impedance: apparent *AC resistance* corresponding to actual *DC resistance*. Measured in *ohms*. Symbol: *Z*.

imported signal—distant signal: *television programming* taken off *air* outside *cable* system's coverage area, for local distribution on *cable*. *FCC* prohibition removed, 1980.

impressions: gross (duplicated) *program* or *commercial* audience. See: *audience accumulation*.

improvise: compose spontaneously. See: *ad lib*.

impulse noise: *audio* noise or *picture* sparkling caused by lightning, *AC* power systems, high voltage coronas, ignition, commutator sparking, etc. See: *S/N*.

in: movement toward. Compare: *out*.

in-betweens: sequential *film animation* drawings between *extremes*. Also: Identical *videotape* effect with *CGI*.

incandescent: inert-gas-filled electric lamp (1879) emitting light (and heat) from excited *tungsten filament*. Compare: *fluorescent*.

inching knob: *editor/projector* control moving *film* one *frame* at a time.

incidence: angle of light striking reflective surface.

incident: light striking subject from any source.

inclining prism: rotating *viewfinder* permitting viewing at awkward *camera* angles.

in-cue: opening words of *cue* line. Compare: *out-cue*.

indecency standard: 1988 *FCC* ruling permitting obscenity *broadcasting*— "depicting or describing . . . sexual or excretory organs or activities"—from midnight to 6:00 A.M.

independent—"indie"—"indy": commercially operated *broadcast station* carrying less than 10 hours of *network programming* a week. Compare: *affiliate, O & O's*.

index: reference number, related to a base.

inductance: electric energy storage in magnetic field, generated by current flow in *conductor,* measured in *henrys*. Compare: *capacitance*.

induction: transmission of electric or magnetic *currents* without direct *connection*.

industrial: media selling industrial (as opposed to consumer) products.

infinity: distance from *lens*—often not more than thirty feet—beyond which *camera* sees all light rays as parallel.

infomercials: informational *commercials*— "minidocumentaries" (two minutes to one hour long)—usually for *cable broadcast*.

infotainment: hoopla *television* news programming. See: *happy talk*.

infrared: *emulsion* sensitive to light waves longer than visible red. Compare: *actinic light*.

infrasonic: below audible (20 *Hz*-up) range. Compare: *sonic, ultrasonic*.

ink: sign contract.

ink-and-paint: completion stage following *pencil test* of full *film animation*.

ink jet: *computer* jet *printing format*. Compare: *ball, daisy wheel, dot matrix, thimble*.

inky—inky dink: tiny 100-to-250 *watt fresnel spotlight.*

inlay: see: *chromakey.*

Inmarsat—International Maritime Satellite Organization: London-based 29-nation ship-to-shore *communications satellite* organization; replaced *Marisat* 1982. *Comsat* is U.S. member. See *OCC.*

in phase: perfect coordination of *film* movement through *gate* with rotation of *camera shutter.* Also: Any electronic *synchronization.*

input: *signal* entering unit or system. Also: *Jack* or receptacle receiving *input signal.* See: gozinta. Compare: output.

input device: keyboard, *keypad,* or touch-sensitive *television screen* communicating with a *computer.*

in safety: within theoretical *overscan* boundaries of superimposed artwork/*titling.* See: *safety.*

insert: portion *matted* into larger television *picture.* Compare: *PIP.* Also: Additional *videotape* or *film* added to previously completed material. Compare: *assemble.* Also: *Close-up* of inanimate object. See: *table top.*

insert camera: small *television camera superimposing* artwork, *titles,* etc. Called *caption scanner* in Britain.

insert editing: replacement *video editing format.* Compare: *assemble editing.*

insertion: individual *commercial* on advertising *schedule.*

insertion loss: *signal* strength decrease when piece of equipment is inserted into *circuit.*

insert stage: small *studio* for minor *(table top)* photography.

in shot—in frame: accidental visual intrusion.

instantlies: *videotape "dailies."*

instant replay: immediate *playback* (often *slow motion* and *freeze frame*) from *video disk recording* of ongoing *live telecast* (usually sports). See: *isolated.*

institutional: "public-image" advertising with no direct product or service "sell."

insulation: *dielectric* protective covering on wire/*cable.*

insurance—cover shot: wide *camera* position, *protection* for *jump cut lip sync close-ups.* Compare: *cutaway.* Also: **Insurance:** *protection* duplicate.

in sync(hronization): *sound/picture* elements aligned exactly.

int.—interior: indoor *set.* Compare: *ext.*

integrated: *commercial* advertising format claiming relationship between two (or more) products made by different corporate advertisers; qualifies for lowered pro rata *time charges*. Compare: *piggyback, split-30*. Also: *Commercial* delivered by program *cast* member(s).

integrated circuit—IC: encapsulated *semi-conductor chip* affixed to tiny *dielectric* base, performing control function. See: *microprocessor, silicon wafer*.

integration: *editing commercials* into body of recorded *(film* or *tape) television program*.

integrity: (in *broadcasting)* "Sufficient to fit in a flea's navel, with room left for seven *network* vice-presidents."—FRED ALLEN.

Intelsat—International Telecommunications Satellite Organization: global *communications satellite* consortium (1964); includes 113 shareholding nations (1987), U.S. *(Comsat)* share 30 + %; utilizes various *satellites* in 6,830 mph *geosynchronous orbits* 22,240 miles above Atlantic, Pacific, and Indian Oceans, with 35,000 *audio/video circuits* to link 658 *earth stations* in 157 countries, territories, and dependencies. Compare: *PAS*.

Intelsat-V: *communications satellite;* lost on *Arianespace* launch 1986.

Intelsat-VII: planned *GE-AstroSpace* international *communications satellite*.

intensity—chroma: measure of color *hue* and *saturation* (undiluted with white, black, or gray). Also: **intensity:** strength of light or sound *wave*, usually measured by its *amplitude*. Also: Strength of light source in particular direction, measured in *candelas*.

interactive: capable of two-way information flow. Also: *microprocessor*-controlled *video disk format* permitting viewer "programming."

interactivity: reciprocal dialogue between technological system and user.

intercom: local voice communication system. See: *headset*. Compare: *PL, talkback*.

interconnect: *broadcasting* units specifically joined for *time sales*. Also: Combination of *cable* system head ends, to sell *time*, etc.

intercut: rapid picture-to-picture alternation. Called *crosscut* in Britain. Compare: *dissolve*.

interface: *connection* point of two discrete systems.

interference: extraneous electronic impulses disrupting normal *signal transmission*.

interlace: *scanning* of alternate lines on *television tube* to create a "complete" *picture* in two passes of 262½ *lines* each; reduces *flicker* potential. See: *positive interlace, random interlace*. Compare: *progressive scanning*.

interline active CCD: improved *CCD chip* utilizing *picture storage elements* adjacent to active *pixels*.

interlock: separated but *synchronized film work picture* and magnetic *soundtrack*. Compare: *composite*. Also: System for projecting above. Called *double head* in Britain.

intermediate: *reversal* color *film* for making *opticals* or *duplicates*.

intermediate film process: *Baird's* pioneering *BBC television camera* technique (1936) utilizing 17.5mm *film* and 67-second-delayed *sound* and 240-line mechanical *disk scanning*. Replaced (1937) by *EMI* instantaneous 405-line electronic *scanning*.

intermittent shutter: rotating prismatic *lens* arrangement replacing normal camera *shutter*. Compare: *mirror shutter*.

intermodulation distortion—IM: generation of spurious *frequencies* during processing, caused by "crossed" *signals*. See: *S/N*.

internal delay: length of time of *signal* passage through equipment.

internegative: *finegrain optical color negative* struck from original *reversal* or *interpositive* materials; used for *release printing*.

interpositive—IP: *finegrain color positive* struck from a selected section of original camera *negative;* used to make *internegative*.

Intersync: *videotape recording* accessory equipment, *synchronizing signals* of *recorders* and *live* cameras.

intervalometer: automatic *motion picture camera shutter*-tripping device, adjustable to various time lapses.

Intervision: East European *television network*.

in the can: recorded *broadcast* material, complete and ready for *air*.

INTV—Association of Independent Television Stations—AITS: trade association representing nonaffiliated *stations*.

inventory: advertising *time* periods available for sale.

inverter: *DC* to *AC* conversion device. Compare: *rectifier*.

ion: atom with net *positive* charge due to *(negative)* electron loss.

ionization: atomic electron loss created by application of energy.

ionized: *positively* charged.

ionosphere: atmospheric band 25 to 250 miles high, "bouncing" *radio waves* (up to 30 *MHz)* back to earth for wider *signal* coverage. Compare: *troposphere*. See: *heaviside layer, skywave*.

ion trap: magnetic field/*aperture* passing electron *beams* but blocking *ions*.

IPA—Institute of Practitioners in Advertising: British agency group exchanging information and establishing general policy and industry standards. Compare: *AA, AAAA, Advertising Council, ANA, ISBA*.

ips—inches-per-second: *tape* travel *speed* measurement. Compare: *frames-per-second.*

IR—infrared: *wavelengths* immediately beyond red end of visible *spectrum.*

IRE—Institute of Radio Engineers: standards-setting professional organization.

iris: *wipe* (in or out) *effect,* generated by a circle.

iris—diaphragm: adjustable *aperture* of overlapping metal leaves controlling amount of light passing through *lens.* See: *stop.*

IRN—Independent Radio News: Britain's *commercial radio* newsgathering organization.

IRTS—International Radio & Television Society: membership group of *broadcast* professionals.

ISBA—Incorporated Society of British Advertisers: client group exchanging information and establishing general policy and industry standards. Compare: *AA, AAAA, Advertising Council, ANA, IPA.*

I signal ("in phase" signal): orange-to-*cyan chrominance sideband* (3.58 *MHz*) produced by *subcarrier modulation* phased 57° from *color burst* reference. See: *Q signal.* Compare: *Y signal.*

island: group of *television station film* and *slide projectors* feeding a *camera chain.*

island position: *commercial* isolated by *program* material from any other *television* advertising.

ISO—International Standards Organization: world engineering standards group. Compare: *ANSI, BSI, DIN.*

isolated: *camera* feeding *instant replay* action only.

Italia-1: Italian *television network.*

I.T. band: European *M & E.*

ITC Entertainment: major entertainment conglomerate.

ITCA: see: *IBA.*

ITFS—Instructional Television Fixed Service: 28 *FCC*-allocated (1971) 6-*MHz channels* (from 2,500–2,690 *MHz*) for *educational*/institutional use. Organized into seven groups (A,B,C,D,E,F,G) of five *channels* each; ten (E,F) groups reallocated 1983 for *commercial* use. 250 *transmitters* on air, 1988.

ITN—Independent Television News: Britain's jointly-*IBS*-owned *broadcast* newsgathering organization.

Itos: Six U. S. (1970–on) low-orbit weather *satellites.* Compare: *Essa, Tiros.*

ITS—International Teleproduction Society: worldwide trade group of *videotape production/post production* facilities (1986). See: *VPA.*

ITU—International Telecommunications Union: established 1865; now a specialized United Nations agency coordinating international electronic communications.

IUS—inertial upper stage: *shuttle orbiter's* spring-loaded space-launch system for *LEO communications satellites*.

J

jack: female plug receptacle for male *input/output circuit plug* of *audio* or *video* device. Standard sizes: phone (¼''); small phone (5.23mm); mini (3.6mm); micro (2.5mm).

jack box: single-plug/multiple-receptacle device.

jackfield: in Britain, temporary *circuit connectors,* often replaced by *switcher.*

Jackson: *(payola)* $20 bill.

Jackson (Richard) distance: *Philips* research scientist's hypothetical U.K. 3 m. (9.8 ft.) *viewer-to-screen* distance. Compare: *Lechner distance.*

jack tube—polecat: telescopic *luminaire* support braced between walls.

jaggies: undesirable jagged edge on *computer-generated* type character. See: *aliasing, stair steps.* Compare: *antialiasing.*

jam: *film camera* pile-up. See: *bird's nest, buckle.*

jamming: extraneous *signal* imposed on operating *radio frequency;* makes original *signal* unlistenable.

jazz: popular music genre encompassing disparate styles—bebop, big band jazz, Dixieland, hard bop, jazz rock, modern jazz, swing, third stream, etc. Also: **all-jazz:** popular music *radio station format.*

JC Sat-1: Japanese *Arianespace*-launched *communications satellite* (1989).

jelly: in Britain, translucent celluloid-like *filter* to alter color characteristics of a light source. See: *color media.*

jenny: power *generator.*

jib: in Britain, cantilevered camera *mount* of varying size and length.

Jicrar—Joint Industry Committee for Radio Audience Research: British *AGB* group compiling weekly radio audience reports. Compare: *Jictar, Radar*.

Jictar—Joint Industry Committee for Television Advertising Research: British *AGB* group compiling weekly television audience reports. Compare: *Jicrar*.

jingle: rhymed advertising *copy* set to music.

jitter: small, rapid *signal amplitude* or *phase* instability.

jog: *frame*-by-*frame videotape* movement during *helical scan editing*.

jogger: control for above movement.

Johnson noise: see: *random noise*.

joiner: in Britain, device for accurately *splicing edited film frames* with transparent tape or *cement*.

Jones plug: polarized multi*connector*.

joystick: vertical hand lever positioning/controlling remote equipment.

judder: in Britain, violent vertical *picture* unsteadiness.

judgment sample: research units subjectively selected for statistical projection.

juice: electric *current*.

jump cut: poor *edit* of interrupted subject movement. See: *frame cut*. Compare: *jump out, match cut*.

jumper: power *cable* extension.

jump out: remove extraneous *frames* within scene without evidence. Compare: *frame cut, jump cut*.

junction box: portable *set terminal* for power *cables*. See: *spider*.

junior: 2,000 *W spotlight*. Also called *two* or *2K*. Compare: *senior*.

junk: inoperative *satellites* still in orbit. Also: Garbled *signals*/data.

junk—dump: destroy.

junket: expense-paid trip exchanged for media publicity. See: *freebie*. Compare: *payola, plugola*.

junkfax: direct mail solicitation by *facsimile*.

justify: set type lines of equal length.

JVC—Japan Victor Corporation: major Japanese electronics manufacturer owned mainly by Matsushita..

J. Walter Thompson: one of seven major (1987 gross *billings* between $3 and $5 billion) worldwide *advertising agencies*.

K

K: see: *kilowatt*. Also: 1,000. Also: west-of-Mississippi station *call letter* prefix.

°K—degrees Kelvin: measurement of light source *color temperature*. 0 °K is −273.15°C; each °K = 1°C.

Ka-band: hybrid *C-band/Ku-band satellite transmission frequency*.

Kahn sideband: Kahn Communications *AM stereo* system. Compare: *C-Quam*.

KB: *kilobytes*.

K-band: 20/30 *GHz satellite transmission frequency*. Compare: *C-band, Ka-band, Ku-band, S-band*.

KDKA: early U.S. commercial *broadcasting station* (Pittsburgh, November 1920).

Kem: horizontal *film-and-sound editing machine*. See: *Steenbeck*. Compare: *Moviola*.

kern: eliminate optical gaps in typographic letter spacing.

key: *insert* one screen image into another. See: *chromakey, matte*. Also: Lead *crew* member.

key in: *matte* an image electronically. See: *plate*.

key (light): apparent principal light source, modeling a subject with shadows and form; usually a single front *spotlight* (placed first). Compare: *ambient, fill light, backlight, rimlight*.

key number: in Britain, multidigit identification number applied on each foot of *negative raw stock*.

keypad: device transmitting instructions to *computer, video disk player microprocessor,* or interactive *cable link.*

keys: important change-of-action drawings in *film animation* sequence.

key stations: *input* stations on multiple-user *computer* system.

keystone: *image distortion* caused by improper *projector*-to-*screen* angle.

kicker: light striking back and side of subject. Compare: *key.*

kideo: children's *VCR cassette/video disk* programming.

kidvid: television *programming* for children.

kill: extinguish or eliminate.

kilobaud: 1,000 *bits* per second.

kilobyte: 1,000 *bytes* (8,000 *bits*) of *computer* information.

kilocycle—kC: *frequency* unit equal to 1,000 *cycles-per-second;* now called *kilohertz (kH).*

kilogram: weight of specific cylinder of platinum-iridium alloy retained at International Bureau of Weights and Measures in Paris; 2.2046 pounds.

kilohertz—kH—kHz: (after discoverer of electromagnetic or *radio* waves) one thousand *hertz. AM radio* operates from 550 to 1,600 *kHz (FM radio* operates in *MHz band).*

kilowatt—kW—K: 1,000 *watts.*

kinescope—kine: poor-quality direct *reversal b/w motion picture film recording* of television *tube picture,* first developed by Hartley and Ives in 1927. Also called *telerecording (TVR).*

kinetograph: *motion picture* strip *film* machine (Edison, 1889).

Kinetoscope (later **Cinématographe**): early *motion picture projector* (Lumière Brothers, 1895).

kit rental: employee compensation for personal equipment use.

klystrode: *UHF television transmitting tube,* combining *klystron* and *tetrode* features; *DC* power output varies with *video signal level.*

klystron: *vacuum tube* generating *ultra high-frequency radio waves.*

knee: characteristic shape of *image orthicon tube* light *pickup* curve.

knockout tab: easily-removed thin plastic "wing" on *audio* and *VHS video cassettes;* protective removal deactivates re-record capability. Compare: *record button.*

knuckle—clamping disk: adjustable *century stand* head, grooved to accept pipe *booms, flag* stems, etc.

Kodachrome: subtractive *16mm* Eastman Kodak *film* stock (Godowsky/Mannes, 1935).

Kodak Special: in Britain, simulated photography with a purposely-empty *camera*.

Kourou: *Arianespace ESA* European *satellite* launch area in French Guiana. Compare: *Balkonur, Cape Canaveral, Plesetsk.*

krypton-86: see: *meter.*

KTLA-TV: Los Angeles *superstation.*

KTUV-TV: Oakland *superstation.*

KTVT-TV: Fort Worth *superstation.*

Ku-band: 11/14 *GHz satellite transmission frequency* (not subject to *microwave interference,* requires no *FCC* clearance). Compare: *C-band, Ka-band, K-band, S-band.*

KW: see: *kilowatt.*

L

lab(oratory): facility for *developing/printing exposed film*.

lace—lace up: *thread film* in *projection path*.

La Cinq: private French *television channel* (1986).

lag—image retention: two (or more) *frame* ''ghosting'' behind fast-moving *television camera* subjects; caused by insufficient illumination (accentuated in low *field*-per-second *television* systems). Eliminated by *solid-state cameras*. See: *bias light*. Compare: *comet tail*.

lambert: light *reflectance* measurement unit = 1 *lumen* per cm^2.

lamp: light-producing device. Compare: *bulb*.

lamphouse: *film projector* light unit, with controls.

lamp lumens: total amount of light available from *lamp*.

landline: telephone or *cable transmission*.

land-mobile: *broadcast frequencies allocated* to *low-power* land installations or vehicle *transmission*.

Landsat (ERTS-1): *NASA* Earth Resources Technology *satellite* (1972) with two *camera* systems for imaging earth.

lantern slide: obsolete glass-mounted 3¼'' × 4'' positive *transparency*.

lap—lap dissolve: fade one *scene* into another.

lapel mike: *microphone* clipped to clothing, leaving performer's hands free. Compare: *lavalier, wireless mike*.

lap switch: imperceptible *dissolve* between two video *signals*, in about 15–20 *milliseconds*.

large scale integration—LSI: measure of *semiconductor* design complexity; up to 20,000 *circuits* on a single *silicon chip.* Compare: *MSI, SSI, VLSI.*

La Sept: French government cultural *television* service.

laser: (from *L*ight *A*mplification by *S*timulated *E*mission of *R*adiation) device generating long, narrow beam of visible electromagnetic *waves* (in *picosecond pulses*), from 80 to 1,000 *terahertz.* Ruby laser developed by Gould in 1957, based on (1917) Einstein theory. Also: *Videotape-to-film transfer* technique (using three laser beams, one for each color). Also: *Video disk recording* technique. See: *LaserVision, Vidtronics.*

LaserVision: *laser*-controlled optical *video disk* system (*Philips,* Pioneer, Magnavox). Compare: *CED, VHD.*

latent: *exposed* but un*developed film image.*

latitude: proper combinations of *shutter* speed and *lens aperture* to expose a particular *film emulsion* (faster *emulsions* permit wider latitudes).

laugh track: *prerecorded* joke response.

lavalier(e): *microphone* hung around the neck, leaving performer's hands free. Compare: *lapel mike, wireless mike.*

lavender: in Britain, colored-netting light *diffuser.* Also: Obsolete *positive film duping stock.*

lay: in Britain, *synchronize* track(s) to *picture.*

lay an egg: fail in performance.

lay back: *transfer mixed elements* to *master.* Compare: *lay down.*

lay down: *transfer* separate *elements* for *mixing.* Compare: *lay back.*

layout: *animator's* guide for plotting *film action.* Also: Editorial plan for *optical* cameraman.

lazy arm: in Britain, small *microphone boom.*

LBO—leveraged buyout: financial (*station*-trading) technique.

LCD—liquid crystal display: temporary visual presentation of stored information. Compare: *CRT, LED.*

LCU—large close-up: in Britain, performer's features. Also called *big close-up (BCU).*

L cut: *VTR* edit to new *picture* with no change in *audio* source.

lead: principal role; most prominent vocal/instrumental part. Also: Wired *connection.*

lead acid accumulator: rechargeable sulfuric acid *storage battery.* Compare: *dry cell.*

leader: non-projected identification and *audio* and/or *video* timing *countdown* at head of *film* or *videotape*, for exact cueing. See: *Academy leader, video leader*. Also: *Head* or *tail* portion of *film/tape* "leading" it from *feed* to *take-up reels* through *projection* or *playback path*. Also: Blank opaque film (black or white) spliced as spacing between sections of *workprint footage;* called *buildup* in Britain. Also: Paper or plastic *audio tape* "spacing."

lead-in: cast introduction to program *commercial*. Also: *Program* preceding.

Leading National Advertisers: see: *LNA*.

lead-out: *program* following.

lead oxide tube: improved *television camera pickup tube* with *lead oxide target*, offering high sensitivity, low *dark current*, 1-*gamma*, low *lag*, uniform *shading* and temperature stability. See: *Leddicon, Plumbicon*.

lead sheet: horizontal "bar graph" showing exact relationship of *animation* action to music beats and voice syllables. Also: All elements of musical composition *(melody, harmony, lyrics)* copied on single sheet of paper.

lead time: period between research and development and initial marketing.

leapfrogging: original *CATV* selection of distant (rather than local) programming; banned by *FCC*, 1972 (reversed 1979).

Learning Channel: see: *TLC*.

LEC—local exchange carrier: *telco* operating subsidiary.

Lechner (Bernard) distance: *RCA* research scientist's hypothetical U.S. 9 ft. *viewer-to-screen* distance. Compare: *Jackson distance*.

LED—light-emitting diode: temporary visual presentation of stored information via glowing crystal *chip semiconductor*. 150,000 *LEDs*—one for each *pixel*—can theoretically create a wall-size *television screen*. Compare: *CRT, LCD*.

Leddicon: improved *lead oxide television camera pickup tube*. Compare: *image orthicon, Newvicon, Plumbicon, Saticon, Trinicon, vidicon*.

leg: *network* interconnection between regional *affiliate stations*.

legs: commercial endurance.

lens: glass optical system focusing light rays to form an *image*.

lens adapter: *camera* device permitting easy *lens* interchange.

lens cap: protective dust (and light) cover. See: *cap up*.

lens extender: device to hold *lens* away from *camera* for *close-up* photography. See: *diopter lens, extension tube, proxar*.

lens hood: tunnel-shaped camera attachment blocking extraneous light sources. See: *matte box*.

lens prism: multiple-*image* attachment.

lens speed: light transmission capability (function of *focal length* to diameter); *faster lenses* = lower *f-stop* numbers.

lens turret: old rotatable *television camera mount* holding up to five *lenses;* obsoleted by *zoom lens.*

lenticular: metallized *projection screen,* embossed with cuplike projections for bright viewing over wide horizontal and narrow vertical angles. Compare: *glass bead, matte.*

LEO: any (retrievable by *shuttle orbiter*) *communications satellite* in Low Earth Orbit—150–500 mile altitude, circling earth every 90 minutes. Compare: *GEO.*

lettering safety: *picture tube* area within which *transmitted titling* is safely clear of *mask* on even slightly *overscanned receivers.* Compare: *cutoff, picture safety.*

letter of adherence: document establishing contractual obligation of hiring *producer* to U.S. *talent* unions. See: *signatory.*

letter quality: *computer printer output* approximating typewriter or printed type.

level: *audio* or *video amplitude* or *intensity.* Also: *Rehearsal* test of that *intensity.*

level cut: see: *level sync.*

level distortion: improper change in *television picture* color *saturation* and *intensity.*

levels: four grades of *video disk* program design sophistication.

level sync(hronization): in Britain, *frame-to-frame synchronization* of *work picture/soundtrack,* with no allowance for *film pullup.* See: *cutting sync.*

lexicographer: harmless *drudge* that busies himself detailing the origin and signification of words.

library footage—stock shot: previously photographed *film footage* licensed for re-use. See: *scratch print.*

library music—stock music: previously *recorded* background music, licensed for re-use. See: *needle drop.* Compare: *original music.*

license: *FCC* authority to operate a *broadcast* facility for a fixed period; increased from three to five years, 1981. In Britain, permission from Minister of Posts and Communications to operate a *broadcast receiver* (1989: color, £65; b/w, £22). Also: Music performance permission.

LIF: see: *Lifetime Cablevision Network.*

Lifestyle: British *cable network.*

Lifetime Cabletelevision Network—LIF: Hearst/*ABC satellite/cable* programming service; erected from *Daytime* and *Cable Health Network* 1984.

lift: material from preceding or longer production. Also: *Cable subscription* cost increase from new programming/additional *tiering*.

lifter: *audio recorder* device removing *tape* from close *head* contact during *fast forward* or *rewind*.

light: visible electromagnetic radiant energy at *wavelengths* between 400 and 750 *millimicrons*.

light bearding—edge beat—twinkle: edge twinkling during sharp *video* transitions.

light box: illuminated translucent (rotating) desk for preparing *animation* artwork. Also: Device for viewing photographic *transparencies.*

light bridge: walkway over *grid*. Called *gantry* in Britain.

light emitting diode: see: *LED*.

light grid: see: *grid*.

lighting: controlled illumination. Compare: *natural light*.

lighting cameraman: in Britain, chief camera technician who determines a *shot's* visual components.

light level: illumination intensity, measured in *candelas*.

light meter—exposure meter: *photoelectric cell* device in various formats, measuring direct or reflected illumination intensity in *candelas*.

lightning stick: hand-operated *arc* light, producing bright flashes.

light pen: photosensitive pointer reacting directly with *CRT* surface, replacing *computer* keyboard control.

light plot: *luminaire* placement plan. Compare: *floor plan, prop plot*.

light-struck: film *footage* inadvertently ruined by *exposure* to light. Called *edge-fogged* in Britain.

light valve: *photoelectric cell* converting electrical *signals* into fluctuations of beam of light, and vice versa. See: *sound head*.

lily: standard color swatch test chart for precise *film printing* control; similar to *television's color bars*. Compare: *china girl*.

limbo: photographic background with no visual frame of reference. See: *noseam, cyc*. Compare: *set*.

limited animation: *frame*-at-a-time *cinematography* of two-dimensional material with slightly altering subject and/or *camera* movement. *Projection* at *speed* (24 *fps*) gives illusion of actual motion. See: *animation*. Compare: *stop motion*.

limiter: device suppressing excessive *signal levels*. See: *compression*.

limiting resolution: perceivable number of *test pattern* horizontal lines.

limpet—sucker: in Britain, rubber suction cup temporarily attaching equipment to any smooth surface.

line: individual *electron beam sweep* across *camera target* or *picture tube* (in 52.3 *microseconds*); in the U.S., 525 such *sweeps* to each *frame*—in Britain, 625. See: *blanking interval*. Also: Material in *transmission*. See: *line check*. Also: Imaginary *tape/film camera* position boundary. See: *crossing the line*.

line amplifier: *amplifier feeding transmission circuit*.

linear: straight-line process. Compare: *non-linear*.

linear speed: *tape* movement past fixed point. Compare: *writing speed*.

linebeat—meshbeat: annoying *moiré* effect caused by certain aberrant linear characteristics of *image orthicon pickup tubes* and *color television picture tubes*. Also caused by horizontal (subject) patterns.

line check: off-the-*line* copy of *air* material prior to *transmission*. Compare: *air check*.

line cord—power cord: electric supply wires.

line feed: *remote signal* transmitted by *cable*.

line frequency: number of horizontal *television frame scans* per second; nominally more than 15,000.

line monitor: *control room monitor* showing *on-air* material. Compare: *preview*.

line-of-sight: high-band *transmission* (such as *television* and *FM*) to *receivers* lying between *transmitting antenna* and its horizon.

line-rate noise: periodic horizontal *television signal interference* occurring at a *frequency* near the *video* line rate (*NTSC* = 15,735 *Hz*). See: *S/N*.

line test: in Britain, rough initial *animation* execution, photographed to check final movement.

line up: adjust proper relationship of elements: *soundtracks,* camera *signals,* etc. Also: 1,000-*Hz audio signal*.

lineup: listing of *stations* carrying program on live or delayed basis.

link: connection.

linkman: in Britain, *documentary*/news presenter or *compere*.

lippy: in Britain, lipstick.

lip sync(hronization): simultaneous *recording* and photography of *on-camera* speaker (or other sound source); crucial during facial *close-up*. Lip sync can be added after *silent* photography by *dubbing* against picture. Also: Mouthing words to *pre-recorded audio* (such as a song). Compare: *wild track*.

liquid gate—wet gate: *printing* process placing tetrachlorethylene coating solution on *negative film* to minimize surface defects.

lissajous pattern: visual *oscilloscope* comparison of *frequency* and sine wave.

live: *broadcast* of something actually happening; not a *recording*. Also: In active use. Also: With *acoustical reverberation*. Compare: *dead*.

live action: normal *motion picture* camera photography.

live announcer: announcer, usually local, adding *tag* to *recorded commercial* message.

live end: studio area of highest sound reflection. Compare: *dead end*.

live fade: sound reduction by studio performer. Compare: *board fade*.

live-on-tape: television *program recorded* to length in *real time*, without pause or later *editing*.

live tag: local *commercial* information (retail store name, price, etc.) at end of *recorded broadcast* advertisement.

LLTV—low-light television: *closed-circuit* systems operating below 0.5 *lumens*/ft^2.

LMCC—Land–Mobile Communications Council: trade association monitoring transmission *spectrum allocation* and use.

LNA: *earth station low-noise satellite signal amplifier*. See: *buttonhook, Cassegrain, dish, prime focus*. Also: **LNA—Leading National Advertisers:** business service reporting *media* activity.

LO—local origination: *cable* community programming.

LOA—local oscillator attachment: *peoplemeter recording/transmitting* device.

load: equipment power consumption. Also: Fill *camera magazine* with *film; recorder* with *tape*.

load in: bring production materials onto *set*. Compare: *strike*.

local: *programming*/advertising generated within *broadcast station's coverage* area. Compare: *network*.

local access: *cable channel(s)* available for public programming (including "blue" material), presumably demonstrating redeeming social communication values.

local advertiser: single-market *client*, usually retail establishment.

local I.D.: local "tag" sponsorship at tail of national *commercial*.

location: non-*studio* photographic site, usually a *background;* avoids *set* construction.

location fee: payment for use of *location* and facilities. Called *facilities fee* in Britain.

location scout—survey: *pre-production* assessment of proposed *remote* broadcast site. Called *recce* or *reccy* (for *reconnaissance*) in Britain.

locked off: see: *tied off.*

lock groove: *phonograph record* run-out.

Loews, Inc.: hotel/*broadcasting* conglomerate. See: *CBS.*

log: *FCC*-required *program,* technical and maintenance record of *station's* daily *broadcast* performance. Compare: *affidavit.*

logo—logotype: concise graphic design, usually incorporating manufacturer's name.

long: *program* material running beyond allotted time. Compare: *short.*

long day: overtime *filming/taping* (beyond eight hours on East Coast; ten on West).

long lens: optical system making distant objects appear near. Called *long focus* in Britain. See: *telephoto.* Compare: *diopter lens.*

Long March: Chinese *satellite*-launching rocket.

long playing—LP: see: *33-1/3 rpm.*

long skip: *transmission signal* multi-reflection (up to 8,000 miles). See: *skip effect.* Compare: *short skip.*

long wave—radio wave: *electromagnetic radiation* over 60 meters long, traveling in space at speed of light. Compare: *short wave.*

look angle: see: *EL.*

loop: length of *film* (or *tape) spliced head*-to-*tail* for continuous *projection* (or *playback*). Also: Purposely slack section of *film* between *projector picture gate* and *sound head,* absorbing shock of intermittent *claw* movement. See: *pullup.* Also: Circular *cable network.*

looping: *recording lip-synchronized* dialogue against existing *film* picture (and often over existing *sound*). (Called *dubbing* on East Coast.) Also: *Coax* termination *circuitry* minimizing *signal distortion.*

loose: camera subject *framing* with considerable top and side room. Compare: *tight.*

LOP—least objectionable program: theory regarding television *viewing* as default rather than design activity.

loran—location and range (system): (1940) navigation system; positioning based on *radio signals* from two known locations. Covers only 10% of earth's surface. Compare: *GPS.*

Lorimar-Telepictures Corporation: major entertainment conglomerate.

lose the light: *control room* switch to another camera (indicated by *tally light*). Also: Have *exterior shooting* halted by darkness.

lose the loop: accidentally shorten the purposely slack section of *film* between *projector picture gate* and *sound head,* resulting in loss of *synchronization.* See: *pullup.*

loss: reduction in *signal* strength *level* during *distribution,* usually expressed in *db.*

lot: large outdoor *studio* area used for *set* construction and *filming.* See: *ext.* Compare: *sound stage.*

loud hailer: see: *bullhorn.*

loudness: subjective measure of *audio playback intensity* that also includes *high-* and *low-frequency equalization.* See: *Fletcher-Munson effect, volume.*

loudspeaker—speaker: originally, *acoustic* "horn" *amplifying* sound from *needle* on *record.* Now—device using *capacitor* plate movement in *transducing* electronic *signals* into *sound waves* (Rice and Kellogg, 1925). See: *tweeter, woofer.*

low band: original *videotape recording* technique utilizing the 5.5 to 6.5 *megahertz band* (with considerable *signal-to-noise ratio*); or, equipment for such *recording.* Compare: *high band.*

low boy: very low *high hat* camera *mount.*

low contrast filter: *lens* filter to mute colors, soften shadows.

low end: bottom of audible *frequency spectrum.* Compare: *high end.*

low-frequency distortion: television *distortion* below 15.75 *kHz.*

low gain—low level: *signal level* of one *millivolt* or less.

low impedance—low Z: 600 *ohms* or less. See: *impedance.*

low key: dim illumination emphasizing lower *gray scale* and producing few or no bright areas. Compare: *high key.*

lows—low frequencies: audible sound *frequencies* starting around 50 *hertz.* Compare: *highs, middle range.*

low Z: see: *Z.*

LP—long playing: see: *33-⅓ rpm.* Also: Greatly extended *VCR cassette record/playback* time mode. Compare: *EP, SP.*

LPFM—low power FM: local *FM* origination, utilizing *translator* equipment.

LPTV—low power television: lottery-allocated *FCC*-licensed "neighborhood" *stations,* ignoring full-power minimum 6 *MHz* geographical *channel* separation (first on air, Bimidji, Minn., 1982; applications frozen 1983). 93 VHF, 258 UHF stations on air, 1988.

LS—long shot: tiny performer(s) against vast *background.* Compare: *FS.*

L-Sat: British Aerospace/*EBU satellite* project, providing *DBS Ku-band* service (*L-Sat-1,* 1984; *L-Sat-2,* 1986).

L-Sat-ESA: cooperative Italian/*EBU* high-power *communications satellite* (1986).

LSI—large scale integration: measure of *semiconductor* design complexity; up to 20,000 *circuits* on a single *silicon chip*. See: *IC*. Compare: *MSI, SSI, VLSI*.

lube tube: epithet for PBS ("petroleum broadcasting system") programming. Compare: *boob tube*.

LUF: lowest usable *frequency* not absorbed in *ionosphere*.

lumen—LM: one *candela* (0.98 *foot candles*) of light covering a square foot of surface. See: *footlambert*.

lumens per watt—LPW—efficacy: number of *lumens* produced by light source for each *watt* of power applied.

luminaire: combination of support, *housing, lens, lamp (bulb)*, and power *connector* of light-producing device.

luminance: measure of light (formerly called *brightness*) leaving a surface in a particular direction, measured in *footlamberts* on a *gray scale*.

luminance noise: *luminance signal interference;* from *line frequency* to 5 *MHz*.

luminance signal: *NTSC* color "brightness" *signal (chrominance signal* supplies *hue* and *saturation*).

luminescence—fluorescence: production of light (and heat) by energy absorption. Compare: *phosphorescence*.

lux: (metric measurement) one *lumen* per square meter of surface; 10 *lux* equal approximately one *foot candle*. See: *candela*.

Lux-Sat: high-power Luxembourg *satellite* (1987).

LV—LaserVision: spinning *video disk* (900 rpm), "read" by *laser beam* reflected from photographically etched microscopic tracking pits; 625 tracks per mm (1972).

LVR—longitudinal video recording: lateral (not *quad, helical*) *videotape recording* technique; one 2-hour configuration utilizes 48 parallel bands of *video/audio signal* at 160 *i.p.s.*, reversing direction (in $\frac{1}{10}$ sec.) along an 8mm *videotape*.

LWT—London Weekend: one of British *IBA*'s *"Big Five"* (the *Central Companies*).

lyrics: words set to music.

M

Ma Bell: Bell System operating companies originally linked through American Telephone & Telegraph Company *(A.T.& T.)*.

MAC—multiplexed analog components: *chrominance—luminance—data* information.

macbeth: glass *filter* converting *tungsten* or *quartz* light source to daylight *color balance*. Also: *Fluorescent* lamp with that characteristic.

McCann-Erickson: one of seven major (1987 gross *billings* between $3 and $5 billion) worldwide *advertising agencies*.

McDonnell-Douglas: *Delta satellite* rocket construction corporation.

macky: in Britain, makeup.

M/A-COM: proprietary *satellite signal scrambling* system.

macro: *computer* program simplifying more elaborate programs.

macrolens: *close-up camera lens*.

made for: *film* made for *television broadcast*. Compare: *MOW*.

Madison Avenue: former location of most major New York *advertising agencies;* figuratively, the "ad game."

Madison Square Garden—MSG: *satellite/cable* sports programming supplier.

magazine: lightproof container feeding *loaded film raw stock* through *motion picture camera* and taking it up after *exposure;* usually 400 or 1,000-foot capacity.

magenta: purplish-red subtractive element of *color negative film;* complementary of (and producing) green. See: *cyan, yellow.*

Magicam: two-*camera computerized chromakey* process; one utilizes miniature *sets*. Compare: *camcorder, Minicam, Steadicam*.

magnetic head: one of three magnetic *gaps (erase head, record head, playback head)* in contact with *tape* in *audio recording*. Also: *Record/playback head*(s) in *videotape recording*.

magnetic recording: (principles developed by Poulsen, 1898) *video* and/or *audio recording* effected by changing polarity of microscopic particles of metallic *oxide* (on *film* or *tape base*) by passing them across modulated *magnetic* field *gap*.

mag(netic) stripe: clear *35mm sprocketed film* with continuous metallic *oxide* strip, *recording* a single (or mixed) *soundtrack*. Called *zonal stripe* in Britain. Compare: *full coat*.

magnetic track: magnetic oxide *soundtrack* on *composite film* (replacing *optical track*). Compare: *mag track*.

Magnetophon: original (German) magnetic *tape recorder* (AEG, 1934).

magnetostatic: field produced by stationary magnet. Compare: *electrostatic*.

Magnum—Vortex: *Titan*-launched U.S. military *satellites* electronically monitoring (since 1978) USSR military and diplomatic conversations.

MagNum—magnetoscope numerique: *EBU digital videotape recording format*.

mag track: loosely, magnetically *recorded soundtrack;* usually on *16mm* or *35mm film base*. Compare: *magnetic track*.

mainframe: *computer central processing unit (CPU)—input, memory, output,* power—serving multiple *terminals*.

mains: in Britain, electric power supply line.

maintained switch: *circuit* that continues its condition when actuating force is removed. Compare: *momentary switch*.

main title: major information on *program* content, at or near beginning of *telecast*. Compare: *credits, subtitle, title*.

major: large Hollywood *film* producer/distributor; Columbia, Disney (Buena Vista), MGM/UA, Paramount, 20th Century Fox, Universal, Warner Brothers. Compare: *mini-major*.

major sponsor: *advertiser* with most *commercials* in multiple-*sponsor* program. See: *alternate sponsorship*.

makegood: free *station rerun* of poorly *transmitted* or omitted *commercial*. Also: gratis advertising, adjusting failure to meet projected *program* audience levels.

makeup: performer's facial "paint 'n' powder," to balance lighting and *camera* requirements.

makeup artist: union craftsman applying above.

male: *connector* insert. Compare: *female.*

mandated: in Britain, *program* whose *transmission* is required of all *IBA* companies.

mandatory: disclaimer or other legally required information in body of *commercial* (usually *video,* in barely legible type). See: *title.*

M & E—music and (sound) effects: *film soundtracks* (separate or combined) of non-*dialog audio* elements, essential for foreign-language *dubbing,* etc.

Marconi, Guglielmo: Italian engineer; pioneered *radio signal transmission* (1895).

Marechal: proprietary French power-cable *connection* system.

Marisat: three-*satellite* shipping/naval communications satellite system operated by *Comsat General* (1976). Replaced by *Inmarsat.*

mark: piece of tape on *studio* floor accurately positioning (or repositioning) *scenery* or performer. See: *hit the mark, miss the mark.*

marketing: all aspects of product distribution and sales.

market profile: characteristics of individuals or *households* purchasing specific categories of brands, services, or products.

"mark it"—"sticks": cameraman's call for *synchronizing clapstick* action.

Markov Noise: see: *random noise.*

Marot-A,B: *ESA* maritime *communications satellite.*

married: in Britain, *composite (picture* with *optical soundtrack) film print.*

Martin-Marietta: *Titan* rocket/*satellite* construction corporation (Denver).

mask: modified rectangular frame with rounded corners, covering *television picture tube* edges. Also: Interchangeable metal cutout to vary size of *film projection gate.* Also: Opaque shape to screen *set* light. See: *flag, gobo.* Compare: *cutter, dot, finger.* Also: Cover unwanted *sound* with another.

mass eraser—bulk eraser—degausser: device demagnetizing all *recorded tape* on a *reel* without unspooling. Compare: *erase head.*

master: final edited *audio/videotape* material for replication. Compare: *dub, dupe, sub-master.* Also: Original *phonograph/video disk,* or molds therefrom. Also: Single *antenna* serving multiple *receivers.*

master control: *broadcast* facility control center. Called *CCR* (central control room) in Britain. Also: Control panel group *fader.*

mastering: *cutting* original *phonograph* or *video disk,* and molding it for reproduction.

master shot: complete *scene* sequence. See: *establishing shot.*

master/slave(s): *re-recording* system playing back *original tape* into *dubbing recorder(s).* Compare: *AC transfer, bifilar, dynamic duplication.*

match cut: *edit* to another *camera* position at identical action moment. Compare: *jump cut.*

match dissolve: *optical* to identical *camera* position.

matching—negative cutting: matching *film negative* material to *edited work print.* See: *pull negative.* Also: **matching:** *impedance alignment.*

matrix: *quadraphonic FM broadcast* and *recording/playback* system, encoding two extra *channels* atop two existing *stereo channels.* See: *SQ, QS.* Compare: *discrete.*

Matrix H: *BBC* compatible *(mono/stereo) quadraphonic broadcast* system.

Matsushita: major Japanese electronic manufacturer; parent company of *Panasonic* and *Quasar,* majority owner of *JVC.*

Matsushita M-II: ½'' replacement for *Type C videotape recording format.*

matte—matteing: optical or electronic insertion of an image into a selected background. See: *chromakey.* Compare: *rotoscope.* Also: **matte:** dull or diffuse, compared to mirrorlike.

matte—matte white: dull-surfaced *projection screen* for even viewing over wide angles. Compare: *glass bead, lenticular.*

matte box: squarish *lens hood* device used for sunshade and wide variety of in-the-camera *optical effects.*

matteing amplifier: television *special effects generator (SEG).*

matteing out: *optically* eliminating an element in the *film frame.*

matte ride: undesirable outlines around *matted* element. See: *ringing.*

MATV—master antenna television system: *antenna* arrangement serving concentration of television *receivers.* Compare: *CATV.* See: *SMATV.*

Mavica: *Sony* video-assisted still camera system.

MAX—Cinemax: *satellite/cable* program service.

maxipay: *cable* service with more than eight hours of programming per day. Compare: *minipay.*

Maxwell: see: *Clerk-Maxwell, James.*

Mayflower Doctrine: 1941 *FCC* decision (reversed eight years later) proscribing *broadcast station* "editorializing."

MB—megabyte: 1,024 *kilobytes.*

MBSA—multiple beam satellite antenna: *earth station* capable of receiving several *satellite signals.*

MC—master of ceremonies: show host. Called *compere* in Britain. Compare: *announcer, narrator.* Also: **MC:** *megacycle.*

MCA—Music Corporation of America: major entertainment conglomerate.

MCI Communications: *communications satellite* operator. See: *SBS.*

MCS—Multichannel Sound Subcommittee: *EIA* group evaluating proposed *television stereo* systems.

MCTV—multichannel television—wireless cable: mixed 2 *GHz microwave* and *cable* instructional/operational fixed service *transmission;* eliminates street *franchise* requirements.

MCU—medium close-up: performers waist-up. Called *close shot (CS)* in Britain. Compare: *MS, CU.*

MD—music director: local *station* executive supervising music selection.

MDR—magnetic disk recorder: early German (156 rpm) *video disk* system (Bogen).

MDS—multipoint distribution service: *FCC*-authorized *common carrier line-of-sight transmission* for *television* program (and business information) distribution.

ME—metal evaporated: *videotape* manufacturing process. Compare: *MP.*

meal penalty: contractual compensation to union *crew* for delayed production lunch or dinner.

media (department): *advertising agency* division recommending *client* purchase of *broadcast time* periods. See: *campaign, schedule, time buyer.*

Media Access Project: Washington public interest lobby.

media buyer: see: *time buyer.*

media market: geographic area defined by *coverage* pattern of market's media (usually television).

media mix: selective use of several *media* in single *campaign.*

media service—buying service: firm purchasing *time* directly for *advertisers.* See: *time buyer.*

medium: means of communicating advertising messages.

medium scale integration—MSI: measure of *semiconductor* design complexity; number of *circuits* on single *silicon chip.* See: *IC.* Compare: *LSI, SSI, VLSI.*

medium wave: *amplitude modulation radio broadcasting.*

megabit: one-millionth *bit.*

megacycle—MC: *frequency* unit equal to 1 million *cycles per second;* now called *megahertz (MHz).*

megahertz—MH—MHz: (after discoverer of electromagnetic or *radio* waves) one million *hertz*. *FM radio* operates from 88 to 108 *MHz* (*AM radio* operates in *kHz band*).

megawatt—MW: one million *watts;* 1,000 *kW.*

melodic range: highest to lowest notes of particular *melody.*

melody: basic sequence of musical notes; for copyright purposes, eight or more *bars.* See: *harmony.*

memory: stored *computer* information; specifically, *semiconductor chip storing computer-bit* information. See: *RAM, ROM.*

menu: *computer* "table of contents" display.

MEOV—Maximum Expected Operating Values: theoretical *broadcast signal transmission* standards.

merchandising: promotional activities complementing product advertising; often provided by media.

MERPS—multi-event record/playback system: *broadcast* multi-*cassette playback* equipment.

meshbeat—linebeat: annoying *moiré* effect caused by certain aberrant linear characteristics of *image orthicon pickup tubes* and *color television picture tubes.* Also caused by horizontal (subject) patterns.

metal halide—MH: *AC*-only mercury arc lamp. See: *halide.*

Meteosat-1,2: *ESA* meteorological *satellites.*

meter: *television* audience research device installed in "sample" homes to measure/record program preference. See: *Audimeter, peoplemeter, SIA.* Also: Instrument measuring level of service or consumption. See: *v.i. meter.* Also: 1,650,763.73 *wavelengths* in vacuum of orange-red spectrum line of *krypton-86.*

metro: standard metropolitan statistical area as defined by U.S. Office of Management and Budget; contiguous counties containing at least one city with 50,000 population. Smallest *ARB* (*radio*) audience research market classification. Compare: *ADI, TSA.*

Metropole TV: private French *television channel.*

Mev: 1 million electron-*volts.* Compare: *Gev.*

MGM/UA—Metro-Goldwyn-Mayer/United Artists: major entertainment conglomerate.

mho: (*ohm* spelled backwards) measurement of admittance (reciprocal of *impedance*).

MHz: see: megahertz.

micro cassette: miniature *audio cassette,* used primarily for dictation. See: *mini cassette.*

microgroove: narrow V-shaped track (approximately 200 per inch) on *long-playing* or *extended play phonograph disk.*

micron: one-millionth *meter;* 40-millionths inch. Equal to 10,000 *ångströms.*

microphone—mike—mic: device *transducing sound waves* into electrical impulses (Berliner, 1878). See: *cardioid, ceramic, condenser, crystal, dynamic, eightball, lavalier, ribbon, rifle.*

microphone noise: *audio frequency* equipment noise caused by mechanical shock or vibration.

microprocessor: tiny *semiconductor chip* containing more than 5,000 *transistors.* See: *integrated circuit.*

microsecond: one-millionth second.

micro video: see: *camcorder.*

microwave: line-of-sight (usually five miles or more) cableless system relaying *broadcast signals* on *wavelengths* of less than one *meter.* First used by Pope Pius XII (15 miles in 1933). U.S. transcontinental *relay* installed 1951. Compare: *coaxial cable, satellite.*

mid-bass: standard *audio frequency* range (60–240 *Hz*). Compare: *bass, mid-range, mid-treble, treble.*

MIDI—musical instrument digital interface: direct electronic equipment connection.

mid-range: standard *audio frequency* range (240–1,000 *Hz*). Compare: *bass, mid-bass, mid-treble, treble.*

midshot: in Britain, performer's whole body in *frame.*

mid-treble: standard *audio frequency* range (1,000–3,500 *Hz*). Compare: *bass, mid-bass, mid-range, treble.*

mil: one-thousandth inch.

military time: 24-hour clock time. See: *GMT, Greenwich time.*

milk sweep: small J-shaped translucent white *scenery* piece, eliminating visual frame of reference. See: *limbo.* Compare: *cyc, no-seam.*

millimicron: one twenty-five-millionth inch.

millisecond: one-thousandth second.

millivolt: one-thousandth *volt.*

mini-brute—nine light: nine grouped 650 *W tungsten-halogen* bulbs.

minicam: *hand-held ENG camera.* Compare: *camcorder, Magicam, Steadicam.*

mini cassette: miniature *audio cassette,* used primarily for dictation. See: *micro cassette.*

mini-hub: *fiber optic transmission cable* substation.

mini-major: secondary Hollywood *film* producer/distributor; Embassy, Orion, Tri-Star. Compare: *major*.

minimum focus: shortest distance at which *lens* is focusable.

minipay: *cable* service with less than eight hours programming per day.

miniseries: single-plot *television* program, split into daily or weekly segments. Compare: *series*.

Minitel: (1987) French Télécom *alphanumeric teletext* information/"lonely hearts" service.

minute: *60-second commercial* message *(television film* allows only 58-second *audio.* See: *pullup).* Compare: *30, split-30, 15, 10.*

MIP–TV—Marché Internationale des Programmes de Télévision: annual Cannes *television* programming exposition.

Mirage: *computerized DVE* system modifying/manipulating *video signals.* Compare: *ADO, Quantel.*

mired—micro reciprocal degree: 1,000,000 divided by appropriate *Kelvin* value, for more workable *color temperature* rating. See: *decamired.*

mirror: plane or curved glass or metal reflective device, concentrating or distributing light *waves.* See: *front surface, back surface.*

mirror ball: reflecting globe covered with tiny mirrored chips; essential to dance marathon photography.

mirror shot: doubling *shot* depth by pointing *camera* at large mirror. Also useful for overhead *POVs.*

mirror shutter: *reflex shutter* system enabling *camera operator* to view *shot* in progress. Compare: *beam splitter, intermittent shutter.*

mispointing: misaligned *satellite/earth station signal loss.*

miss the mark: move to predetermined *set* point—and miss. Compare: *hit the mark.*

Mitchell: workhorse *35mm motion picture camera.* Most common model (non-*reflex) BNC.*

Mitsubishi: major Japanese electronics manufacturer.

mix: session in *re-recording studio.* See: *audio mix.* Also: To *dissolve.* Also: Optimized media selection.

mixed feed: *television camera scene* lineup technique; one camera's *output* is fed into another's *viewfinder.*

mixer: engineer handling *mix* control *console.* Called *recordist* in Britain. Also: The *audio* or *video mixing console* itself.

mixing studio: *recording* facility equipped to electronically combine two or more *audio* elements into single final *sound-track,* usually against picture *projection.* Compare: *worldize.*

mm—millimeter: one-thousandth meter.

MMDS—multichannel multipoint distribution service: *on-air/cable* programming operation. See: *MCTV.*

MNA—multi-network area: *Nielsen*'s group of 30 major markets where programs of all three *networks* can be received over local *television stations.*

mnemonic: easily recalled image or word representing difficult-to-recall image(s) or word(s).

mobile unit: vehicle or equipment *recording/transmitting television signals* from *location.*

mob scene: group of actors acting as crowd.

mockup: imitative section of a large scenic *prop,* built full scale rather than in miniature.

mode: electronic setting activating specific *circuit(s).*

modeling—counter key: illumination directly opposite to *key light.*

model sheet: *animation* cartoon drawings showing character in various poses See: *animation designer.*

modem—modulator/demodulator—acoustic coupler: telephone *terminals* translating (and re-translating) *binary computer* data into *analog tones* for voice line, *transmission* between *peripherals.* See: *fascimile.*

modulate: vary amplitude, *frequency,* or *phase of carrier* wave with *signal.* Compare: *unmodulated.* Also: Convert *digital signal* to *analog.* Compare: *demodulate.*

modulation: recorded *analog audio signal* patterns; called *mods* in Britain. Also: Musical change of key.

modulator/demodulator: see: *modem.*

module: interchangeable electronic component.

moiré: undesirable optical effect caused by one set of closely spaced lines improperly imposed over another. In *television, picture* disturbance caused by *interference* beats of similar *frequencies.*

mole: amount of a substance containing as many elementary units (atoms, molecules, ions, electrons, *photons,* etc.) as there are carbon atoms in 0.012 *kilograms* of carbon-12.

Molevator: 6- to 14-ft.-high power-operated extensible stand for *brutes* and other large *spotlights.*

Molinya: USSR domestic *communications satellites* in *Orbita transmission* program (1965); four non*geosynchronous satellites,* 25,000 miles high, cover Soviet polar areas.

momentary switch: *circuit* reversion to original condition when actuating force is removed. Compare: *maintained switch.*

monaural: single sound source intended for both ears. Compare: *binaural.*

monitor: *television receiver* (often without *channel* selector or *audio* components) connected to *transmission* source by wire. Also: To check *recording* in progress.

mono: see: *monophonic.*

monochromatic: tones or gradations of a single color or *hue.*

monochrome: black, grays, and white.

monochrome transmission: *signal* wave representing *brightness* components of a *television picture* but not its *color (chrominance)* values.

mono conversion: electronically converting *color* image to *black-and-white.*

monophonic: single-channel ¼″ *audio tape recording, full- or half-track.*

monopod: single-leg camera support.

montage: visual blending of several *scenes.* Also: In Europe, the *film editing* process (from Fr. *monter* = to set up). Also: **Montage:** *computerized effects* storage system for *videotape editing* convenience.

Montreux: biannual Swiss International Television Symposium and Technical Exposition.

MOR—middle of the road: popular music *radio station* hit *format,* avoiding stylistic extremities.

Morse code: "dot-dash" *radiotelegraphy* (letter symbols developed 1838 by telegraph inventor).

MOS—mit-out sound: *silent film* shooting mythically requested by Hollywood German Refugee director. Also: Metal oxide *semiconductor* image-sensing *chip.* Compare: *CCD.*

mosaic: *dve* reduction of screen image to hundreds of tiny colored squares. See: *pixellization.* Compare: *posterization.*

mosaic—target: light-sensitive *camera pickup tube* surface (over 350,000 *photosensitive* dots) *scanned* by *electron beam.*

motif: short sequence of notes characterizing musical theme.

motion control: *computerized camera* movement on various axes. See: *Skycam.*

motion picture: varying-width (measured in *mm*'s) band of flexible transparent sequential-image *film,* punched with *sprocket holes* for advancement through *projector.* Makes possible connected series of *still* images, presenting illusion of movement on *screen* (or *television tube*).

motorboating: rapid succession of *audio* "pops"; usually caused by *film sprocket hole* misalignment over *projector sound drum.*

mount: *camera lens* or *luminaire socket.* Also: *Earth station* support.

mouse: hand-operated *computer cursor* positioning device.

Moviecam: *35mm motion picture camera.*

Movie Channel: see: *TMC.*

Movietime: *satellite/cable* programming service (1987) with *MSO* majority interests.

Moviola: horizontal/vertical *film-* and *sound-editing* machine. Compare: *Kem, Steenbeck.*

MOW—movie of the week: theatrical *motion picture* broadcast on *television.* Compare: *made for.*

MP—metal particle: *videotape* manufacturing process. Compare: *ME.*

MPA: multiple product *television commercial.*

MPPAA—Motion Picture Association of America: trade association of *motion picture* producers and distributors.

mps: miles per second.

MRA—metro rating area: *ARB* audience research classification of U.S. metropolitan markets.

MS—medium shot: performer's whole body in *frame.* Also called *midshot* in Britain. Compare: *FS, MCU.*

MSG: see: *Madison Square Garden.*

MSI—medium scale integration: measure of *semiconductor* design complexity; number of *circuits* on a single *silicon chip.* Compare: *IC, LSI, SSI, VLSI.*

MSO: firm operating multiple *cable* systems.

MTBF—mean time between failures: random equipment reliability measurement.

MTS—multichannel television sound: stereo sound transmission.

MTV—Music Television Network: Viacom music video satellite/cable programming service. Also: **MTV—Magyar Televizio:** Hungarian government *television* network.

MTV-Europe: London-based European *satellite/cable* programming service.

MTV/YLE-I, II: Finnish government *television networks.*

M-II: *Matsushita ½" studio/location video recording format.* See: Compare: *Type C.*

muddy: lacking adequate *signal* information vs. *noise.*

mug: facially overreact.

multi-camera: simultaneous *filming/taping* from two or more *camera* positions.

Multichannel News: weekly *broadcast* industry newspaper.

multichannel television: see: *MCTV*.

multievent record/playback system—MERPS: *broadcast* multi*cassette play-back* equipment.

multipath: *broadcast signal* reflection from tall objects; results in *static*, fading, and cancellation. See: *ghost*.

multiplane: layered *cel animation* technique.

multiple beam satellite antenna: see: *MBSA*.

multiple image: *frame* composed of several different picture sources.

multiple interference: cancelled sound *frequencies* from two *microphones* in close proximity.

multiple sub-Nyquist encoding: see: *MUSE*.

multiplexed analog components: see: *MAC*.

multiplexer—film chain: *television master control room* mirror/prism device; allows selective *projection* of *film* or *slide* material into *camera chain*.

multiplexing—duplexing: accepting two different *signals* for *transmission* in one or both directions on single *conductor*.

multi-plug: *connector* feeding (press conference/public speech) *signal* to several *pickups*.

multipoint distribution service: see: *MDS*.

multitap: passive device feeding distributed *cable signal* to subscriber's *dropline*.

municipal access: see: *local access*.

Muppets: *Jim Henson*'s *television* puppet characters. See: *CTW, Sesame Street*.

MUSE—multiple sub-Nyquist encoding: operational *NHK* 1,125 *lines*/60 *Hz ATV/HDTV* system with 9 *MHz* bandwidth, 2:1 *interlace*, 16:9 *aspect ratio*. Compare: *Del Rey, Farjouda, NBC, NYIT*.

MUSE-6—narrow MUSE: 6 *MHz MUSE* system adaptated to *NTSC*.

MUSE-9: 9 *MHz MUSE* system *transmitting* to 6 *MHz NTSC receivers;* theoretically adaptable to *cable transmission*.

Museum of Broadcast Communications: Chicago *broadcast* history archive.

Museum of Broadcasting: New York City *broadcast* history archive.

Music Box/Super Channel: British *cable network*.

Music Channel—MTV: *Warner/Amex music video satellite/cable* programming service.

music video—video: *video* scenes edited to popular music song track.

Must Carry I: *FCC* ruling requiring *cable transmission* of all local *television broadcast signals* within 120-mile radius (vacated by Federal Appeals Court 1985 as First Amendment violation). See: *Quincy*.

Must Carry II: compromise *FCC* ruling requiring *cable transmission* by 20 + *channel* systems of all local television broadcast signals within 50-mile radius; expires 1991. See: *A/B switch*.

mute: in Britain, *silent film*.

Mutoscope: early *motion picture* "peepshow" viewer (Casler, 1894).

Mutual Broadcasting System, Inc.: U.S. *radio* (news) *network;* 700 + *affiliates*.

M-wrap: *VHS recording/playback head videotape* configuration.

N

NAB—National Association of Broadcasters: standard-setting *broadcast station* organization. Compare: *AA, AAAA, Advertising Council, ANA, IPA, ISBA*.

NAB Code: former minimum programming and advertising standards for *NARTB* member *stations: radio* = 18 *commercial* minutes per hour; *television* = 16 *commercial* minutes per hour. Suspended by U.S. district court, 1984.

NAB curve: *audio playback equalization* standard.

NABET—National Association of Broadcast Employees and Technicians: *broadcast* technicians' union.

NAC: *Nielsen* 13-week written *diary*. See: *NTI*.

nadgers: in Britain, equipment trouble.

NAEB—National Association of Educational Broadcasters: educational *station* operators' membership organization.

naff—US: in Britain, useless, no good. Compare: *NG*.

Nagra: high-quality portable ¼" *audio tape recorder* for *location production*.

nanosecond: one-billionth (i.e., one-thousand-millionth) second.

NAPTE—National Association of Television Program Executives: trade organization of program suppliers/purchasers.

NAPTS—National Association of Public Television Stations: membership organization of *noncommercial stations*.

NARB—National Advertising Review Board: self-regulatory industry group.

narrator: "neutral" *on-* or *off-camera* performer telling *program* story. Called *commentator* in Britain. Compare: *announcer, MC.*

narrowband: *rf transmission* on minimal number of *frequencies.* See: *bandwidth.*

narrowcast: public *signal transmission* by any other mass medium than *broadcast.* Also: **narrowcasting:** targeting specific audience *demographics.*

narrow-gauge—substandard: *film* less than *35mm* wide.

NASA—National Aeronautics and Space Administration: government agency overseeing *communications satellite* program. See: *ATS-6.*

Nashville Network: Gaylord Broadcasting satellite/cable country music programming service (1983).

NATAS—National Academy of Television Arts and Sciences: trade membership organization bestowing program awards.

national: higher rate charged more-than-one-market advertisers by stations also offering *local retail rate.*

National ARBitron: audience survey technique utilizing mailed-in listening *diaries.* See: *ARB.* Compare: *Pulse.*

National Black Network: ethnic U.S. *radio network;* 94 *affiliates.* Compare: *BET.*

National Broadcasting Company: see: *NBC.*

National Exchange, Inc.: *communications satellite* operator. See: *SpotNet.*

National Public Radio: see: *NPR.*

NATPE—National Association of Television Program Executives: *broadcasting* trade organization of *program* supplier/purchasers.

NATTKE—National Association of Theatrical, Television and Kine Employees: in Britain, trade union representing studio *carpenters, prop* men, *grips, projectionists, wardrobe, makeup,* etc.

natural light: daylight. Compare: *lighting.*

Navstar: 13-*satellite* (1979) global navigation system; initial launch 1978. See: *GPS.*

NBC—National Broadcasting Company: U.S. *broadcasting conglomerate;* owned by *General Electric Company.* 207 *affiliates.* Occasionally known as "Nothing But Commercials." See: *Thirty Rock.* Also: Experimental *AT/HDTV* system. Compare: *Del Rey, Farjouda, MUSE, NYIT.*

NCGA—National Computer Graphics Association: industry membership organization.

NCTA—National Cable Television Association: *cable* system operators' membership organization.

NEC—Nippon Electric Company: major Japanese electronics manufacturer.

Nederland 1, 2, 3: Dutch government *television network.*

needle: *meter* dial indicator. Also: *Stylus* element of *phonograph* arm, *tracking record grooves.*

needle drop: single use of *licensed stock music* composition.

needletime: in Britain, *broadcasting recorded* music.

negative: *film* image or television *signal* with opposite tonal (and color) values to original subject material. Also: Lower electrical *potential.* Compare: *positive.*

negative cost: finished *film production* cost, before *release printing.*

negative cutting—pulling: matching *film negative* material to *edited work print.* Compare: *conform.*

negative transfer: (positive) *videotape* created from *film negative.* Compare: *positive transfer.*

nemo: early acronymically derived telephone company designation: *"not em-anating main office,"* hence any *remote* broadcast *signal* origination point. See: *pickup.*

net: metal or gauze *spotlight diffuser;* also called *lavender* in Britain. Also: A *network.*

NET—National Educational Television: *educational television programming* organization. See: *ETV, CPB, PBS.*

net rating points—NRP: total number of *rating points* for specific *television advertising schedule,* eliminating *duplicated* viewing. Compare: *gross rating points.*

net weekly circulation: audience survey estimate of unduplicated *households* viewing a *television station* for at least five consecutive minutes at least once a week.

network—net: one of three important entertainment/news/public affairs con-glomerates *(ABC, CBS, NBC),* supplying programming and advertising material to *affiliated* U.S. *broadcast stations.* Initial *network* develop-ment *(radio)* via telephone lines, 1922. Compare: *independent, local.* Also: *Station* interconnection to *broadcast* a program, or *cable* system for similar purpose. Also: *Computer interconnection.*

network feed: programming *transmitted* (usually from New York, Chicago, or Los Angeles) to *affiliate stations* across U.S. by *satellite, AT&T* cables, and *microwave* link. Compare: *bicycling, DB.*

networking: assembling program/*station lineup.*

neutral density filter—ND: *lens filter* reducing transmitted light without af-fecting color, *contrast,* or *definition.* Used on excessively illuminated subjects, such as exterior windows.

never-never: in Britain, consumer installment purchase of *radio/television* equipment.

New Age: avant-garde popular music *radio station format.*

Newhouse Broadcasting: major *MSO* (with between one and five million *subscribers,* 1988).

news block: extended news *programming.*

newscaster: reader/presenter of news items. Compare: *anchorman, commentator.*

Newvicon: improved *television camera pickup tube.* Compare: *image orthicon, Leddicon, Plumbicon, Saticon, Trinicon, vidicon.*

NG: no good!

NHK—Nippon Hoso Kyoka: Japan Broadcasting Corporation.

nibble: four *bits;* one-half *byte.*

niche strategy—segmentation: targeting specific audience in a market.

Nick at Night: *Nickelodeon* evening *transmission* for teenagers.

nickel-cadmium—NiCad: portable heavy-duty rechargeable *storage battery.* See: *power pack.*

Nickelodeon: *Warner/Amex/Viacom* children's *satellite/cable* programming service (1979).

(A.C.) Nielsen: *television* audience survey service utilizing *peoplemeters* (formerly *Audimeters)* to record viewing habits in U.S. sample homes; sold to Dun & Bradstreet, 1984. Publishes *NTI (Nielsen Television Index)*—biweekly *station*/program audience measurement. See: *SIA.* Compare: *AGB, ARB.*

nighttime: *broadcast time* period, 7:00–11:00 P.M.

NIK: see: *Nickelodeon.*

9 KHz: proposed separation standard between Western Hemisphere *AM broadcast frequency allocations.* See: *NRSC.* Compare: *10 KHz.*

nine light—mini-brute: nine grouped 650 *W tungsten-halogen lamps.*

976: *telco* exchange for sexually explicit message services.

nitrate: see: *base.*

nixie: *computer* light indicating electronic information.

NLRB—National Labor Relations Board: government agency overseeing union-management relations. See: *AFTRA, IATSE, IBEW, NABET, SAG, SEG.*

NOB—Nederlands Omroepproduktie Bedrijf: technical production arm of Dutch *broadcasting networks.*

nod shot—noddy: in Britain, cutaway shot of interviewer, to avoid *jump cut* of interviewee.

no fax: *rehearsal* without technical *facilities*.

noise: random energy generated by unwanted *voltages* within (or external to) electronic device, reducing its performance. See: *snow*.

noise bar: picture *breakup* on *helical scan videotape playback*, usually during *still framing*.

noise gate: *audio signal* switch, controlled by adjustable *level* detector.

non-air commercial: *broadcast advertising* message specially prepared (at lower *talent* fees) for various non-*broadcast* audience research techniques. See: *black box*.

non-commercial: *broadcasting* minus major *advertising* support; approximately 10% of all U.S. *radio stations*, 35% of all *television stations*.

non-compatibility: inability of one system to *retrieve* information stored by another. Compare: *compatibility, interface*.

non-composite: *video signal* lacking *synchronization* information. Compare: *composite*.

non-directional: *microphone* with uniform areas of sensitivity. Compare: *directional*.

non-duplication: *FCC* prohibition on identical *programming* over twin *AM/FM* facilities.

non-linear: sequencing in and out of order. Compare: *linear*.

non-segmented—single-scan: *"Type C"* 1" *videotape format (Ampex, Sony) recording* one complete *television field* during each *head* pass; permits *freeze-framing*. Compare: *segmented*.

Nord-Sat: cooperative Scandinavian high-power *communications satellite* (1987). See: *Tele-X*.

northlight: *luminaire* using four indirect *1K quartz-iodine lamps* for *diffused fill* illumination.

NOS—Nederlandse Omroep Stichting: Broadcasting Foundation of the Netherlands; government-subsidized *broadcasting* group.

no-seam: very wide paper background in various colors, unrolled to provide no frame of photographic reference. See: *limbo*. Compare: *cyc, milk sweep*.

notch: shallow *cue* cut in edge of *film negative* for *print timing* purposes. Compare: *tab*. Also: *Film emulsion* edge marks for *darkroom* identification.

notch filter: electronic device removing specific *signal frequencies*.

NPACT—National Public Affairs Center for Television: Washington-based *PBS*-controlled *television* program *production* unit.

NPR—National Public Radio: partially government-funded Washington-based national *radio* programming organization (1971); 260 member *stations* (1988).

NRBA—National Radio Broadcasters Association: industry trade association; merged with *NAB,* 1986.

NRK: Norwegian government *television network.*

NRSC—National Radio Systems Committee: U.S. industry group supporting Western Hemisphere *AM bandwidth* reduction from 15 to *10 KHz.* See: *9 KHz.*

NSI—Nielsen Station Index: audience rating survey.

NSRC—National Stereophonic Radio Committee: *radio* engineering group formed (1959) to recommend *FM stereo broadcast* standards to *FCC.*

NTAs—Nielsen Television Areas: standard U.S. market areas established by *Nielsen* survey service.

NTI—Nielsen Television Index Rating: biweekly *television* audience size (only) *rating* report, based on *Audimeter* records from 2,000+ *households;* industry standard for national *network* audience estimates, available a few weeks after each *telecast.* See: *diary, NAC, SIA.*

NTIA—National Telecommunications and Information Administration: agency created (1978) from White House Office of Telecommunications Policy, and Department of Commerce *(OT) Office of Telecommunication.* Recommends telecommunications technology policy/legislation; monitors government utilization of *radio frequency spectrum.*

NTSC—National Television Systems Committee: *television* industry engineering group, established early 1940s to recommend final *b/w transmission* standards (525-*line,* 60-*field,* 6 *MHz bandwidth)* to *FCC.* Reactivated early 1950s to recommend color standards (two *color difference* signals—*R-Y, B-Y—quadrature-*modulating 3.58 *MHz carrier; carrier phase* determines *hue, amplitude* determines *saturation).* Unlike *PAL* and *SECAM color* systems, *NTSC phase/amplitude* relationships are easily distorted—hence, "Never Twice the Same Color." 140 million U.S. receivers in use (1988).

NTV: Nippon Television Network.

NUJ: in Britain, National Union of Journalists.

null: *dead microphone* area.

null detector: *circuitry* detecting absence of *signal.*

number board: in Britain, several *frames* of small blackboard indicating full *scene* information, photographed at head of each *take;* hinged *clapstick* provides visual/sound *synchronization.* Also called *take board.*

number crunching: see: *crunch.*

NYIT—New York Institute of Technology: experimental *ATV/HDTV* Vista system. Compare: *Del Rey, Farjouda, MUSE, NBC*.

Nyquist, Harry: *television* theorist; inventor of Nyquist *filter*, propounder of Nyquist limit, Nyquist rule. See: *MUSE*.

Nyquist noise: see: *random noise*.

O

O&O's: *broadcast stations* owned and operated by *network;* limited by *FCC* (1984) to 12 *VHF*/12 *UHF*/12 *radio,* traditionally located in highly profitable U.S. markets, with combined maximum coverage (special provision for *UHF*'s) set at 25% of U.S. *television households; FCC* limits for independent *station* groups are higher. Compare: *affiliate, independent.*

OB: in Britain, outside *(remote* location) *broadcast.* See: *recce.*

objective lens—projection lens: convex lens (or system) projecting enlarged *screen* image.

OB van: in Britain, self-contained *control room*-and-equipment *broadcast* vehicle, often with *microwave/satellite* capability.

OC—on camera: *television* performer both heard and seen. Compare: *off camera.*

OCC—Operations Control Center: *Inmarsat* London headquarters.

OCR—optical character recognition: direct *computer* input from printed characters.

octave: doubling of original *frequency*—25 *Hz* to 50 *Hz,* 50 *Hz* to 100 *Hz,* etc. (highest octave of audibility is 10,000 *Hz*–20,000 *Hz).*

odd line field: first half of *interlaced television frame transmission.* Compare: *even line field.*

OEM—original equipment manufacturer: basic equipment supplier.

Øersted, Hans Christian: *magnetic recording* theorist, 1819. See: *Poulsen.*

øersted: unit of *tape recording* magnetic field strength. See: *coercivity.*

OF: optical fibers. See: *fiber optics*.

off camera—VO—voice over: *television* performer heard but not seen. Called *commentary over, out-of-vision, OOV* in Britain. Compare: *OC*.

off-line: (less expensive) use of non-standard *production* equipment. Compare: *on-line*.

off mike: speech directed away from *microphone*, simulating ''distant'' sound. Compare: *on mike*.

off-network: former *network* programming, *syndicated* for local market presentation. Compare: *first-run*.

offset: *sound* overlap from previous or following *scene*.

offstage: anywhere outside *camera* view. Compare: *onstage*.

Oftel—Office of Telecommunications: U.K. government supervisory agency.

Ogilvy & Mather: one of seven major (1987 gross *billings* between $3 and $5 billion) worldwide *advertising agencies*.

Ohio State Award: annual University recognition for distinguished *educational broadcasting* achievement. Compare: *Peabody Award*.

ohm—O: basic unit of electrical *resistance*. Compare: *ampere, mho, volt, watt*.

Ohm's Law: (1827) *voltage* (E) = *amperage* (I) × *resistance* (R).

oink: *demographic* family, one-income-no-kids. Compare: *dink*.

OIRT—International Radio and Television Organization: world telecommunications standards group.

olivette: obsolete *floodlight*.

omega wrap: *Beta videotape wind* configuration around *helical scan drum*. Compare: *alpha wrap, M-wrap*.

omnidirectional: *microphone pickup* from any direction.

omnies: non-identifiable crowd *extras*, or their murmuring voices. Called *rhubarb* in Britain. See: *crowd noise, walla-walla*.

on-air: *program* being *broadcast* or *recorded*.

½": see: *VHS*.

1.5 head system: *SONY helical videotape* design utilizing separate *head* for *vertical interval signals*.

1"—one inch: see: *helical scan*.

one light: *positive film print* made without *intensity* or *color correction* for initial *editorial* work. See: *dailies, rushes*.

1-Plus: Munich-based European *satellite/cable programming* service.

one shot: single performance not scheduled for re*broadcast*. See: *special*. Compare: *across the board, strip*.

one-step: *phonograph disk duplication* method, using backed silverplating of original *acetate recording* for low-quantity vinyl *pressings*. Compare: *two-step*.

1,000 Hz pulse: standard *audio reference tone signal*. See: *beep(s)*.

1,000 Hz system: automatic *projector* advance, triggered by recorded *1,000 Hz pulse*.

on-line: use of standard *production* equipment. Compare: *off-line*.

on mike: speaking directly into *microphone*. Compare: *off mike*.

onstage: within camera view. Compare: *offstage*.

on the air: *broadcasting*.

on the fly: choosing *video edit* point while *tape* is moving.

on the nose: to exact time.

On-TV: *subscription-television* program *network*.

on two's: economical *animation film* technique exposing same *frame* art twice, with unnoticeable effect.

OOP: out-of-pocket (expense).

OOT: out of town.

opaque: not transmitting light.

opaque projector: device reflecting opaque graphic materials onto close-by screen. Compare: *overhead projector*.

opaquer: *animation* artist applying paint to inked backs of *cels*.

open call: nonrestricted *audition*.

open channel: local *television channel* unused *on-air;* utilized for *VCR, video game,* etc.

open door: in Britain, minority viewpoint *programming* over standard *broad-casting facilities*.

open end: *program* with no specific scheduled completion time. Also: *Commercial* with space and time for added local material.

open mike: live *microphone*.

open rate: maximum rate charged by *broadcasting* facility for one-time *advertising* message.

open reel—reel-to-reel: *tape transport* system with separated supply *(feed)* and *take-up reels*. Compare: *cartridge, cassette*.

open-up: enlarge *camera lens aperture*.

operations department: *broadcast station scheduling* group.

operations sheet: daily *station broadcast schedule*.

operator: franchised company administering *cable* system(s). Compare: *programmer*. Also: In Britain, technician actually operating (and usually loading) *camera*.

optical effect—optical: artificially produced *camera effect: fade, dissolve, wipe, superimposition*, and other transitional devices. Also: Similar *digital video effect*.

optical fibers: see: *fiber optics*.

optical glass: high-quality *lens* material.

optical house: facility for processing final *film negative* to include selected *optical effects* and *titling*.

optical negative: final *printing negative (picture)*. Compare: *optical track*.

optical printer: *optical house printing* machine producing final *optical negative*.

optical sound: *recorded audio* material, *printed* on *motion picture film;* reproduced by *projecting* an *exciter lamp* beam through the *soundtrack* to a *photoelectric cell/amplifier*. See: *variable area, variable density*. Compare: *magnetic track*.

optical track: final *soundtrack printing negative*. Compare: *optical negative*.

optical transfer: duplication of fully *mixed audio tape track* into a *negative film soundtrack*.

optical view finder: device permitting *operator* to see and *frame picture that camera* is taking.

optical wand: see: *wand*.

optional cut: predetermined deletion.

Oracle—Optional Reception of Announcements by Coded Line Electronics: British *(IBA)* system for *digital transmission* of *alphanumeric* information, utilizing *television signal blanking intervals* at seven *megabits* per second. See: *Ceefax*. Compare: *Antiope, Slice, Teletext, Viewdata*.

Orbita: USSR domestic *communications satellite* program (1965); four nongeosynchronous *Molinya satellites*, 25,000 miles high, cover Soviet polar areas.

Orbital: planned *DBS satellite* operator (1993).

orbiter: see: *satellite, shuttle orbiter*.

orchestra: group of musical instrumentalists, usually 18 or more, with *conductor*.

orchestrator: *copyist* inscribing scored parts of composition for instrumental performance. Compare: *arranger*.

ORF-I, II: Austrian government *television networks*.

original: initial *camera negative* (or *videotape recording*) before *post production.*

original music: new creative composition. Compare: *library music.*

origination: U.S. *network feed* point, usually New York, Chicago, Los Angeles.

ORTF—Office de Radiodiffusion-Télévision Française: French government *broadcasting network,* dismembered in 1974 into seven separate entities. Compare: *BBC, FCC, RAI.* See: *SFP.*

orthicon: see: *image orthicon.*

Oscar: Academy (of Motion Picture Arts and Sciences) Award statuette. Also: In Britain, adjustable quartered *luminaire diffuser.* Also: *O*rbital *S*atellite *C*arrying *A*mateur *R*adio; first (of seven) launched 1961.

oscillator: electronic device producing specific *frequencies.*

oscilloscope—scope: *cathode-ray tube* device for visual electronic *signal* analysis.

OT—Office of Telecommunication: U.S. Department of Commerce unit. See: *NTIA.*

OTO: *broadcast* material for one-time-only *transmission.*

OTS—Orbital Test Satellite: developmental *ESA satellite* (#1 destroyed in 1977 launch; #2 launched 1978). See: *ECS, H-Sat, Sirio, Symphonie.*

out: movement from. Compare: *in.*

outage: electric power failure.

out-cue: closing words of *cue* line. Compare: *in-cue.*

outgrade: eliminate *commercial player* in *editing.* Compare: *downgrade.*

outlet: female *connector* (usually for *power*). Also: *Network-affiliated station.*

outline: brief written summary of proposed *program* idea.

out of focus: distorted or fuzzy *picture.*

out of frame: not in *camera* view. Also: Faulty *projection* of portions of two *frames* at once. Called *out of rack* in Britain.

out of safety: superimposed artwork/*titling* extending beyond theoretical *overscan* boundaries. See: *safety.*

out of sync: mis*aligned sound* and *picture* elements. Compare: *in sync.* Also: Absence of *synchronization* between *television receiver* and *transmitted signal,* causing vertical *roll* or horizontal displacement.

out of vision—OOV—commentary over: in Britain, performer heard but not seen.

output: *signal* leaving unit or system. Also: *Jack* or receptacle source of *output signal.* See: *gozowta.* Compare: *input.*

outs: see: *outtake.*

outtake: *taped/filmed* material discarded in final *edit*. See: *trim*. Compare: *selected take*.

overbuilds: competing *cable* systems serving same area.

overcrank: operate *motion picture camera* at faster-than-normal *frame speed*, producing "slow-motion" effect with normal *projection*. Called *turn fast* in Britain. Compare: *undercrank*.

overdub: add new *elements* to existing *recording*. See: *sel-sync*.

overexpose: too-slow *shutter speed* or overwide *aperture* matched to *film emulsion* characteristics; results in undesirable "dark" *negative* (or *reversal)* and "light" *print*. Compare: *underexpose*.

overhead projector: device projecting manually placed transparent graphic sheets onto close-by screen. See: *slinky*. Compare: *opaque projector*.

overlap: cemented *film splice*. Compare: *butt splice*.

overload: *input* of power or *signal* beyond equipment's capability to distribute or reproduce, causing *distortion* or failure.

overmodulation: *audio overload*.

overnight: earliest *NTI* program *rating* compilation.

overscale: *talent* fee in excess of union minimums.

overscan: *television picture* area beyond normal *receiver mask*. See: *bezel*.

over-the-air: *broadcast signals*.

overtime: extension of normal work period. See: *golden time, long day*.

oxide: microscopic oxidized metallic particles (usually about 400 millionths of an inch thick) coated onto *base* to form *magnetic tape* or *film track*.

P

P: indication to *film laboratory* to *print take*.

PA—public address system: local *microphone/loudspeaker* system. Compare: *PL, talkback*.

Pacifica Broadcasting: listener-supported U.S. *FM network*.

Pacifica Decision: 1978 Supreme Court ruling prohibiting *on-air* use of seven "dirty words."

package: *element* combination. Also: Completely prepared *program* or series offered for sale. See: *syndication*.

package plan: *broadcast station*'s specially priced *spot time* combination sale offer, usually on weekly or monthly basis.

packager: company producing *program package*.

packed: tightly wound *tape*.

packet: short *transmitted* information block.

packing density: amount of magnetic information potentially *recordable* in given linear dimension. See: *recording density*.

pack shot: in Britain, product *close-up*.

pad: concrete *earth station* base. Also: Innocuous music behind dialog. Also: Lengthen program material to fill time. Compare: *bumper, cushion*.

page: screenful of *teletext/videotex* information.

page turn: screen image rotation on vertical axis. See: *dve*. Compare: *door swing*.

Paintbox: *computer*-driven *videotape* graphics *editing* system. See: *Harry*. Compare: *ADO*.

paint pots: *console* color control *rheostats*.

pairing: *interlace* failure where alternate *scan lines* fall too close to each other.

PAL—phase alternate line—phase alternation by line: *color television transmission* system (625-*line*, 50-*field*, 6 *MHz bandwidth*) developed 1967 by Bruch; used in Britain, Western Europe, Scandinavia, Africa, Asia, South America, etc. Technically more complex than *NTSC* system, requiring millionth-second accuracy; *R-Y* and *B-Y* signals used to *quadrature*-modulate 4.3 *MHz carrier*. Less subject to color *distortion; carrier phase* reverses with each *scan line,* minimizing *hue* error—hence, "Peace At Last." Compare: *SECAM*.

Palapa-1,2: Indonesian *LEO satellites* at 277° and 283° W (malfunctioning *Palapa 1* retrieved by *NASA shuttle* Discovery, 1984).

palette: *CGI* color chart.

Panasonic: Japanese electronics manufacturer (division of *Matsushita).*

Panavision: *16/35mm motion picture camera.*

Panavision 35: *wide-screen film* process; 2.35:1.

pancake: water-soluble *makeup*. Also: Very low *set* support box. Compare: *apple, riser.*

panchromatic: *b/w film emulsion,* sensitive to all colors of visible spectrum.

pan(chromatic) glass: *filter* originally used for *eyeball* evaluation of *monochromatic* values; still useful for calculating sun vs. cloud movement, or light path centers.

pan(chromatic) master: positive *b/w finegrain* made from *color negative,* used to make *b/w dupe negative.*

P&W—pension and welfare: *talent* union retirement benefits, usually paid by *producer.*

panel show: *broadcast* discussion with several interviewees.

pan handle: handle controlling *camera mount* movement.

pan head: *camera mount* permitting even, controlled *panning*. See: *friction head.*

pan(oramic): *camera* swivel from fixed position along horizontal *arc.* Compare: *tilt, track.*

panstick: grease-based *makeup.*

pantograph: overhead *spotlight* suspender.

papering: in Britain, visual identification—with inserted paper strips—of portions of *film footage.*

paper tape: punched-hole information *storage* medium.

parabolic—beam projector—sun spot: *spotlight* projecting narrow, almost parallel light *beam*.

parabolic antenna: focusable concave reinforced-plastic, metal, or mesh *dish, transmitting/receiving line-of-sight signal.*

parabolic (reflector) microphone: concave *dish*-mounted *microphone focusing* distant *sound waves* without *distortion*.

parallax: angle of divergence between *camera lens* and its *viewfinder*. Can cause *framing* error.

parallels: temporary steel-tube-and-wood high *camera* platform. Compare: *cherry picker, crane.*

Paramount Pictures Corporation: major entertainment conglomerate.

parity: transmitted-data error check.

park: maneuver *geosynchronous satellite* into final orbit.

participation: *program* accepting noncompetitive *commercial insertions*. Compare: *wild spot.*

PAS—Pan-American Satellite Corporation: *Arianespace*-launched international *communications satellite* operator; six-beam PAS-1 at 45°W (1988). Compare: *Intelsat.*

passive: equipment incapable of power generation or *amplification*.

patch: temporary electronic *circuit connection*.

patch bay—patchboard: see: *patch panel.*

patch cord: short *cable* with *jacks* at both ends.

patch panel: temporary *circuit connectors*, often replaced by *switcher*. Called *jackfield* in Britain.

patch plug: *console*-mounted male *cable connection*.

path: *signal* route. Also: *Film/tape* route. See: *lace up.*

path loss: attenuation in *signal* medium.

pause: control halting *audio/videotape* movement past *playback head* (without switching off *capstan* motor).

pay cable: wired *subscription television*, with surcharge for optional programming; 29% U.S. penetration, 1988. See: *premium television, see/fee.* Compare: *pay-per-view, pay television, STV.*

payola: coercion (usually bribery) to secure additional *air play* for competitive material; made illegal (by 1960 amendment to *Communications Act of 1934*) when not disclosed. Loosely, a bribe for any illegal service rendered. See: *freebie, junket, plugola.*

pay-per-view: *cable* on per-program rather than monthly basis; available on 240 *addressable* U.S. systems, 1988. See: *Home Premiere Television, Request TV, Viewer's Choice*.

pay television: initiated in New York (1950); *scrambled* over-the-air *broadcast* television *programming* made available by *decoder*. See: *premium television, STV*. Compare: *pay cable, see/fee*.

PBS—Public Broadcasting Service: ''interconnection'' supported by government, corporate, and personal funding; via 3.25 *transponders* on *Westar IV satellite*, distributes programming to 225 *noncommercial* U.S. television stations. System occasionally identified as ''Plenty of British Shows,'' or ''Petroleum Broadcasting System'' (from substantial gasoline company underwriting). See: *CPB, ETV, NET, NPR*.

PC: general-use office or personal home *computer*. Also: *Printed circuit*. Also: see: *planoconvex*.

PCA—promotion consideration allowance: *television* program prize/gift manufacturer identification.

PD—public domain: uncopyrighted creative work, or one whose copyright restriction has expired. Compare: *license, permission, royalty*. Also: **PD— program director:** local *station* executive supervising *broadcast* scheduling.

(George Foster) Peabody Award: annual University of Georgia recognition for distinguished *broadcasting* achievement. Compare: *Ohio State Award*.

pea bulb: small *lamp* inside *motion picture* camera; produces *flash frame edit cue*.

peak: maximum *positive* or *negative signal* excursion (excluding *spikes*); *voltage* difference = peak-to-peak.

pedestal—set up: electronic calibration (interval between *blanking* and *black level pulses*) of *television picture black levels (brightness* control on home *receivers)*. See: *blacker than black, reference black*. Also: **pedestal:** *television camera dolly* support.

peg bar—peg board—animation board: studded drawing board (or *light box*) accurately aligning sequential *animation cels*.

pel: see: *pixel*.

penalty: see: *meal penalty*.

pencil test: rough *animation* execution, photographed to check movement. Called *line test* in Britain.

penetration: proportion of equipment use to potential users. Also: Ratio of households with *television* to total households (now too high in U.S. to be meaningful statistic). See: *cable penetration*.

penthouse: *film projector magnetic sound head*.

pentode: *amplifying vacuum tube* with three variably charged wire mesh *grids* controlling electron flow between *negative filament (cathode)* and *positive plate*. Compare: *diode, tetrode, triode*.

peoplemeter: *Nielsen* and *AGB* "electronic diary"—*television* audience measuring device (1987) installed in sample U.S. homes; AGB service discontinued 1988. Compare: *diary*.

per diem: daily food/room expense allowance.

perforations: *sprocket* holes. See: *single, double perf.*

performance credit: *ASCAP/BMI* composition usage payment.

periodic noise: *picture noise* unrelated to *AC* power lines. See: *S/N.*

peripheral: device connected to and under control of basic equipment.

permanent set—standing set: *set* in continuing *production* use. Compare: *strike*.

permission: use of copyright material. See: *license, royalty*. Compare: *PD*.

persistence: *phosphor* glow following excitation.

persistence of vision: phenomenon of image retention (enunciated 1824 by Peter Mark Roget of *Thesaurus* fame) upon which all *film* and *television* motion illusion is based. Occurs when succession of static but slightly different images is displayed at greater frequency than either the brain or optic nerve can comprehend (in excess of 10 times per second), creating visual inertia.

perspective: *audio* matching apparent distance of sound source.

perspective rotation: *dve* turning generated 3-D object naturally in screen space.

phase: coincidence of *color burst* and *reference signal*.

phase distortion: changes in proper *television picture color*.

phase modulation: *color television transmission* information (phase shift rate = *frequency;* phase shift degree = *amplitude*).

phasing: standard *television camera* and *VTR alignment* process.

Phenekistoscope: slotted disk animation viewer (Plateau, von Stampfer, 1832). Compare: *Praxinoscope, Thaumatrope, Zöetrope*.

(N.V.) Philips Gloeilampenfabrieken: Eindhoven-based giant Netherlands electronics manufacturer.

Phillips screw: standard wood or machine screw with indented "cross" head (requiring Phillips screwdriver). Compare: *Allen screw*.

phon: unit of *loudness,* equal to *decibel* at 1,000 *Hz*.

phoneme: basic language element.

phonograph: *audio disk* player. Called *gramophone* in Britain. Invented by Edison (or Charles Cros) in 1877.

Phonoscope: (1927) *Baird* invention, recording primitive *television signals* (30 lines at 12½ *fps*) on wax *disk.*

phosphor: chemical coating inside *picture tube,* luminescing when struck by *electron beams.*

phosphorescence: production of light (without heat) through energy absorption. Compare: *fluorescence, luminescence.*

photo: from Greek, ''a light.''

photoconductor: *conductor* permitting variable *current* flow when exposed to light *(photons).* See: *dark current.*

photodiode: *video disk signal detector.*

photoelectric cell—photocell: selenium device converting light variations into electrical impulses. See: *exposure meter.*

photoelectric effect: emission of electrons from specific elements struck by visible light.

photoflood: high-*wattage* (standard light socket) *bulb.*

photography: formation of optical image on sensitized surface by action of light or other radiant energy.

photon: variably sized discrete bundle of energy in electromagnetic wave.

photonics: optical-electrical technology.

photoplastic: image-recording technique utilizing light and heat to deform surface of special plastic film. Compare: *thermoplastic.*

photoresist: material reacting to light by hardening.

photosensitive: reactive to light.

photostat—stat: inexpensively processed photographic reproduction, usually enlarged or reduced from original to match available space.

physical edit: mechanical *splice* in *videotape* (obsolete practice).

p.i.—per inquiry: *station* (fee-per-order) direct response *broadcast advertising.*

pickup: *remote broadcast.* Also: *Microphone* sensitivity area. Also: *Phonograph needle* arm (''tone arm''). Also: *Insert* shot. Also: Increase pace of performance. Also: *Television camera tube* converting optical images into electrical *signals* by electronic *scanning* process. See: *iconoscope, image isocon, image orthicon, Leddicon, Newvicon, Plumbicon, Saticon, SEC, SIT, Trinicon, vidicon.*

picosecond: 1/1,000,000,000,000 second.

picture: portion of composite *television video signal* above the *blanking signal;* contains the *picture* information. Also: Loosely, sequential *film frames.*

picture safety: *picture tube* area within which all significant *picture* detail is safely clear of *masks* on even slightly *overscanned receivers*. Compare: *cutoff, lettering safety.*

picture stop: embedded *video disk addressability* code.

picture tube: television *receiver* (or *monitor) cathode ray* component converting electronic *signal* to fluorescent optical image by *scanning beam intensity* variations. Compare: *camera tube.*

piezoelectricity: ability of certain crystals to generate *voltage* under pressure; or undergo mechanical stress in electric *field*. See: *ceramic.*

pigeons: *monitor noise* in *pulses* or short bursts.

piggyback: *broadcast commercial* combination presenting different products (originally defined by *NAB* as ''not related and interwoven'') made by same corporate advertiser. Compare: *integrated.*

pilot: initial program of proposed *broadcast* series, prepared as demonstration for potential advertising *sponsors*. Also: **pilot—clip roll—four-framer:** in Britain, laboratory *film* test strip of *color balance* range, determining final *printing light* selection.

pilot pins: see: *pins.*

pilot tone: see: *sync tone.*

PIN—personal identification number: *computer* recognition signal.

pinch roller—pressure roller—puck: rubber idler wheel holding *recording tape* against *capstan spindle* during *transport.*

PIN diode: *optical fiber detector*. Compare: *APD.*

ping-pong: *stereo microphone* separation for maximum *audio channel* difference.

pinning: *audio recording volume overload,* causing *v.i. meter needle* to bang against upper pin-limiter.

pin rack: sorting bar above editing *bin* for hanging ends of *film* lengths. Called *bin stick* in Britain.

pins: teeth engaging *sprocket* holes, centering and pressing each *motion picture film frame* rock-steady in *camera/projector gate*. See: *pressure plate.* Compare: *claw.*

PIP—picture in picture: small screen insert of additional *on-air television* program.

pipe: wire *hookup* for *television* or *radio program transmission.*

piracy: illegal *signal tap* or *descrambling.*

pirate: unlicensed *broadcaster.*

pitch: *frequency* location in audible range. Also: Distance between two successive *sprocket* holes.

pix: see: *picture.*

pixel: *television pic*ture *el*ement forming *scan line, transmitted* at 8½ million per second; standard *television picture tube resolution* is 256 horizontal elements × 192 vertical.

pixellization: *dve* breakup into irregular groups of *pixels,* creating mosaic or posterized look.

pixlock: adjusted *color synchronization* between two *videotape recorders.*

PL—party line: wired on-*set* communication system. See: *headset.* Compare: *PA, talkback.*

plain lighting: artificial light approximating normal sunlight angle.

planoconvex—PC: simple *lens* with one flat, one convex side. Also: *Spotlight* with such *lens.*

plant: physical facilities of *broadcasting/cable* operation.

plate: *rewind disk* supporting *film* wound on *core.* Also: Base *insert* shot. Compare: *external key.* Also: *Positively* charged *vacuum tube* element.

platen—frame glass: optically clear hinged glass plate holding *cels* flat during *animation* photography.

platter: horizontal *projection reel;* contains up to 25,000 feet (4½ hours) of *film.* Also: *Phonograph disk.*

playback: *reproduction* of previously *recorded* material. Also called *playout* in Britain. Also: *Circuitry* permitting field review of *tape production.* See: *confidence head.*

playback—guidetrack: *prerecorded* music or speech, cueing *MOS action.*

Playboy Channel: *satellite/pay cable* programming service (1982).

players: principal *talent* in a *commercial.* Compare: *extras.*

Players' Guide: directory of performing *talent.* Compare: *Spotlight.*

playlist: *broadcast* musical *recordings.*

playout: in Britain, *reproduction* of previously *recorded* material.

pledge week: public *television* viewer-donation period.

Plesetsk: USSR *satellite* launch area, 300 miles NE of Leningrad. Compare: *Balkonur, Cape Canaveral, Kourou.*

plop—pip: in Britain, audible *cue* hole or *sync pulse* in *film soundtrack.*

plot: story development. Also: See *light plot, prop plot.*

plug: *conductor* inserted into *jack.* Compare: *socket.* Also: *on-air* promotional mention.

plugging box: stage light inter*connector.*

plugola: excessive *on-air* promotion in covert exchange for merchandise. See: *freebie.* Compare: *junket, payola.*

Plumbicon: improved Philips *color television camera tube* (30:1 contrast range) with lead oxide *target* surface coating, affording linear *video output* (1974). Also: *Camera* containing this *tube.* Compare: *image orthicon, Leddicon, Newvicon, Saticon, Trinicon, vidicon.*

pocket: permanent *female* stage light receptacle.

pocketpiece: handy *NTI* pamphlet containing biweekly *rating* review.

pod: *television* multi-*commercial break.* Also: Equipment housing/container.

point—rating point: *broadcast* audience size standard. See: *gross rating points, net rating points, share.*

polar curve: graph showing light source intensity, distribution, and emission characteristics.

polarity: *positive* or *negative picture* characteristics of *b/w* television *image.* Can be electronically reversed.

polarization: see: *circular/horizontal polarization.*

polarized light: light passed through lenses or plates of millions of tiny needle-shaped crystals; blocks all *waves* except those vibrating in same direction (thus controlling undesirable glare and reflection).

polar mount: *earth station mounting* system, parallel to earth's poles (less stable than *Az-El*).

Polaroid filter—pola screen: light-*polarizing lens filter* to reduce glare, reflection, or *highlights.*

pole attachment: *cable* use of telephone wire support(s).

polecat—jack tube: telescopic wall-braced *luminaire* support.

(George) Polk Award: annual recognition for distinguished *broadcast* news-gathering.

polyester: *recording tape base* of polyethylene glycol terephthalate.

polyphony: two or more musical *melodies* played simultaneously.

polytonal: music played simultaneously in two or more keys.

poop sheet—fact sheet: *copy* points for *announcer*'s *ad-lib* use; opposite of prepared *script.*

pop: contemporary music. Also: Explosive hard consonant (usually ''p'') in voice *recording.*

pop filter: internal *microphone* device to limit above. Compare: *windscreen.*

Popoff: Russian *radio* pioneer.

pop-on—pop-off: instantaneously add or subtract new *optical picture* information (usually *titles)* to *frame.* Called *bump-in, bump-out* in Britain. Compare: *fade.*

Popov, Aleksandr Stefanovich: early Russian *radio* experimenter (1895).

population: see: *universe.*

porch displacement: *level* difference between *front* and *back porch signals.*

porky: in Britain, exaggerated performance.

port: electronic *input/output* point.

portal-to-portal: pay period, including transportation time to job site.

Portapak: early portable (over-the-shoulder) battery-powered miniaturized camera/*recording deck* ensemble. Compare: *backpack, camcorder.*

position: *commercial* location within *program* format. Also: Location of *recorded* material on *tape.* Also: Competitive *advertising copy platform.* See: *purchase proposition.*

positive: *projectible film* with color and/or tonal representation of original subject. Also: Higher electrical *potential.* Compare: *negative.*

positive interlace: exactly spaced sequential *scanning* of *picture tube field lines.* Compare: *random interlace.*

positive transfer: *videotape* made from *film negative.* Compare: *negative transfer.*

post—post production: *film/videotape editing*/completion.

postcode: *time code* for *pre-recorded videotape.*

post dubbing: see: *post* production.

posterization: *analog* or *digital video* effect producing overlapping areas of *color saturation.* Compare: *mosaic, pixellization.*

post score: compose/*record* music to existing *picture.* Compare: *pre-score.*

post sync(hronization): later addition of *synchronous sound* to *silent* picture.

potential: difference in electrical charge between two points in *circuit.*

pot(entiometer): round control *console rheostat* raising or lowering *audio* or *video levels.* See: *attenuator.* Compare: *fader.*

Poulsen, Valdemar: successful *magnetic recording* and *playback,* 1893; narrow band *FM* theory, 1903. See: *Armstrong, Faraday, Henry, Øersted.*

POV: (*camera's*) point of view.

power: *broadcast transmitter output* (in *watts*).

power cord—line cord: electric supply wires.

powerhouse: *radio station* operating at 50 *kw* on *frequency* assigned to no other full-time *FCC* licensee. Compare: *CH, clear channel, daytimer, PSA.*

power pack: rechargeable portable battery power supply for *film* or *tape camera* or *tape recorder,* often belt-mounted. See: *battery belt, nickel-cadmium.*

PPV: see: *pay-per-view.*

p.r.: public relations activity.

practical: *set* piece or *prop* that works; *practical lamps* may or may not affect actual *set* illumination.

Praxinoscope: mirrored-drum animation viewer (Reynaud, 1877). Compare: *Phenakistoscope, Thaumatrope, Zöetrope.*

preamp(lifier): electronic equipment boosting weak *signal voltages* to useable *amplifier levels,* without additional *S/N deterioration.*

pre-emptible: discounted *station commercial broadcast time;* subject to "re-capture" if *station* finds *advertiser* willing to pay full *rate.* Compare: *pre-emption.*

pre-emption: optional "recapture" of *network time* by *affiliate* (or of other-wise-scheduled *network time* by *network* itself) for special, usually last-minute *programming.* Compare: *acceptance, pre-emptible.*

pre-light: arrange *set lighting* in advance of actual *production.*

Premiere: British *cable network.*

premium rate: *station*'s extra charge for specially requested *commercial time position.* Compare: *ROS.*

premium television: any *television transmission* system charging for *program viewing.* See: *pay cable, pay television, see/fee, STV.*

pre-mix: preliminary *audio mix;* reduces quantity of sound elements.

pre-production: planning activity prior to actual *production.*

pre-record: prepare material for later *playback* during *production.*

pre-score: *record* final *sound* or music *track,* before *filming* or *videotaping* to *playback.* Compare: *postscore.*

presence: apparent closeness and fidelity of *live* or *recorded audio.*

preset: store control data for automatic *retrieval.*

pressing: *phonograph/video disk,* mass produced from molds.

pressure pad: pad holding *tape* against *record/playback heads.*

pressure plate: *camera* or *projector gate* unit holding *film frame* flat on *pins* in *focal plane.* Compare: *claw.*

pressure roller—pinch roller—puck: rubber idler wheel holding *recording tape* against *capstan spindle* during *transport.*

Prestel: British *videotex* system (Fedida, 1971). See: *Bildschirmtext, Captain, Teletel, Telidon.*

presynchronization: usually, *prerecording* voice *tracks* for lip-movement *animation.*

preview: *control room monitor* showing upcoming *scenes, effects, titling,* etc. Compare: *line monitor.*

primary colors: (not the artist's opaque pigments red, yellow, and blue, but optically—and electronically) red-orange, green, and blue-violet. No mixture of any two can produce the third. See: *additive primaries, RGB, triad.* Compare: *subtractive primaries.*

prime focus: *dish LNA feed* system. Compare: *buttonhook, Cassegrain.*

prime lens: *lens* of fixed *focal length.* Compare: *zoom lens.*

prime time: four hours of *television station's schedule,* traditionally 7 to 11 P.M. (advanced one hour in Central/Mountain time zones); under 1971 *FCC* ruling, only three hours of this period (generally 8 to 11 P.M.) may be utilized for *network-fed* programming excepting news. See: *prime time (network) programming, time.*

Prime Time Access Rule (I, II, III): 1971 *FCC* regulation reducing *network prime time feeds* (for top-50 market *affiliates* to three hours per weekday exempting news evening, theoretically forcing more local *television* programming; subject to waivers. After 1972, local programming could not include *network* or *film re-runs* (creating *game show* explosion); see: *Westinghouse Rule.* Modified 1974 to return 7:00–7:30 P.M. as previously for *network feeds.*

prime time (network) programming: *network-produced prime time* material; *FCC*-limited to non-*syndicated* programming three hours per week (by 1990, five hours).

print: *positive* copy from *film negative,* duplicating original subject tonal values and/or colors. Also: *Film director*'s call to include completed *take* in next day's *rushes.* See: *buy.* Also: Space advertising in newspapers/magazines.

printed circuit: metal *conductor path* etched onto laminated plastic base.

printer: optical duplicating machine exposing *positive film print* stock to light through *negative image,* or vice versa. Also: *Computer hard copy* machine.

printing light: calibrated amount of illumination used to print particular *film scene.* See: *cinex.*

printing sync: *synchronization* of *picture* and *soundtrack* to allow for *pullup track* delay. Compare: *cutting sync.*

printout: electronic information converted to paper. See: *hard copy.*

print-through: excessive magnetism transferred from one *audio tape* layer to the next, producing "ghost" sound. Usually caused by *overloaded recording levels,* high *tape* storage temperatures, or physical shock.

print-up (print-down): decreasing (increasing) density of *optical soundtrack* for dramatic *volume* increases (decreases).

prism block: compact *color-separating optical* unit.

prism lens: *optical* device producing "in *camera*" multiple images.

probability sample—random sample: research units mechanically selected for statistical projection.

proc amp—video processing amplifier: electronic device altering *video signal (sync, picture, color)* characteristics.

processing: *developing,* fixing, washing, drying, and *printing negative film.* See: *laboratory.*

process shot: optical combination of several *film images,* making them appear photographed by single camera. See: *blue matteing, rotoscoping.* Compare: *chromakey.*

Prodigy Computer Services: see: Trintex.

producer: in-charge person preparing project for *broadcast production* and directly responsible for its economic success or failure.

production: preparation of *program* or *commercial* material for *broadcast.*

production assistant: *producer's* general assistant. See: *gopher.*

production house: specialist facility preparing *film* or *videotape commercials.*

production secretary: in Britain, *director's* personal assistant.

product protection—commercial protection: formal minimum time interval between competing *commercial* messages. See: *separation.*

profile—demographics: breakdown of *broadcast* audiences by varying statistical characteristics, such as sex, age, family size, education, and economic level. See: *audience composition.* Compare: *psychographics.* Also: **profile:** dimensional free-standing piece of "landscape" *scenery.* Compare: *drop.* Also: Minute-by-minute *program* audience *viewing* pattern.

program: *computer* processing instructions. Also: *Sponsored* or un*sponsored broadcast* presentation.

programmer: *program producer* or *syndicator.*

progressive scanning: 1/30 second *television frame scanning* where one *scan line* follows the next. Compare: *interlace.*

projectionist: *projector* operator. Compare: *VTR operator.*

projection lens—objective lens: convex *lens* (or system) *projecting* an enlarged *screen* image.

projector: machine passing *focused* high-intensity light beam through *motion picture film* onto distant reflective *screen,* usually simultaneously reproducing *film's synchronized soundtrack.* Compare: *VTR.*

Project Pisces: abandoned version of *ELF Project Sanguine,* utilizing *radiated transmission* from 400,000V *DC* Pacific Intertie linking Bonneville Dam and Los Angeles.

Project Sanguine: abandoned plan for 20,000 sq. mi. underground *antenna* plus 100 buried *transmitters* to bounce *ELF waves* off the *ionosphere* and into the ocean for emergency U.S. Navy communication with submerged nuclear submarines.

Project Seafarer: abandoned half-billion dollar version of *ELF Project Pisces,* establishing 3,500 sq. mi. buried *antenna* with seven above-ground *transmitters.*

Project Shelf—super hard extremely low frequency: abandoned version of *ELF Project Sanguine* utilizing underground tunnels several thousand feet deep.

Project Tacamo (Take Command and Move Out): U.S. *VLF* submarine communications system utilizing two C-130s flying continuous random Atlantic Ocean patterns, trailing lightweight six-mile-long *antennas.* Compare: *ELF.*

Project Westford: (1963) *NASA* stratospheric *grid* of 400 million copper wires for reflective space communication.

promo(tional announcement): *network* or *station commercial* announcement of forthcoming *program.* See: *clutter.*

prompter: *cueing* device rolling up or electronically projecting *script* material in performer's view. Mounted on *camera* or on either side of dais. Called *autocue* in Britain. See: *TeleprompTer.* Compare: *cue card, deaf aid.* Also: In Britain, *microphone/speaker* system connecting *studio* to control room.

prop list—prop plot: list of required *production properties.*

props—properties: owned or rented non-structural *set* furnishings.

pro-sumer: electronic equipment theoretically designed for both professional and non-professional use.

protection: reproducible *duplicate,* in event of damage to *master.* In *film, interpositive* struck from *optical negative;* in *videotape,* first *duplicate* off air *master.* Called *backing copy* in Britain. Compare: *composite master.* Also: Wide *camera* position to cover *jump cuts* of *lip-sync close-ups.* See: *insurance.*

protocol: rules governing exchange of data between *computer* systems.

Proton: Soviet *satellite*-launching rocket.

proxar: supplemental screw-on *close-up* element(s) to shorten *lens focal length.* See: *diopter lens, extension tube, lens extender.*

PSA—public service announcement: *broadcast time* contributed by *station* for messages of noncommercial nature. Also: **pre-sunrise authority:** special *FCC* authorization to *daytimer radio station* for early *sign-on.*

PSSC—Public Service Satellite Consortium: non-profit organization (1975) utilizing *NASA satellite transmissions* for public service. See: *ATS-6.*

psychographics: research on personality characteristics and attitudes affecting audience's life style and purchasing behavior. Compare: *demographics.*

PTAR: see: *Prime Time Access Rule.*

PTL—Praise the Lord—People That Love: 24-hour *satellite/cable* religious programming service. Renamed *Heritage Ministries* (1988).

PTT—Posts, Telephone & Telegraph: European government-monopoly communications systems.

public access: *FCC*-mandated *channel* for *cable* systems with more than 3,500 *subscribers;* set aside for public community or individual programming (including "blue" material) at minimal facilities fees. In Britain, *on-air* version called *open door.*

"public interest, convenience and necessity": traditional catchwords of Federal *Communications Act of 1934;* describes operational standard for U.S. *broadcast station licensees.*

(music) publisher: owner/licensee of musical composition copyright.

puck—pinch roller—pressure roller: rubber idler wheel holding *recording tape* against *capstan spindle* during *transport.*

pull back: *dolly camera* away from subject. Compare: *push in, zoom.*

pull down: *camera/projector* action, moving *film* into *gate* one *frame* at a time by means of *claw.* Compare: *pullup.*

pull focus: in Britain, alter *focus* to another subject.

pull negative: *match original negative film* to *edited work print.*

pull the breakers: in Britain, go on strike.

pullup: *loop* of *film* (approximately one second long) in *film projection path,* to snub intermittent jerking through *picture gate* into required smooth flow over *sound head:* 20-frame *loop* in *35mm;* 26 *frames* in *16mm (optical:* 28 *frames magnetic);* 52 *frames* (2.17 seconds) in *8mm;* 22 *frames* in *super 8 (optical:* 18 *frames magnetic).* Compare: *pull down.*

Pulse: in-home aided recall *radio* audience survey service. Compare: *National Arbitron.* Also: Weekly trade news magazine. Also: **pulse:** electronic *signal* variation of finite *amplitude* and duration, generated for control reference or *circuit* activation.

pulsed magnetron: British (WW II) *radar* device generating *microwaves* 10 centimeters long, at 3,000 *megacycles.*

pulse track—click track: *conductor's* audible music scoring beat, based on *film speed* (24-*frame pulse* = one second; 12-*frame pulse* = ½ second; etc.).

pulsing: augmenting normal *flighting* base with burst of heavy advertising pressure.

pumpkin: *animation stand* projection of *television picture safety* area.

punch: *film cue* created by hole-punch, used visually when *recording* against *picture*. Compare: *beep*.

punch up: switch to specific *feed*.

pup—baby: 500 *W spotlight*. Also: **PUP:** *Ku-band* portable *satellite uplink*.

PUR: person using radio. Compare: *PUT*.

purchase proposition: creative *copy* summarizing putative product differences. See: *position*.

pure tone: single *frequency* sound, without overtones.

purity: degree of *video* color separation; registration maintained by tricolor *beam* control coil.

push—force: develop *film emulsion* beyond recommended *exposure rating*, usually half or full *stop*.

push in: *dolly* camera toward subject. Compare: *zoom*.

PUT: person (using) viewing *television*. *Compare: PUR*.

put-put: small (location) electric power generator.

PVC: see: *vinyl*.

Q

QS: *CBS matrix quadruphonic* system. Compare: *SQ*.

Q signal ("quadruture" signal): purple-to-yellow/green *chrominance sideband* (3.58 *MHz*) produced by *subcarrier modulation* phased 147° from *color burst* reference. See: *I signal*. Compare: *Y signal*.

quad—quadruplex: original four-unit *videotape recording/playback headwheel* system, rotating at 14,400 rpm at right angles to transported *2″ tape*, "writing" *video* information in successive, almost-vertical stripes (1,2,3,4,1,2,3,4, etc.) First U.S. *network transmission* November 30, 1956. Called *4-H* in Britain. Compare: *helical scan*.

quadlite: unit containing four 500 *W floodlights*.

quadruphonic: *FM broadcast* or home *recording* system utilizing four *loudspeakers*, two in front and two behind listener. Compare: *stereophonic*.

quadruture error: *video recording head* misalignment.

Quantel: computerized *DVE* system for modifying/manipulating *video signal*. Compare: *ADO, Mirage*.

quantity discount: see: *frequency discount*.

quartz-iodine—Q-I: *tungsten-halogen lamp* (3,200–3,400K°) containing iodine gas in a quartz envelope; 650 *W*, 750 *W*, 1K *(redhead)*, 2K *(blonde)*.

Quasar: Japanese electronics manufacturer (division of *Matsushita*).

quasi-DBS: 9 *W* low power *satellite transmission* (3.7–4.2 *GHz*) to 6–15 ft. *backyard/cable* system *antennas*. See: *dish*. Compare: *early entry DBS, true DBS*.

Qube: discontinued (1983) *Warner/Amex* Columbus, Ohio, *interactive* (two-way) *cable* system.

quick cuts: instantaneous *picture* changes (without *dissolves*).

quick study: performer able to memorize lines rapidly.

Quincy (Mass.): 1986 Supreme Court decision striking down *Must Carry I*.

quintile: standard audience research division; $^1/_5$th of total *reach*.

quiz show scandals: rigged audience participation programming, and subsequent Congressional investigation (1968).

quonking: accidental sounds picked up by open *microphone*.

QVC: *satellite/cable network* home shopping service (1986).

R

==

RAB—Radio Advertising Bureau: *broadcast* industry marketing organization. Compare: *TVB*.

rabbit ears: V-shaped in-home *television antenna*.

raceway: recessed *cable* channel.

rack: pivot a *camera lens turret*. Also: Mount *reels* and *thread film* in *projection path*. Also: In Britain, register *film* in *projector gate*. Also: Sorting *pin* bar above editing *bin*. Also: Instrument or equipment mounting frame. See: *bay*.

rack and pinion: pinion gear engaging toothed rack bar, converting rotational to lateral movement (*lens* focussing, etc.).

rack focus: alter *focus* to another *camera* subject. Called *pull focus* in Britain.

rack over: shift non-*reflex camera lens* to *viewfinder* position.

radar: (*ra*dio *d*etecting *a*nd *r*anging) device generating *microwaves* reflected by target (first moon contact January, 1946: $384{,}402 \pm 1.5$ km).

Radar—Radio's All-Dimension Audience Research: British *radio* audience survey. Compare: *Jicrar*.

radiant energy: energy (usually electromagnetic) traveling in *waves*.

radiate: *transmit* electromagnetic *signal*.

radiation: energy emitted as *waves* or particles.

radiator: licensed/unlicensed *rf* device; unlicensed *field* strength *FCC*-limited to 40 μV/m at 3 *meters*.

radio: (Latin: "to radiate"; called "*wireless*" in Britain) *sound transmission* technique based on *wave* theories originated by *Clerk-Maxwell*, 1867;

demonstrated by Thomson, 1875; developed by *Hertz*, 1885; applied by *Marconi*, 1895; utilized in *De Forest*'s pioneer Caruso *broadcast*, 1910. Second only to *television* as most effective means of modern mass communication. See: *AM, FM*.

Radio Act: first U.S. government legislation to control domestic *radio* (1912). Compare: *FCC, Federal Radio Act*.

Radio Beijing: see: *RBI*.

Radio Canada: *CBC* French-language service (Quebec).

Radio Caroline: Europe's oldest *pirate radio;* uses floating North Sea *transmitter*.

Radio Denmark: Danish government *television network*.

Radio Free Europe—Radio Liberty: Munich-based news and analysis *broadcasting* in 25 languages aimed at the Soviet bloc. Convertly financed until 1960s by *CIA*.

radio frequency: see: *rf*.

radio home: *household* containing one or more *radio receivers*.

Radio Martí (after 1895 Cuban revolutionary Jose Martí): Florida Keys 50 *kw AM* station, *transmitting* Cuba-oriented *USIA/VOA* programming; has provoked retaliatory Cuban 50 *kw clear-channel interference*. See: *TV Marti*.

radio mike: in Britain, performer's concealed *microphone broadcasting* voice *signal* directly to *receiver/recorder*.

Radio Moscow: world's most powerful *broadcasting station*. Compare: *Radio Beijing*.

radio spectrum: *frequencies* from 25,000 to 50 billion *Hz*, equivalent of 21 octaves (visible light covers one octave).

radiotelegraphy: *Morse code broadcasting*, initiated by *Marconi* with one-mile *transmission* (1895).

radiotelephony: speech *broadcasting*, initiated with *De Forest*'s *audion tube* (1915).

radio telescope: giant *dish antenna*, intercepting weak extraterrestrial *radio signals*. See: *SETI*.

Radiovision: early 1920s *GE* experimental 30-*line television* system.

radio wave—long wave: *electromagnetic radiation* over 60 meters long, traveling in space at speed of light. See: *short wave*.

RAI I, II, III—Radiotelevisione Italiana: Italian government *broadcasting* facilities. Compare: *BBC, FCC, ORTF, RIAS*.

RAM—random access memory: stored *computer* data obtainable without sequential search.

random: uninfluenced by past behavior.

random access: instantaneous retrieval of recorded information.

random interlace: obsolete, imprecise sequential *scanning* of *picture tube field lines.* Compare: *positive interlace.*

random noise: series of nonpredictable narrow *pulses.* See: *S/N.*

random sample—probability sample: research units mechanically selected for statistical projection.

range: lowest to highest performable note by particular instrument or singer.

range extender: see: *extension tube.*

Rank: workhorse *flying-spot scanning* equipment.

raster: *picture tube scanned* area, partly hidden behind *receiver mask.*

raster graphics: *CGI,* defined by on-screen *pixel* selection.

raster scan: image-building from varying intensity *phosphor* dots.

rate base: projected *broadcast* facility *viewer* total, for *commercial rate card* structure.

rate card—card rate: *broadcast station*'s standard advertising charges, broken down by *time* of day, length of message, and *frequency* of *insertion.* Loosely, to pay this full *rate* with no discount.

rateholder: minor advertising announcement, *broadcast* only to maintain *sponsor*'s weekly *schedule* continuity and discount structure. See: *short rate.*

rating: size of potential or actual *broadcast* audience. (*ARB* Rating Number totals estimated local *households* viewing *telecast* during an average quarter hour of reported *transmission* period; *AA Rating* is percentage of *television homes viewing* average *telecast* minute.) See: *hypo.* Compare: *share.* Also: *Film emulsion speed* index number. See: *DIN, A(N)SI.* Also: *Circuit* or equipment *load* design capacity.

rating book: biweekly subscription booklet containing audience measurements. Loosely, the biweekly period itself. See: *Nielsen, NTI.*

rating point—point: *broadcast* audience size standard; 900,000+ *television homes* (1988). See: *gross rating points, net rating points.*

rating service: research organization offering periodic audience survey measurements.

ratio—editing ratio: relationship of *exposed film stock* to final *edited footage;* average around 7 to 1 (far higher for television commercials). Called *cutting ratio* in Britain. Also: see: *aspect ratio.*

raw stock: unexposed *negative film* or *virgin videotape.*

RBI—Radio Beijing International: world's second most powerful *broadcasting station.* Compare: *Radio Moscow.*

RBOC: see: *BOC*.

RBV—return beam vidicon: *Landsat* imaging device.

RCA Americom: see: *GE Americom*.

RCA Corporation (formerly Radio Corporation of America): U.S. electronics industry conglomerate; owned by *General Electric Company*. See: *Sarnoff Research Center, Satcom*.

RDD—random digit dialing: telephone audience survey technique, presumably unweighted because of random access to unlisted subscribers.

RDSS—radio determination satellite system: U.S. over-the-road truck location system; utilizes *Geostar* and *Loran-C* navigation *networks*.

reach—cumulative audience—cume: number of unduplicated *broadcast program* (or *commercial*) viewers over specific number of weeks. Compare: *frequency*.

reaction shot: cut to performer's emotional facial response. Compare: *cutaway*.

(sound) reader: *editing* device with *speaker/synchronizer playback head* reproducing *magnetic soundtrack*.

reading: actors' first script rundown. Also: *Animation frame* count.

read only: able to play back; unable to *record*. See: *ROM*.

read only memory: see: *ROM*.

readout: *retrieval* of stored information, usually in visual display form (see: *nixie*) or *hard copy*.

real estate: available *unrecorded* space on *video disk*.

real time: original time span, without compression or selective condensation. Compare: *subjective*. Also: Happening now.

rear projection: inverted (right for left) *film print, projected* through *translucent screen*.

rear (screen) projection—RP: *projection* of *still* or *motion picture* as scenic *background*. Normally used for scenes where background area is relatively small—e.g., looking through a car or room window. Called *back projection* in Britain. Compare: *background projector, front (axial) projection*.

rebroadcast: repeat performance. Also: *Relay* a *signal*.

recall interview: telephone audience survey technique researching recent *viewing*/listening. (Misses homes without phones.)

recce—reccy: (for *reconnaissance*) in Britain, *pre-production* assessment of proposed *remote broadcast location*.

receiver: combination of electronic equipment to *view* and/or hear *broadcast*. See: *set*. Compare: *amplifier, tuner*.

receptacle: power/*signal* outlet.

record: store electromagnetic *signals* for later *retrieval.* Also: *Grooved phonograph disk.*

record button: red plastic "lock" *U-matic* every *video cassettes;* its removal deactivates *re-record* capability. Compare: *knock-out tabs.*

record changer: see: *changer.*

record head: *magnetic gap(s)* in *tape path,* recording picture and/or *sound* information by realigning magnetic particles. Compare: *erase head.*

recording density: ability to *record* greater or lesser amounts of electromagnetic information. See: *packing density.*

recording engineer—recordist: *audio* or *VTR* technician.

recording studio: soundproofed room for *audio recording.*

recordist: in Britain, *audio* engineer in charge of *mixing* session.

rectifier: *AC* to *DC* conversion device. Compare: *inverter.*

Red Channels: *broadcasting*'s notorious 1950s political blacklist.

red gun: device emitting electrons at *picture tube* red *phosphors.* Compare: *blue gun, green gun.*

redhead: 1*KW quartz-iodine lamp.*

Red Lion (Pa.): 1969 Supreme Court decision affirming *FCC Fairness Doctrine.*

Red Network: early *NBC radio station affiliation.* Compare: *Blue Network.*

red pencil: eliminate air material. Compare: *blue pencil.*

reduction print: sub*standard*-width *film print,* projected down from larger *negative*—usually *35mm* to *16mm.* (Accompanying *soundtrack* is usually *contact-printed* from a same-sized *track negative.*)

redundant: backup equipment capable of performing identical function.

reel: flanged metal/plastic hub for winding and storing *film/tape.* Reel capacity usually 1,000 feet for *35mm film,* 400 feet for *16mm* (both slightly over 11 minutes). Standard 2″ *videotape* reel holds 4,800 feet (64 minutes). Standard ¼″ *audio tape* reels hold 2,400 feet (10″ reel), 1,200 feet (7″ reel), 600 feet (5″ reel). Called *spool* in Britain. Also: *Commercial production* house sample presentation.

reel-to-reel—open reel: tape *transport* system with separated supply *(feed)* and *take-up reels.* Compare: *cartridge, cassette.*

re-entry: production of additional *switcher effects* as part of original *effect.* See: *double re-entry.*

Reeves, Hazard: *digital signal* theorist, 1939.

reference black: darkest part of *television picture;* minimal (0.014 *V*) signal separating *black picture levels* from *sync signals.* Compare: *black level, reference white.*

reference white: brightest part of television picture, *transmitted* at 100% *voltage* (1.0 *V*) with recommended maximum reflectance value of 60%. See: *white clip.* Compare: *reference black.*

reflection: indirect illumination made visible by secondary surface.

reflection angle: angle at which indirect light leaves surface.

reflector: large mirror-like device (with different reflective characteristics on opposite sides) redirecting *location* sunlight. Compare: *butterfly.*

reflectoscope: see: *opaque projector.*

reflex: optical mirror system permitting through-the-camera-lens viewing of *filmed* subject.

reflex (axial) projection: in Britain, scenic *background* effect, achieved by low-intensity *projection* of *location slides* or *film* along taking-*lens* axis (by 45° half-silvered mirror) directly on performers, and on huge *Scotchlite* screen behind them. Compare: *back (screen) projection.*

regeneration: *signal* reconstruction/magnification.

regional: *network feed* to and within a specific U.S. geographical area, usually sponsored by advertisers with products not yet in national distribution. Compare: *basic network.*

registration: proper *alignment* of (1) visual elements, (2) separate *images* of a color television camera, (3) *animation cels,* etc.

registration pins—pilot pins: see: *pins.*

rehearse: practice performance.

relay: point-to-point *pickup* and *retransmission* system, usually *amplifying* original *signal.*

release: legal permission (or form on which it is executed). Also: News information provided by subject.

release print: *duplicate tape* or *film* for *air* use. Called *show print* in Britain. Compare: *answer print.*

reluctance: durable but low-quality *microphone.*

Rembrandt lighting: in Britain, 45° angling of *key light* to subject.

remote: *location broadcast.* See: *nemo, survey.* Called *OB* in Britain.

remote truck (van): self-contained *control room*-and-equipment *broadcast* vehicle, usually with *microwave* capacity. Called *OB van* in Britain.

renewal: contract extension on or before expiration. Also: Regranted *FCC station license.*

rental: lease of required production equipment. Called *hire* in Britain.

rep(resentative): see: *station rep.*

repeat: *rebroadcast program* or series. Also: Re-exposure of *animation cel cycle;* walking, running, etc.

repeater—booster: low power *transmitter,* improving inadequate *station signal* on same *channel.* Compare: *translator.*

replication: *duplication* of *master* material.

reportage: blend of *documentary* and *cinéma vérité* production.

report sheet: in Britain, camera operator's *take-by-take* record, with instructions to *laboratory.* Also called *camera sheet, dope sheet.*

reprint: make ("strike") additional *positive film print* from *negative; duplicate tape* from *master.*

reproducer: obsolete term for *phonograph pickup.*

reproduction: transformation of *recorded signals* into audible *sound.* Also: Generally, *duplication* of original material.

Request TV: Reiss Media *pay-per-view cable programing* service.

RER—Radio Expenditure Reports: trade organization measure of *radio advertising* dollar levels.

re-record: *duplicate* (or *record* over) previously *recorded* magnetic impulses.

re-run—rebroadcast: repeat *program* material.

reset: begin again.

residual: talent or musician *re-use* payment. Compare: *buyout, session fee.*

resistance: opposition in *conductor* to passage of steady electric *current.* See: *impedance, ohm.*

resistor: electrical *circuit resistance* component.

resolution: distinguishable *television picture* detail.

resolution chart—chart: standard *camera*-test artwork.

resonance: sound tone reinforcement by identical *frequency* from another source. Also: Natural *frequency* of vibrating body.

response: equipment *output* characteristics.

restore the loop: see: *lose the loop.*

resumé: personal employment history.

retail rate: lower *broadcast advertising time rate* for local merchants. Compare: *national.*

retained image: see: *burn-in.*

re-take: reshoot rejected material.

Rete-A: private Italian *television network.*

retention: *cable* system *subscriber* renewal.

reticulation: undesirable *film emulsion* wrinkling.

reticule: etched indications on camera *viewfinder* glass indicating un*masked projection* (or television *transmission*) "safe" areas. See: *Academy aperture, safety.* Compare: *cutoff.*

retrace: *scanning beam*'s left-to-right return for each successive *horizontal scan line* (in 10.5 *microseconds*).

retrieval: recovery of stored magnetic information.

return: 90° *(scenery) flat* angle.

re-use: see: *residual.*

Reuters: subscriber news service for *broadcast stations,* newspapers. Compare: *AP, UPI.*

reveal: widen (pull back from) camera position to include additional picture information.

reverb(eration): multiple echo effect added electronically (or acoustically) to *audio signal.*

reverberation time: time in which *sound level* diminishes to one-millionth of original intensity.

reversal—direct positive: *camera-original film* producing *positive* image when developed; eliminates intermediate *negative* and *printing* steps.

reverse action: shoot or print normal *film* action "backwards," *frame-by-frame,* for special visual *effect.* See: *scratch off.*

reverse compensation: non-traditional *affiliate* payment for *network* membership.

rewind: high-speed return of *film* or *tape* from *take-up* to *feed reel.*

rewinds: pair of geared hand-cranked devices spooling off or rewinding *film reels.* See: *tightwinder.*

rf—radio frequency: *waves* transmitting *video* and/or *audio* electronic *signals.* Compare: *af, if.*

RFI: *radio frequency interference* (eliminated with *fiber optics*).

rf modulator: portable-*VTR* device *feeding recorder playback signal* into locally vacant *television receiver channel.*

rf pattern: "herringbone" *television picture distortion* created by high-frequency *interference.*

RGB: television's red-orange, green, and blue-violet channels. See: *additive primaries, primary colors, triad.*

rheostat: wire coil tappable at any point to adjust *circuit resistance.* Compare: *SCR.*

rhubarb: in Britain, crowd murmurs.

rhythm & blues: *radio station format* featuring contemporary music with emphasis on black performers.

RIAA—Recording Industry Association of America: music *recording* trade association.

RIAS: *R*adio *I*n the *A*merican *S*ector (of Berlin). Compare: *RAI*.

ribbon: obsolete (delicate) *microphone* containing thin metal ribbon suspended between two magnetic poles. Bi- and unidirectional *pickup* pattern.

Richeouloff: *tape recording* experimenter, 1927.

Richter Ciné: *16mm motion picture camera.*

ride gain—ride the needle: *monitor recording* or *transmission levels.*

ridgepole—clothesline: *television* programming technique; schedules popular *network* shows at 9:00 P.M. throughout the week.

rifle—shotgun: long, highly *directional microphone.*

rig: set up equipment. Also: *Mobile unit.*

rigging: unfairly acquiring or disclosing bid information.

rights: creative or performance equities. See: *license, royalty.*

Rikisutvarpid-Sjonvarp: Icelandic government *television network.*

rimlight: high illumination from behind camera subject. See: *backlight.* Compare: *key, fill light.*

ringer: *teletype* news bulletin, heralded by machine "bells."

ring flash: axial light source fitted over *lens* barrel.

ringing: dark outlines around (usually *matted*) elements in *television picture.*

ringout: decay time of final musical note.

rip 'n' read: read *teletype* news material directly on air.

ripple: *optical effect* producing wavy or "melting" *film dissolve.* Also: *Amplitude* variations in power supply *output.*

ripple tray: shallow reflecting pan containing water and bits of broken mirror.

riser: low *set* platform. Called *block* in Britain. Compare: *apple, pancake.*

rise time: period required to charge electrical *potential.*

roadblocking: *scheduling* identical advertising message on all local *broadcast* facilities in same *time* period. Compare: *counterprogramming, horizontal* and *vertical saturation.*

robotics: automated process/movement control. Also: Remote-controlled studio equipment.

rock: to move *tape* manually back and forth across *playback head*, locating specific *recorded* material. Also: Popular music genre, originating in

1950s and including *country rock,* folk rock, *hard rock, MOR* rock, rock-a-billy, *soul* rock, etc.

Rockefeller Center Television—RCTV: abandoned *cable* service providing cultural programming.

rock 'n' roll: in Britain, *film audio mixing* equipment permitting easy forward/backward movement without complete rewinding of *mix* materials.

Roget, Peter Mark: *Thesaurus* compiler and developer of theory of *persistence of vision* (1824).

roll: aberrant vertical *television picture* movement. Also: Voice *cue* to start *film* or *tape* (''Roll 'em!''). Also: Length of *raw stock* on *core,* usually 1,000 feet of *35mm* or 400 feet of *16mm* film. Also: In Britain, drum-mounted *program credits.*

roll off: eliminate *high* or *low frequencies* (or both) from an *audio signal.* Called *cutoff* in Britain.

roll out: move product (and advertising) into new markets.

roll over: aberrant *television picture* effect of *unsynchronized edit.* Also: Replacement of *cable network feed* by local programming.

ROM—read only memory: *memory circuit* retrieving—but unable to process—information.

room tone: recorded ambient noise, used when spacing (opening up) *soundtracks.* Called *buzz track* and *atmosphere* in Britain.

ROS—run of schedule: *broadcast* advertising *scheduling* left to *station* discretion. *Rates* are lower, but *spots* are *preemptible.* See: *BTA.*

rostrum: in Britain, *motion picture camera* mounted vertically over horizontal subject table for single-*frame exposures;* movements of both *camera* and table are carefully coordinated. See: *animation camera.*

rotary: original telephone dial *input.* Compare: *touch-tone.*

rotation: see: vertical saturation.

rotoscope: individually inked ''traveling action'' *film,* changing shape from *frame* to *frame.* Compare: *blue matteing, traveling matte.*

rough: *demonstration* of proposed creative work. Compare: *final.*

rough cut: initial *work picture assembly* in approximate length and order, with *opticals* indicated with *china marker.* Compare: *fine cut.*

royalty: compensation for use of creative *equity.* See: *license, permission, rights.* Compare: *PD.*

royola: *payola* derived from interlocked business interest.

RP: see: *rear (screen) projection.*

rpm—revolutions per minute: *disk* rotation speed.

RTBF-I,II: Belgian government *television networks.*

RTE-I,II: Irish government *television networks.*

RTI—radiation transfer index: relative loss of transmitted *fiber optics* light *level,* after coupling and propagation.

RTL—Radio-Télévision Luxembourg: government *broadcasting network.*

RTL-Plus: Cologne-based European *satellite/cable* programming service.

RTL-TV-1: Belgian government *television* programming (1987); *transmitted* via *RTL.*

RTNDA—Radio Television News Directors Association: industry group of broadcast news supervisors.

RTP-I,II: Portuguese government *television networks.*

RTS—Royal Television Society: British professional membership organization.

rubberbanding: screen image contraction/expansion.

rumble: motor vibration transmitted at low *frequencies* from *phonograph turntable* through *pickup.*

run: schedule or *transmit program.*

runaway: *production* specifically organized to escape normal union *talent* or *crew* jurisdiction.

rundown: program event order.

runners: in Britain, metal girders suspending lights, etc., over *set.* See: *gantry.*

running part: continuous role in daily dramatic *television program.*

running shot: *camera* and subject maintain same relative motion against background.

running time: *broadcast* length.

run-through: cast *rehearsal* without technical *facilities.* Compare: *dry run, dress.*

run-up: *film reel projection* changeover procedure. Also: In Britain, time required to bring *film cameras* or *tape recorders* up to normal operating *speed.*

rushes—dailies: *film positives* processed overnight from previous day's original *negative* photography. See: *one-light.*

RUT: (hotel/motel) room using *television.*

RX: receive.

R-Y: *video color difference signal* obtained by subtracting *luminance signal* from red *signal.* See: *B-Y.* Compare: *Y.*

S

Saatchi & Saatchi: one of seven major (1987 gross *billings* between $3 and $5 billion) worldwide *advertising agencies*.

SABC—South African Broadcasting Corporation: government *broadcasting network* (English/Afrikaans language).

Sabre—Steerable Adaptive Broadcast Reception Equipment: low-*interference* British *UHF* receiving antenna.

sad: sex-and-drug oriented popular song *lyrics*.

safelight: *darkroom* illumination *wavelength* not affecting photographic *emulsions*.

safety: *unmasked* area of *transmitted television picture;* less critical *picture safety* denotes slightly larger area than *lettering safety*. See: *Academy aperture, reticule*. Compare: *cutoff*. Also: *Protection* copy.

safety tab: see: *knockout tab, record button*.

SAG—Screen Actors' Guild: *film* performers' union. Compare: *AFTRA*.

sales: *broadcast station*'s marketing group.

SAMPAC—Society of Advertising Music Producers, Arrangers & Composers: *commercial* music trade organization.

sample: elementary units selected from statistical population for research projection.

sampling error: slight, projectible difference between *sample* and actual *universe* survey results.

sampling frequency: discrete per-line sampling rate during *analog-to-digital conversion*.

sandbag: sand-filled heavy canvas bag used to weight *set*-stand legs, etc. Compare: *water bag*.

Sanyo: major Japanese electronics manufacturer.

(David) Sarnoff Research Center: (former *RCA*) electronic research laboratory.

Satcom: *RCA Americom* (now *GE Americom*) *C-band/Ku-band geosynchronous communications satellite* program; extensively used by *cable networks, superstations*. Compare: *sitcom*.

Satcom F-I: *RCA Americom communications satellite* (first to carry a *superstation—WTBS-TV*, 1976), retired from 139° W, 1984.

Satcom I-R: *GE Americom 24-transponder C-band communications satellite* at 139° W (1983).

Satcom II-R: *GE Americom 24-transponder C-band communications satellite* at 72° W (1983).

Satcom III: *RCA Americom communications satellite*, lost on launch, 1979.

Satcom III-R: *GE Americom 24-transponder C-band communications satellite* at 131° W (1981); carries *CNN*.

Satcom IV: *GE Americom 24-transponder C-band communications satellite* at 82° W (1982).

Satcom V (now Aurora I): *GE Americom 24-transponder C-band communications satellite* at 143° W (1982).

Satcom K-1: *GE Americom 16-transponder Ku-band communications satellite* at 85° W (1986).

Satcom K-2: *GE Americom 16-transponder Ku-band communications satellite* at 81° W (1985).

Satcom K-3: planned *GE Americom Arianespace*-launched *16-transponder Ku-band communications (Crimson) satellite* for 99° W (1990).

Satcom K-4: planned *GE Americom 16 Ku-band/24 C-band transponder communications satellite* for 101° W (1991).

satellite: orbiting space station 22,240 miles high relaying up to 40 *uplink C-band* and *Ku-band television signals* back to earth in ¼ second. Initiated with *Telstar*, 1962. Average life ten years; average cost, including launch, $50 million. See: *Comsat, earth station, Intelsat*. Compare: *antenna, balloon, microwave*. Also: Separate *television broadcast* facility *retransmitting* nearby *station's* air material, increasing local *coverage*.

Satellite Business Systems: see: *SBS*.

satellite finder: device orienting *dish* for *satellite reception*.

Satellite News Channel: abortive (1981) Westinghouse/*ABC* all-news *satellite/ cable* programming service; sold to *TBS* 1983.

Saticon: improved *television camera pickup tube* with selenium/arsenic/tellurium *target* surface coating; offers low *lag, 1-gamma sensitivity.* Compare: *image orthicon, Leddicon, Newvicon, Plumbicon, Trinicon, vidicon.*

SAT-1: Mainz-based European *satellite/cable* programming service.

saturation: heavy bombardment of *broadcast* audiences with advertising message. Also: *Intensity* of picture color. See: *autochroma, chroma.* Compare: *brightness range, contrast, hue.*

Saturday morning: traditional children's *television* program *scheduling.*

SAWA—Screen Advertising World Association: trade group promoting *film* advertising in theatres; conducts annual festival.

S-band: 2.5/2.6 *GHz satellite transmission frequency.* Compare: *C-band, K-band, Ka-band, Ku-band.*

SBCA—Satellite and Broadcasting Communications Association: *satellite* operators' trade and *signal* protection organization.

SBRTC—Southern Baptist Radio and Television Conference: former *ACTS* operator.

SBS—Satellite Business Systems: *Ku-band geosynchronous* business *communications satellite* program. Coestablished by *IBM/Comsat General/*Aetna Insurance; now owned by *MCI/IBM.* Handles 64 million *computer bits* per second.

SBS I: *Comsat* 10-*transponder Ku-band communications satellite* at 99° W (1980). Now out of fuel.

SBS II: *Comsat* 10-*transponder Ku-band communications satellite* at 97° W (1981). Now out of fuel.

SBS III: *MCI* 10-*transponder Ku-band communications satellite* at 95° W (1982).

SBS IV: *IBM* 10-*transponder Ku-band communications satellite* at 91° W (1984).

SBS V: *IBM Arianespace*-launched *communications satellite* (1988).

SBS VI: planned *IBM Arianespace*-launched *communications satellite* (1990).

SBT—Show Business Today: planned *HSN satellite/cable* entertainment programming service (1989).

SC—Sports Channel: Cablevision *satellite/pay cable* service programming East Coast collegiate/professional sports events.

scale: minimum union contract pay rates.

scallop: wavy *television picture distortion* caused by improper *quad VTR* vertical *vacuum guide alignment.*

scan: (principle enunciated by LeBlanc, 1880) horizontal *electron beam sweep* across *television camera target* or *picture tube* in $\frac{1}{15}$ *millisecond.* Full vertical *scan* in U.S., $\frac{1}{60}$ second; in Britain, $\frac{1}{50}$.

ScanAmerica: *Arbitron*/TIME, Inc., *peoplemeter*/marketing methodology; uses *UBC scanning wand.* Compare: *AGB, NTI.*

scanner: *shortwave receiver monitoring* police/fire *wavelengths.*

scanning: converting image to electronic *signal.*

scanning disk: mechanical *television* system invented by Nipkow, 1884.

scan(ning) line: single horizontal *path traced* across *television picture tube* by *electron beam.* See: *blanking interval.*

scanning spot beam: experimental *satellite communications* system *broadcasting* "bursts" of information at 600 million *bits* per second over multiple 10,000 sq. mi. areas.

scatter market: national advertising *time* unsold after *up-front* buying period.

scatter plan: carefully random *broadcast advertising schedule* for audience maximization.

scene: *setting* for particular piece of *action,* usually with single *camera set-up.*

scenery: *set* pieces suggesting real (usually interior) *location.*

SCG—Screen Cartoonists Guild: *animation* workers' union.

schedule: dates and *times* of *advertiser*'s *broadcast* commitments. See: *media, time buyer.* Compare: *campaign.*

schematic: electronic equipment wiring diagram.

Schlieren lens: optical device for *video projection.*

Schmidt mirror: optical device for *video projection.*

schtick: unusual personal routine. See: *gimmick.*

Scientific Atlanta: major *dish* manufacturer.

sciopticon: theatrical device projecting moving *slide.*

scoop—basher: 500-*watt* circular *floodlight.*

scope—oscilloscope: *cathode-ray tube* device for visual electronic *signal* analysis. Also: *Cinemascope.*

score: compose music against *picture.* Also: Musical portion of *program.*

Scotchlite: proprietary highly reflective *background* sheeting.

scouting—location scouting—survey: *pre-production* assessment of proposed *remote broadcast* site. Called *recce* or *reccy* (for *reconnaissance*) in Britain.

SCR—silicon-controlled rectifier: *solid-state semiconductor;* basis for most luminaire *dimmers.* Compare: *rheostat.*

scramble/unscramble: *encode*/*decode* electronic *signal transmission.*

scrambled: jumbled *pay-television transmission.*

scraper: knifelike *splicer* device removing *film emulsion* preparatory to applying *cement*.

scratch: transverse mechanical damage to *oxide* coating of *videotape*, resulting in *playback dropouts*. Also: Similar vertical damage to *negative* (white *scratch*) or *positive* (black *scratch*) *film*.

scratch off: *animation film effect,* photographed (not *printed*) backwards to make removed material ''appear.'' See: *reverse action.*

scratch print: sample *positive stock shot* deliberately damaged to prevent illicit *duplication,* with original *negative* maintained intact for subsequent *print* order and *duplication.*

scratch track—guide track: temporary *soundtrack* prepared to assist *editing* or subsequent *silent camera work.*

screen: reflective surface for *film projection.* Also: *Phosphorescent* inner surface of *CRT* or *television picture tube.*

screen ratio: see: *aspect ratio.*

Screen Sport: British *cable network.*

scrim: gauze (or metal) light *diffuser.* See: *butterfly, silk, spun.* Also: Gauze stage curtain.

script: material written for *broadcast* performers to read or act.

script girl: see: *continuity clerk.*

scriptwriter: professional *broadcast* writer. See: *continuity.*

scroll: vertical *crawl.*

SCSA—Standard Consolidated Statistical Area: Federal Office of Management and Budget population *coverage* designation.

SE—SFX: *sound effects.* Compare: *effects, FX, special effects.*

SEC—secondary electron conduction: *television camera pickup tube* designed for low light *levels.*

SECAM—séquential couleur et mémoire: French, Eastern Europe, Soviet, and Middle East *color television transmission* system (625-*line,* 50-*field,* 6 *MHz bandwidth*). Operationally the world's simplest system, less demanding in terms of timing accuracy and least subject to *color signal distortion; modulates* different *carriers* for *R-Y* (4.4*MHz*) and *B-Y* (4.25 *MHz*), *transmitting* them on alternate *scan lines*—hence, ''System Essentially Contrary to American Method.'' Compare: *NTSC, PAL.*

second: duration of 9,192,631,770 cycles of radiation associated with specified transition of atom of cesium, $\frac{1}{60}$ minute.

secondary service: see: *skywave.*

second generation: see: *generation.*

Section 315: see: *Equal Time.*

Section 326: "free speech" portion of Federal Communications Act of 1934, prohibiting *FCC censorship.*

see/fee: pay (per *program) cable television.* See: *pay cable, premium television.* Compare: *pay television, STV.*

SEG—Screen Extras Guild: *film extras'* union. Also: *Special effects* generator. See: *matteing amplifier.*

segmentation—niche strategy: targeting specific audience in a market.

segmented: *"Type B"* 1" *videotape* format (*Bosch*) recording each *television frame* in 51 short tracks; *freeze-*framing only with *frame-store* attachment. Compare: *non-segmented, single-scan.*

segué: (musical term = "follow up.") "dissolve" from one *audio* element into another. Compare: *cut.*

SelectaVision: *RCA* trade name for both *VCR* and (discontinued) *CED video disk* equipment.

selected take: approved version of *taped* or *filmed scene.* See: *buy.* Compare: *hold, outtake.*

selectivity: *receiver (tuner)* discrimination between two adjacent *broadcast signals.*

SelecTV: *satellite/cable* programming service.

selenium: light-sensitive element (electrical properties discovered by May, 1873).

self-matteing: *film optical* process utilizing color *mattes* to eliminate *rotoscoping.* Compare: *chromakey.*

sel-sync—self-synchronous: *servo* control maintaining two motors at identical speed. Also: *Overdub* new elements on existing *recording.*

semiconductor: element (silicon, germanium, etc.) with electrical properties between *conduction* and *insulation,* capable of electron transfer (by free electrons in molecular structure) on application of tiny *voltages.* See: *chip, integrated circuit, microprocessor.*

senior: 5,000 *watt spotlight.* Also called *five* or *5K.* Compare: *junior.*

sensitivity: index of equipment *signal response.*

sensitometer: *film emulsion speed* measurement device. Compare: *densitometer.*

separation: protective *time* period between competitive *commercials.* See: *product protection.* Also: Breakdown into *primary colors.* Also: *Decibel* ratio between *speaker channels.* Also: *Frequency* spacing; $TV = 6MHz$, $AM = 15 KHz$, $FM = 200 KHz.$

separation positives—color separations: individual b/w record of each of the three *primary* components of *color negative film,* for *optical* work for future *print (color shift)* protection. See: *prism block, Technicolor, Vid-tronics.*

sequential scanning: see: *progressive scanning.*

serial: *across-the-board soap opera.*

servo: "closed" system utilizing *output* to control *input.*

SESAC: (originally *S*ociety for *E*uropean *S*tage *A*uthors and *C*omposers) trade guild protecting musical performance rights. Compare: *ASCAP, BMI.*

Sesame Street: long-lived *CTW* program (features Jim *Henson's Muppets*).

session—date: *audio recording booking.*

session fee: talent payment for initial *filming* or *recording* services. Compare: *residual.*

set: see: *receiver.*

set(ting): *studio* construction suggesting real (usually *interior*) *location.* Compare: *cyc, limbo, no-seam.*

set-and-light: prepare *studio production.* See: *dress.*

Seti—Search for Extraterrestrial Intelligence: *NASA* program continuously broadcasting Earth information into space.

set light: *background* (opposed to subject) illumination.

sets-in-use—audience potential: obsolete research survey count of home *receivers* actually switched on during specific time period. See: *HUR, HUT.*

setup: position of *camera* and *recording* equipment, *scenery,* and *props* at start of *shot.*

set-up—pedestal: electronic calibration (interval between *blanking* and *black level pulses*) of *television picture black levels (brightness* control on home *receivers*). See: *blacker than black, reference black.*

7½ ips: (usually nonprofessional) *audio tape recording speed.* Compare: *15 ips.*

750: baby *spotlight.*

78 rpm: obsolete *phonograph disk* rotation speed. See: *shellac.*

SFP—Société Française de Production: French government *television* production facility (derived from *ORTF*) feeding *channels* TF1, A2, FR3.

SFX—SE: *sound effects.* Compare: *effects, FX, special effects.*

shade: degree of black mixed into pure *hue.*

shader—video engineer: technician controlling *television picture* quality *(black level, color balance, exposure gamma, video gain)* for *switcher.*

shading: *television picture contrast* adjustment.

shadow mask: perforated *mask* directly behind face of *color television picture tube,* separating *RGB* electron *beams.* Compare: *faceplate.*

share—share point: audience survey percentage of *households* actually *viewing station*'s *programming* during average broadcast minute. Compare: *rating.*

shared I.D.: *station identification* formerly added to *commercial copy* on *slide,* card or *film.*

shared time: simultaneous *computer* usage by two or more *terminals.*

share the boob: enjoy equal *exposure* on *television.*

sharpness: apparent *image resolution.*

shash: in Britain, *television picture breakup* caused by weak *video signal* reception.

shellac: obsolete *78 rpm phonograph disk pressing* material.

SHF—super high frequency: *wavelengths* 3-30 *GHz.*

shielded cable: inner *signal conductor* protected (from stray *signal interference*) by outer *grounded* metallic braid.

SHO—Showtime/The Movie Channel: *Warner/Viacom/TCI satellite/cable* programming service.

shoot: *film* or *videotaping;* possibly derived from Marey's 1882 photographic "rifle." See: *shot.*

shoot and protect: *framing film* or *tape action* for one *aspect ratio,* while anticipating *projection* in others.

shooter: *cameraman.*

shooting date: scheduled day of *filming/videotaping.*

shooting script: numbered *scenes* with technical instructions.

shootoff: excess artwork border, insuring *bleed* of camera *image.*

shop steward: on-site union spokesman for management discussions.

short: *program* material hardly filling allotted *time.* Compare: *long, tight.* Also: Accidental electrical *circuit grounding.*

short end: un*exposed film* at *tail* of *exposed reel.*

short rate: additional charge when advertiser fails to fulfill contract *rate.* Compare: *rateholder.*

short skip: minimal *transmission signal* reflection (100 to 1,000 miles). See: *skip effect.* Compare: *long skip.*

short wave: *electromagnetic radiation* up to 60 meters long, traveling in space at speed of light. Compare: *long wave.*

shot: individually photographed *scene.* See: *shoot.*

shot box: preset device controlling *zoom lens* system.

shotgun—rifle: long, highly *directional microphone.*

shot list—shot sheet: *live television cameraman's* card, listing his shots. Called *crib card* in Britain.

shoulder brace: hand-held body-conforming *camera* support.

shouter: presidential press conference with helicopter motor background.

Show Business Today: see: *SBT.*

show print: in Britain, *duplicate tape* or *film* for *air* use.

Showtime: *Viacom satellite/pay cable* feature *motion picture programming* service.

shunt: divert power/*signal.*

shutter: rotating, segmented *disk* in both *film camera* and *projector.* Also: *Spotlight intensity* control.

shutter bar: horizontal line area moving upward, in *television picture* of *film screen* projection (and vice versa). Called *bar line* in Britain.

shutters: vertical slat *diffusers* affixed to *brute.*

shuttle: *videotape fast-forward* or *rewind mode.*

shuttle orbiter: 200-ton rocket-launched 7-astronaut ''space glider''; can deploy/retrieve *communications satellites.*

SI: *I*nternational *S*ystem of measurement.

sibilance: voice *tape hiss.*

sideband: *rf-modulated* area above (or duplicated below) *carrier frequency.* Note: In single *sideband transmission,* one *sideband* is suppressed at *transmitter.*

sidebar: secondary event.

sidelobe: spurious *antenna* response, reducing efficiency.

SIGGRAPH—Special Interest Group on Computer Graphics: industry conference organization.

Sigint: U.S. *satellite* interception of Soviet military intelligence.

signal: electric impulse derived from and convertible to visible *picture* and/or audible *sound.*

signal generator: *television test signal* device.

signal piracy: override *television transmission* with stronger, illegitimate *signal.*

signal-to-noise ratio—S/N—snr: *signal* strength (expressed in *db's*) as function of extraneous *interference* induced by *transmission* system itself. The higher the *S/N* the better the sound.

signatory: *producer* formally adhering to *talent* union contract. See: *letter of adherence.*

signature: unique musical device denoting specific product or *advertiser*.

sign-on—sign-off: *station identification* information *broadcast* at beginning and end of daily *transmission*.

silent: *film* prepared or *projected* without *soundtrack*. Compare: *sound*.

silent speed: 16 *frame-per-second film exposure* rate (meets *persistence of vision* requirements). Compare: *sound speed*.

Silicon Valley: epithet for 25-mile Santa Clara, California, area producing major U.S. share of metal oxide *semiconductor memories* and *silicon chip microprocessors*.

silicon wafer: ingot base for *integrated circuits;* sliced into individual *chips*.

silk: gauze light *diffuser*. See: *butterfly, scrim, spun*.

silver-oxide battery: button-sized, low-power *dry cell* (characterized by long life, sudden failure).

simulcast: simultaneously *broadcast* complementary *signals* on two different *transmitters*.

SIN—Spanish International Network: U.S. Spanish-language program *network*.

single broad: box-shaped 2,000 *watt fill light*.

single perf(oration): *16mm film* with *soundtrack* along one edge, *sprocket* holes along the other. Compare: *double perf*.

single rate card: *broadcast station*'s identical charge for both *national* and local advertising. Compare: *retail rate*.

single-scan—non-segmented: *"Type C" 1" videotape* format *(Ampex, Sony) recording* one complete *television field* during each *head* pass; permits *freeze-framing*. Compare: *segmented*.

single sprocket: see: *single perf*.

single-strand: successive *negative* sequences *optically printed* on one piece of *film*.

single system: *picture* and *sound* simultaneously *recorded* (and *developed*) on same piece of *film; pullup* requires audio pauses at *edits*. Compare: *double system*.

siphoning: *fee-cable transmission* of program also available by free *broadcast*. Practice banned by FCC, 1972; reversed 1979.

Sirio: developmental *ESA satellite* (1975). See: *ECS, H-Sat, OTS, Symphonie*.

SIT—silicon-intensified target: *television camera pickup tube* designed for low light *levels;* offers low *lag*, high *sensitivity*, good *resolution*.

sitcom—situation comedy: popular U.S. *television* program genre. Compare: *Satcom*.

SITE—Satellite Instructional Television Experiment: educational *transmission* by *satellite* (first used over India, 1974).

625-line: standard number of *horizontal line sweeps* per *frame* in all Eastern Hemisphere (except Japan) *television transmission* systems (offering better *picture resolution* than U.S. *525-line*).

16mm: *film stock 16mm* wide (for safety reasons, purposely sized less than half of older inflammable *35mm nitrate stock*), adopted as international standard 1923; 40 *frames* to foot, 0.6 *feet per second* at *sound speed* (24 *fps*). Compare: *8mm, Super 8, 35mm.*

60: see: *minute.* Compare: *30, split-30, 15, 10.*

$64,000 Question: see: *quiz show scandals.*

skating: unequal *phonograph record groove* wear.

skew: zig-zag *television* picture *distortion* caused by improper *quad VTR* horizontal vacuum guide *alignment.*

skip effect: long-distance reflection of *radio waves* (sometimes erratic) from *ionosphere*. See: *long skip, short skip.*

skip frame: *printing* every other *frame* to double apparent speed of action. Compare: *double print.*

Skyband: (former Inter-American Satellite Television) Murdoch-proposed *Ku-band DBS* programming service, abandoned 1983. See: *Sky Channel.*

Skycam: proprietary remote-controlled cable-suspended electronic *zoom camera* for sports stadium overhead photography. See: *motion control.*

Sky Channel: London-based European *satellite/cable* programming service; replaced *Skyband.*

sky filter: see: *haze filter.*

sky pan: *cyc floodlight.*

skywave: secondary portion of *broadcast signal* radiating skyward *(AM* reflects from *ionosphere)*. Compare: *groundwave.* See: *heaviside layer.*

slant track: see: *helical scan.*

slap: in Britain, performer's *makeup.*

slash print: in Britain, quick non*balanced print* from newly completed *optical picture negative* to check mechanical *printing* errors. Often used for *dubbing.*

slate: several *frames* of a small blackboard with chalked *scene* information, filmed at start of each *take;* often a hinged *clapstick* provides *double-system synchronization.* Called *ident board, number board, clapper board,* or *take board* in Britain. See: *end slate.* Also: Equivalent verbal recorded identification on original *soundtrack;* called *announcement* in Britain. Compare: *electronic slate.*

slave(s): *recorder(s) dubbing playback* from a *master.* Also: *Videotape* so used.

SLD—superluminescent diode: *fiber optic* light source.

sled: *set luminaire* support.

Slice—Source Label Identifying and Coding Equipment: in Britain, *IBA* equipment for *transmitting* non*program* data during *television vertical blanking interval.* Compare: *Antiope, Ceefax, Oracle, Teletext, Viewdata.*

slice (of life): *television commercial* creative technique; purports to reflect conversation of real people.

slide: small transparent photograph, mounted in *drum* and projected on *camera chain* for *television broadcast.*

slide film: sequence of individual frames in *cartridge, slide projector;* with or without separate *synchronized soundtrack.* Compare: *filmstrip.*

slide projector: light source/*lens* system, projecting individual sequential materials (usually $2'' \times 2''$ 35mm *transparencies*).

slider: see: *fader.*

slinky: large *transparency* for *overhead projector.*

slop print: see: *check print.*

slot: one of only ninety possible equatorial orbit positions (with 4° separation, 1988) for *geosynchronous satellites.* Also: Recurring program period.

slow (fast): *emulsions* less (or more) *sensitive* to light. (Slow *emulsions* tend to be less *grainy.*)

slow-mo: *video disk* equipment (recording 30 seconds of *real time*) for speed-up, *slow motion, freeze frame,* or *reverse action* effects (introduced in 1961). See: *super slo-mo.*

slow motion: apparent slowing of action by *film overcranking.* Called *turn fast* in Britain.

slow scan: simplified *television transmission* system for *still* subjects (also used in space exploration).

SLR—single lens reflex: *35mm still camera* through-the-*lens viewing/focusing.*

Slugger—Small Lightweight GPS Receiver: hand-held battery operated military position indicator. See: *GPS.*

small scale integration—SSI: measure of *semiconductor* design complexity; number of *circuits* on single *silicon chip.* Compare: *LSI, SSI, VLSI.*

SMARTS—Selective Multiple Address Radio and Television Service: *satellite/cable* programming system.

smart terminal: *receive/process/send* unit. Compare: *dumb terminal.*

SMATV—Satellite Master Antenna Television: *direct satellite transmission* to apartment project, hotel, etc., *master antennas.* Avoids municipal street *franchise* requirements. See: *MATV.*

smear: see: *comet tail.*

Smith, Oberlin: *magnetic sound recording* experimenter (*"Some Possible Forms of Phonograph,"* 1888).

SMPTE—Society of Motion Picture and Television Engineers—"Simpty": standards-setting professional engineering group. Compare: *IEEE.*

SMPTE standard test bars: see: *color bars.*

SMSA—Standard Metropolitan Statistical Area: Federal Office of Management and Budget market designation.

S/N: see: *signal-to-noise-ratio.*

sneak: slow *sound* or picture *fade-in* or *-out.*

SNG—satellite newsgathering: *uplinked* local news coverage. See: *Conus, SNV.* Compare: *ENG.*

SNV—satellite newsgathering vehicle: *television station* mobile *uplink.* See: *SNG.*

snoot—funnel: cone or tubelike attachment pinpointing spotlight *beam.*

snorkel: inverted periscopic *lens* system, permitting unusual *close-up camera* perspectives.

snow—visible noise: *television picture breakup,* caused by weak *video signal* reception. Called *shash* in Britain.

soap (opera): (from traditional detergent sponsorship) daytime *broadcast,* usually sexual or melodramatic.

soapdish: *audio cassette* plastic container.

Société Française de Production et de Création Audiovisuelles: major French *film/videotape production* organization.

socket: mechanical *circuit* inter*connector (female).* Compare: *plug.*

sodium thiosulfate—hypo: photo-developing fixative.

SOF—sound-on-film: *footage* accompanied by *sound,* usually *filmed* by *16mm single-system* camera.

soft: unintentional or deliberate lack of sharp *focus.*

soft copy: *CRT* display. Compare: *hard copy.*

soften: lose *focus.* Compare: *harden.*

softlite—softlight: *luminaire* providing bright, diffused illumination.

software: *computer* programming. Also: *Broadcast* programming. Compare: *hardware.*

solar array: *communications satellite* cylindrical/sail panel area of sunlit *photoelectric cells,* charging storage *batteries.*

solenoid: electromagnetic switch.

solid state: *transistorized circuit;* replaces *vacuum tubes.*

SOM—share of market: competitive brand sales evaluation.

sonic: in audible range (20–20,000 *Hz*). Compare: *infrasonic, ultrasonic.*

sonic cleaner—ultrasonic cleaner: *ultra high-frequency sound wave film*-cleaning device.

sonovox: device coupling speech with *sound effects.*

Sony: (from Latin *sonus* = "sound") major Japanese electronics manufacturer.

Sony Decision: 1979 California U.S. District Court ruling (sustained 5 to 4 by U.S. Supreme Court, 1983) that "noncommercial home use *(Betamax)* recording of material broadcast over public airwaves does not constitute copyright infringement."

SOT: start of *tape.* Compare: *EOT.*

soul: popular music genre; includes elements of gospel, *rhythm and blues,* etc.

sound: *film* prepared or projected with *soundtrack.* Compare: *silent.* Also: See: *sound wave.*

sound bite: *edited* fraction of *television* news interview. Compare: *vidclip.*

sound drum: flywheel insuring smooth *film* movement over *projector sound head.*

sound effects—SE—SFX: *recorded* or *live audio* effects creating illusion of realistic or symbolic sounds. Compare: *EFX, FX.*

sound filmstrip projector: *frame*-at-a-time *film projector* with built-in *synchronized audio* source. Compare: *filmstrip projector.*

sound head: *film projector* system "reading" *optical* or *magnetic soundtrack.*

sound (effects) man: technician providing realistic or stylized *broadcast sound effects.*

sound reader: *film editing* device *playing back optical* or *magnetic soundtracks.*

sound report: *film sound* recordist's *take-by-take* record.

sound speed: *(film)* 24 *frame-per-second exposure* rate, offering *high-fidelity sound playback.* Compare: *silent speed.* Also: (Physics) 1,100 feet per second.

sound stage: soundproofed *filming/videotaping* area in *studio* or *production house.* See: *int.* Compare: *lot.*

soundtrack—track: *audio* portion of *film/videotape.*

sound wave: area of air pressure created by any kind of mechanical vibration.

soup: *film developing* solution.

South Pacific: *communications satellites;* #1 at 70° W; #2 at 119° W.

SOV—share of voice: individual brand sales evaluation.

SP—standard play: *VCR cassette record/playback* time *mode.* Compare: *EP, LP.*

SPACE: *satellite* industry trade association.

Spacenet I: *GTE Spacenet* 6 *Ku-band/*18 *C-band transponder communications satellite* at 120° W (1984). See: *Spacenet IV.*

Spacenet II: *GTE Spacenet* 6 *Ku-band/*18 *C-band transponder communications satellite* at 69° W (1984). See: *Spacenet V.*

Spacenet III: *GTE Spacenet* 6 *Ku-band/*18 *C-band communications satellite;* lost on *Arianespace* launch, 1985.

Spacenet III-R: *GTE Spacenet* 6 *Ku-band/*18 *C-band communications satellite* at 87° W (1988).

Spacenet IV: planned *GTE Spacenet* 22 *Ku-band/*24 *C-band transponder communications satellite* at 120° W (1993, will replace *Spacenet I*).

Spacenet V: planned *GTE Spacenet* 22 *Ku-band/*24 *C-band transponder communications satellite* at 69° W (1993, will replace *Spacenet II*).

Spanish International Network: see: *SIN.*

Spanish windlass: in Britain, chain or cable anchoring *tripod* to *stage screw.*

sparkle: white *print* specks=*film negative* dirt; black *print* specks=*film print* dirt.

sparks: *set* electrician. See: *gaffer.*

speaker: see: *loudspeaker.*

spec(ulation): creative work, anticipating acceptance/payment.

special: *one-shot* major *television program.* See: *blockbuster.* Compare: *across the board, strip.*

special effects: camera illusions. Also: Electronic generation of graphic elements; *wipes, dissolves, inserts,* etc. See: *matteing amplifier, SEG.* Compare: *sound effects.*

spec(ification) sheet: technical equipment information.

spectrum: full *broadcast frequency range.* See: *electromagnetic spectrum.*

spectrum allocation: international/national designation of certain *bandwidths* at certain *frequencies* for specific purposes.

spectrum fee: proposed annual government charge for private commercial use of *broadcast frequencies;* estimated value (U.S. Senate, 1988) = $500 billion.

specular: mirror-like reflectance from performer's eyes (or teeth). See: *eye light*.

speed: *film emulsion* light *sensitivity*. Also: Call when *camera* or *recording* equipment reaches proper operating rate. See: *tape*.

speed up: hand *cue* to increase *talent* performing speed.

spherical: *earth station antenna* (spherical in both horizontal and vertical planes) *receiving* several *satellite signals* simultaneously. Compare: *torus*.

spider: multi-outlet electrical *cable* box. Also: In Britain, metal floor brace for *film camera tripod*. Also: see: *spyder*.

spigot: in Britain, threaded *luminaire mounting* pipe.

spike: *signal peak transient*. Also: *Voltage surge* affecting delicate electronic *circuitry*.

spill: undesirable illumination.

spill-in: percentage of home market audience viewing outside-market *station*.

spill-out: percentage of outside market audience viewing home market *station*.

spindle: rotating shaft in *tape transport* system. See: *capstan*.

splice: joint between two separate pieces of *tape* or *film*. Called *join* in Britain.

splicer: device for accurate joining of *edited film frames,* using transparent tape or *cement*. Called *joiner* in Britain.

splicing block: grooved device to cut and join *audio tape*. Compare: *Gibson Girl*.

splicing tape: specially formulated, noncreeping pressure-sensitive tape, applied to *base* side of *audio tape splice*.

split focus: approximated *focus* between subjects at varying distances from *camera*.

split reel: reel with screwable flange for removing *cored film* without unspooling. Called *split spool* in Britain.

split screen: divided *frame* containing two or more *image* areas.

splitter—directional coupler: device dividing *signal input* equally between two or more *outputs*.

split-30: two *15-second commercial* messages for one *advertiser*. Compare: *minute, 30, 10*.

sponsor: *broadcast advertiser*. See: *account, client*.

spool: in Britain, flanged metal/plastic hub for winding and storing *film* and *videotape*.

Sports Channel: see: *SC*.

spot: colloquial term for broadcast *commercial* (from days when *networks* sold *sponsorships;* only local *stations* sold individual "on the spot" *com-*

mercials). Also: (Spotlight) directional *luminaire* with variable-angle, *focusable* beam.

spot beam: section of *satellite signal* directed to area outside normal *footprint*.

Spotlight: in Britain, four-volume directory of performing *talent*.

spotlight: see: *spot*.

SpotNet I: planned *National Exchange* 18 *Ku-band "spot beam" transponder communications satellite* 101° W.

SpotNet II: planned *National Exchange* 18 *Ku-band "spot beam" transponder communications satellite* 93° W.

spot television—spot radio: *commercial* time purchased market by market by *advertiser* with national or regional product distribution.

spotter: sports *announcer*'s assistant.

spray: reduce reflected glare with aerosol *matte* finish. Also: Special *laboratory film developing* process.

spread—stretch: slow down *broadcast* presentation. Also: Unplanned increase in running time. Also: **spread:** diffuse *luminaire beam*.

sprocket: toothed gear in *film* transport system, engaging symmetrical edge *perforations (sprocket holes)* of varying dimensions. See: *double perf, single perf*.

sprocket holes: see: *sprocket*.

spud: *luminaire* pipe support. See: *turtle*. Compare: *century stand*.

spun: gauze light *diffuser*. See: *butterfly, scrim, silk*.

Sputnik I: initial (*transmission* only) global *satellite*, launched by U.S.S.R. October 4, 1957. Compare: *Explorer I*.

sputtering: (obsolete) gold surfacing of *acetate phonograph disk recording*, prior to *pressing;* replaced by silverplating. Compare: *one-step, two-step*.

spyder: small *camera dolly*. Compare: *crab dolly*.

SQ: Sansui-pioneered *matrix quadruphonic* system. Compare: *QS*.

squeegee: wiping device in continuous *film processor*.

(un)squeeze: (de)*anamorphize* a *film image*.

squelch: *receiver* "gate" *circuitry;* eliminates un*modulated signal*.

SRA—Station Representatives Association: trade organization of local *station* national *advertising representatives*.

SRG: Swiss government (three-language) *television network*.

SSI—small scale integration: measure of *semiconductor* design complexity; number of *circuits* on a single *silicon chip*. Compare: *IC, LSI, MSI, VLSI*.

SSL: *satellite*-to-*studio link*.

SSPD: self-scanned *photodiode* array.

stability: continuous operating *balance*.

stabilizer: anti-vibration camera *mount*. See: *Steadicam, Tyler mount*.

stage: *studio* production area.

stage brace: *scenery* support strut.

stagehand: general *set* worker. See: *grip*.

stage right, stage left: movement from point of view of performer facing *camera*. Compare: *camera right, camera left*.

stage screw: *set* floor anchor for *tripod* chain, etc. See: *Spanish windlass*.

stagger through: in Britain, first *rehearsal* without *costumes, facilities*, etc.

staircase: *video test signal* measuring differential *gain, phase luminance signal* regularity, and *burst phase* errors.

stair steps: undesirable jagged edge on type character. See: *aliasing, jaggies*. Compare: *anti-aliasing*.

STAM—Sequential Thermal Anhysteric Magnetization: abandoned high speed (5 to 1) *helical scan videotape contact printing duplication* technique. Compare: *AC transfer*.

stand alone: non-*satellite* local *cable* service.

standard: *35mm film*. Also: Adjustable height *set* support. Also: *AM broadcasting*.

standard error: amount of survey error arising from sampling technique.

standards conversion: see: *converter*.

stand by: *action* warning *cue*.

standby: contingency replacement performer (or *program*). Also: *VTR mode; tape* stationary, *record head(s)* in motion.

stand-in: substitute performer, not recognizable as such when photographed. Compare: *extra, understudy*.

standing set—permanent set: *set* in continuing *production* use. Compare: *strike*.

stand-upper: *television* news presentation without *cutaways*.

star—star filter: line-engraved *lens* filter, transmitting light source as pointed star effect.

start mark: *synchronization* indication at *head* of *film* and/or *soundtrack*.

stat—photostat: inexpensively processed photographic reproduction, usually enlarged or reduced from original.

state-of-the-art: most recent technical improvement.

static: *random noise* associated with atmospheric or solar activity.

station: *broadcasting* facility assigned specific *frequency*. First U.S. government authorization *(radio)* issued to WBZ, Springfield, Mass., Sept. 15, 1921. Over 10,000 U.S. *radio stations;* 1,050 *television* (1988).

station break: pause in *program transmission* for *FCC*-required *call-letter* identification, usually at half-hour intervals.

station identification—ID: originally, *10-second commercial* announcement, *audio* limited to 8 seconds or less to allow for shared station identification. Now any *10-second broadcast advertising* message.

station rep(resentative): group representing local *stations* in sale of *broadcast time* to national *advertiser*.

STC—Satellite Television Corporation: *Comsat* subsidiary proposing six-*satellite* high-power *DBS transmission* service.

Steadicam: proprietary gyroscopic *servo*-controlled body-mounted *film/television* camera. See: *enhanced hand-held*. Compare: *camcorder, Magicam, minicam*.

Steenbeck: German horizontal *film/sound editing* machine. See: *Kem*. Compare: *Moviola*.

steerable: capable of controlled movement along two axes. See: *AZ, EL*. Compare: *fixed*.

steerable antenna: *earth station* capable of picking up various *satellites*.

step: *frame*-at-a-time *video* advance.

step framing: *frame* removal within sequence, creating irregular movement.

step on: overlap another performer's lines.

step printer: *film laboratory* machine *printing optical picture negatives*. Compare: *continuous printer*.

steps—test bars: bar-shaped pattern in *videotape recording* for *playback alignment*. See: *bar test pattern, color bars*.

step wedge—wedge—step tablet: length of *motion picture negative* for *processing* control; each *frame* progressively darker. Compare: *camera test, cinex*.

stereo(phonic): "dimensional" *sound* reproduction achieved by two separated *recording microphones* matched to similarly separated *playback speakers;* developed by *EMI*, 1931. Compare: *quadruphonic*.

stereo FM: dual-*channel broadcasting*, approved by *FCC* (1961) on recommendations of *National Stereophonic Radio Committee*.

Stereoscope: "depth" *slide* viewer (Wheatstone, 1838).

"sticks": *cameraman*'s call for *clapstick sync* action.

stilb: one *candela* (0.8 *foot candle*) of light covering square centimeter of surface.

still: individual photograph.

still store: long- or short-term *digital storage/retrieval* of individual *video* images. See: *frame store.*

sting: strongly accented note of musical composition. Compare: *button.*

stirrup: device suspending overhead *set luminaire.*

STL: *studio*-to-*transmitter link.*

stock—raw stock: unexposed *negative film* or *virgin videotape.*

stock music—library music: previously *recorded* background music, licensed for *re-use.* See: *needle drop.* Compare: *original music.*

stock set: standard *scenic background.*

stock shot—library footage: previously photographed *film footage licensed* for *re-use.* See: *scratch print.*

stop: *aperture* opening controlling amount of light passing through *lens* (usually calibrated from 1.5 to 22). See: *f, diaphragm.*

stop down: reduce *aperture* opening.

stop leader: blank *film* indicating *projection* interruption on single *reel.*

stop motion: *frame*-at-a-time cinematography of three-dimensional subjects moved slightly between exposures; *projection* at *speed* (24 *fps*) gives illusion of actual motion. See: *animation camera.* Compare: *limited animation.*

storage: information *recording.*

storage battery: see: *battery.*

Storer Cable Communications: major *MSO* (with between one and five million *subscribers,* 1988).

storyboard: inexpensive stylized format reviewing *audio* and representative *video* portions of planned *television commercial;* usually drawn on cardboard in separated *frames.*

straight across: non-*equalized audio recording.*

straight cut: edit *scene*-to-*scene;* no intervening *optical* device. Compare: *transition.*

straight up: clock second hand at 12.

Strap—Simultaneous Transmission and Recovery of Alternating Pictures: two *television signals* carried on same *channel* with independent *receiver* reconstruction.

Stratovision: obsolete wide-area *television signal* distribution technique, utilizing airborne *transmitter/antenna.* Compare: *balloon.*

stray light: see: *ambient light.*

streaking: *television picture distortion;* extends objects horizontally beyond normal boundaries.

streamer: *editor*'s diagonal *china marker* indication on *work print* (in *projection,* appears to move across *frame*).

stress marks: in Britain, random vertical black stripes in *film print,* caused by overtight *negative* winding damage.

stretch: slow down *broadcast* presentation. Also: Exaggerated *animation change.*

stretch print: upgrade *silent footage* to 24 *fps sound projection speed* by *printing* every other *frame* twice.

strike: dismantle *set* or equipment after *production.* Compare: *load in.* Also: Print *positive film* from *negative;* less often, make *dupe* from *master tape.* Also: Appeal to *FCC* to cancel *allocation* application for cause.

stringer: *free-lance* local journalist.

strip: *program broadcast* at same time each weekday. See: *across the board.* Compare: *one shot, special.* Also: Row of lights, usually containing five 1,000-*watt bulbs.* See: *bank.* Also: Remove *insulation.*

stripe—mag(netic) stripe: clear *35mm sprocketed film,* with magnetic *oxide* stripe for *recording* single *soundtrack.* Called *zonal stripe* in Britain. See: *balance stripe.* Also: Coat *film print* with narrow *oxide* band for *track recording* on *single-system playback.*

striped tube: *television camera color filter;* consists of alternating *RGB* stripes (111 to *mm.*) breaking up component image light without *dichroic mirrors.*

stripping: *syndicating* accumulated weeks of former *network* programs for daily (usually non-*prime time*) local *broadcast.*

strobing: transverse or rotary movement of object in *film frame* at speed undesirably counteracting phenomenon of *persistence of vision* (also results from too-rapid *panning*).

stroboscope: device emitting bursts of illumination at controlled intervals.

stroboscopic disk: cardboard rotation-speed test device.

studio: soundproofed room for creating *broadcast* material. Also: Generally, premises of large *film/television* facility.

studio zone: union-negotiated distance covering permanent-to-*location* work area.

stunting: flamboyant *network* programming; usually attempt to dominate *rating* periods.

STV—subscription television: *transmission* (for a monthly fee) of *scrambled* over-the-air *television signals* to home *receivers.* Launched in California

1964; killed immediately by popular referendum. See: *premium television, pay television*. Compare: *pay cable, see/fee*.

STV/Channel 1: Swedish Broadcasting Corporation *network;* "the Stockholm channel."

STV/Channel 2: Swedish Broadcasting Corporation *network;* "the peasant channel."

stylus: *needle* for *phonograph disk cutting* or reproduction. Also: A *video disk tracking* technique. Also: Electronic "pen" drawing freehand artwork (or initiating *computer* system commands) on *touch screen* or *digitizer tablet*.

subcarrier: 3.58 *MHz NTSC color television signal*. See: *black burst, color burst*. Also: any auxiliary information *carrier* added to *baseband signal* before *modulation*.

subjective: time duration felt by audience. Compare: *real time*.

subliminal: *broadcast advertising* allegedly below normal visual perception threshold.

submaster: *first generation* copy of *master*.

subreflector: *earth station* device concentrating *satellite signals* on *feedhorn*. See: *dish*.

subscriber: *cable* service home.

subscription TV: see: *STV*.

substandard—narrow-gauge: *film* less than *35mm* wide.

substrate: thin slice of *semiconductor* ingot, usually *silicon*.

subtitle: explanatory *caption* (often a translation of foreign *soundtrack*) at bottom *frame*. Compare: *title*.

subtractive: *color film processing* system; removes components from *emulsion* layers during *development*.

subtractive primaries: *cyan, magenta, yellow*.

sucker—limpet: in Britain, rubber suction cup temporarily attaching equipment to smooth surface.

sum: *stereo signal* adding right to left *channels* (L + R).

sun gun: small portable high-intensity *luminaire*.

sunk up: *sound synchronized* to *picture*.

sunshade: see: *matte box*.

sun spot—beam projector—parabolic: *spotlight* projecting narrow, almost parallel light *beam*. Also: **sunspot:** vast cyclic disturbance on sun's surface, creating severe *radio wave* disruption on earth.

super(imposition): electronic addition of one picture information source (usually *titling*) over another.

super band: *television frequencies* from 216 *MHz* to 318 *MHz*.

Superchannel: London-based European *satellite/cable* programming service (1987).

Super 8: enlarged-frame version of older *8mm motion picture film;* 72 *frames* to the foot, 0.325 *feet per second* at *sound speed* (24 *fps*). Compare: *8mm, 16mm, 35mm*.

superimpose: overlap pictures from two *cameras*.

superluminescent diode: see: *SLD*.

Super NTSC: *(Faroudja)* improved *television resolution* system; uses adaptive bidimensional *comb filtering* before *signal transmission*. See: *NTSC*.

SuperScope: 35mm *anamorphic film* system with 2:1 or 2.35:1 *aspect ratio*.

super slo-mo: specially engineered 1″ *type-C VTR* using *HDTV bandwidth* at 90 *fps;* generates *NTSC*-compatible *slow motion picture* with sharply reduced blurring.

superstation: local *broadcast* facility utilizing *satellite* for nationwide program *transmission;* e.g.: *KTLA* (LA), *KTUV* (Oakland), *KTVT* (Ft. Worth), *WGN* (Chicago), *WPIX* (NY), *WTBS* (Atlanta), *WWOR* (NY).

Super VHS: improved ½″ *component videotape recording* system; 400 *lines* additional *resolution*.

supply reel: see: *feed reel*.

suppression: reduction of objectionable *frequencies* to acceptable level.

surface: extraneous *phonograph record* noise.

surge: *transient* increase in supplied *rated* power.

surge suppressor: device to dampen above phenomenon.

surround sound: spectacular method of artificial *quadruphonic audio recording,* effectively "seating" listener in mid-orchestra.

survey—location scout: *pre-production* assessment of proposed *remote broadcast* site. Called *recce* or *reccy* (for *reconnaissance*) in Britain.

survey area: see: *TSA*.

sustainer: unsponsored *network* or local *station broadcast*.

SWABC—South West Africa Broadcasting Corporation: government *broadcasting network* (English/Afrikaans language) serving S.W. Africa/Namibia.

swarf: in Britain, filament thrown up by *disk*-cutting *stylus*.

sweep: electronic *picture tube scan*. Also: Small J-shaped *scenery* piece, usually translucent (see: *milk sweep*), eliminating visual frame of reference.

Also: Periodic 4-week-long measurement of television market audiences.

sweetening: addition of new or variant singing to existing music track. Compare: *double tracking*. Also: Addition to *soundtrack* of *canned* audience reaction.

swinger—flapper: *flat* swung out of path of camera *dolly*.

swish pan—zip pan: image-blurring *pan* shot, usually transitional. Called *flash pan, whip (wizz) pan* in Britain.

switch: see: *A/B switch*.

switcher: *television input* control *console* to select or mix *video output*. Also: Technician *(technical director—TD)* operating this equipment. Called *vision mixer* in Britain.

Symphonie: developmental *ESA satellite:* #1 at 49° E (1974); #2 at 11.5° W (1975). See: *ECS, H-Sat, OTS, Sirio*.

sync generator: electronic pulsing device controlling *television picture scanning*.

sync(hronization): exact *alignment* of *sound/picture* elements. Called *laying* in Britain. See: *edit sync, printing sync*. Compare: *wild*. Also: *Television signal* control.

synchronization rights: permission to *animate* to previously *recorded* musical composition.

synchronizer: greared table device for simultaneously *editing film* and *soundtrack*. Called *four way* in Britain.

synchronous demodulation: *color set*'s *I & Q signal* detection.

synchronous motor: *AC* motor with speed exactly governed by *frequency* of applied *voltage*.

Synclavier: proprietary musical composition and *audio* modification device.

sync mark: *editor*'s *synchronizing* point indication.

Syncom: initial experimental *Hughes geosynchronous satellite*, launched in a 6,830 mph, 22,240-mile high orbit, February 14, 1963.

sync pulse: *voltage pulse* (4.77 *microseconds* long) introduced into *video signal* during *blanking interval* to insure exact *transmission/reception synchronization*. Also: *Camera* device using inaudible *sound frequencies* to control *recorder speed*. See: *crystal sync*. Also: see: *sync tone*.

synch punch: hole punched in *film soundtrack* as audible *cue* mark. Called *sync plop* in Britain.

sync roll: *cueing* two *videotape feeds* for coordinated *recording*. See: *backspacing*. Also: Vertical *television picture rollover*, caused by *circuit* interruption.

sync tone: 60 *Hz signal* added during *audio tape recording* to control identical *playback* speed.

syndex—syndicated exclusivity: *FCC*-mandated elimination of *syndicated* programming from *distant-signal feeds* (*superstations*, etc.) when it duplicates local *broadcast* material (abandoned 1980, restored 1988).

syndication: independently produced or former *network* programming distributed in local markets. See: *first-run, off-network, package.*

synex: see: *cinex.*

synthesizer: keyboard instrument processing voltage-generated *waveform* musical composition. Also: Device for manipulating *color television signals* for striking visual effects.

system: *closed-circuit television transmission/reception.*

—

T

T: see: *T-stop*.

tab: foil-faced sensor attached to *film negative* for *print timing* purposes. Compare: *notch*.

table top—insert: *close-up camera* work with inanimate objects.

tachometer: *camera frame-speed* indicator.

tag: brief *live* announcement added to *recorded commercial*. See: *open end*. Compare: *cut-in*.

tag line: performer's final line, often humorous.

tail—tail leader: end portion of *film* or *tape reel*. Compare: *head*.

tails out: *film/tape reel* requiring *rewinding* before *projection/playback*. Compare: *heads out*.

take board: see: *number board*.

"take it away!": traditional *remote audio broadcast cue*.

takes: consecutively numbered attempts at most effective *film/tape* performance. See: *buy, hold, selected take*.

take sheets: detailed *production* records kept by *continuity clerk* or *audio engineer*.

take-up: *reel* spooling *tape* or *film* from *feed reel*.

take-up plate: *editing table* horizontal *take-up reel*.

talent: *broadcast* performer(s).

talent agent: *broadcast* performer's booking representative; usually taking 10% of fee.

talent union: performers' labor organization. See: *AFTRA, SAG, SEG.*

talkback: private *microphone/speaker* system connecting *control room* to *studio*. Also called *prompter* or *fold back* in Britain. Compare: *PA, PL.*

talking book: recorded literary work.

talking clock: obsolete *videotape* (one-second *audio* counts) *cueing* method. Compare: *time code.*

talking heads: poorly produced *television* discussion.

talk show: *broadcast format* consisting of celebrity conversations, panel discussions, telephone interviews, etc. Also called *chat show* in Britain.

tally light: red light atop *television camera;* indicates when its *shot* is being *transmitted;* often used to *cue* (when extinguished) *camera* moves. Also called *camera cue* in Britain. See: *lose the light.* Compare: *camera light.*

T&A—tits and ass: trade epithet for sex-oriented programming. See: *bimbo programming.*

tap: *cable* system *feeder-dropline connection.*

tape: non-sprocketed plastic ribbon base $\frac{1}{1,000}''$ thick and $\frac{1}{8}''$ to $2''$ wide, coated with metallic *oxide* and *transported* past magnetic *field* for electronic *recording* of *sound* and/or *television picture* patterns. *Audio tape recording speeds are $1\frac{7}{8}$, $3\frac{3}{4}$, $7\frac{1}{2}$ and 15 inches per second (ips); $1''$ and quad videotape speed, 15 ips.*

tape counter: see: *counter.*

tape deck: see: *deck.*

tape guide: metal alignment post on either side of *magnetic head.*

tape hook: *camera* attachment used when measuring *lens* distance to subject.

tape life: degree of *tape* degeneration from *recording/playback* passes.

tape lifter: metal arm removing *audio tape* from *record/playback heads* in *fast forward/rewind modes.*

tape recorder: electronic/mechanical device for *recording magnetic audio/video* information on *tape* for instantaneous *playback.*

tape speed: see: *tape.*

target: imaging surface of *television camera pickup tube.* Also: **target—dot:** metal disk used as *flag.* Also: **target—mosaic:** light-sensitive *camera pickup tube* surface (over 350,000 *photosensitive* dots) *scanned by electron beam.*

target audience: primary *demographic* to whom *program* or *commercial* is directed.

target ring: *camera circuit* draining electrons from conductive layer of *pickup tube.*

Tarif—Technical Apparatus for Rectification of Inferior Film: *BBC* device comingling *film* and *videotape* sources without *color shift.*

tariff: *FCC*-approved *common carrier* fee schedule.

TAT-7: 1983 trans-Atlantic seabed wire *cable* carrying 9,000 simultaneous voice, *video,* and data *transmissions.* Operated by 29 companies, led by *AT&T.*

TAT-8: planned trans-Atlantic seabed *fiber optics cable* carrying 37,000 simultaneous voice, *video,* and data *transmissions;* to replace *TAT-7.*

TBA—to be announced: undetermined action for specific time.

TBD—to be determined: undetermined time for specific action.

T-bone: in Britain, *luminaire mount* on flat metal base.

TBS—Turner Broadcasting System: U.S. *television* programming/*transmission* conglomerate; major stake held by *TCI.* See: *CNN, WTBS-TV.*

TCI—Telecommunications Inc.: major *MSO* (with between one and five million *subscribers,* 1988).

TD—technical director—switcher: *television video control console* engineer. Called *vision mixer* in Britain.

TDF-1: high-power *Télédiffusion de France DBS* (1988).

TDF-2: planned French *DBS* (1989).

TDRSS—Tracking and Data Relay Satellite Service: *NASA K-band* system; built by *Western Union.*

Teac: major Japanese electronics manufacturer.

tearing: *horizontal picture aberration* caused by lack of *sweep synchronization.*

technical director: see: *TD.*

technical manager: in Britain, "in-charge" *television studio* technician.

Technicolor: *film color separation* process using three *black/white negative* components. See: *Vidtronics.*

Telaction: *satellite/cable network* home shopping service; uses touchtone phone return (1988).

telco (patch—line—feed): telephone company *cable* connection.

TelDec: early British-German (Telefunken/Decca) 8″ *video disk* system (1975).

telecast: *television broadcast.*

teleciné—T/C—T/K: *television station film* and *slide projection chain.*

Télécom 1-C: French-administered *communications satellite; Arianespace*-launched 1988.

telecommunications: *transmission/reception* of images/*sound*/text etc. either by *radio frequency,* wire, or *fiber-optic cable.*

Tele-Communications, Inc.: major *MSO*.

Telecommunications Subcommittee: House of Representatives Commerce Committee subcommittee overseeing U.S. domestic and international *broadcast* activity. Compare: *Communications Subcommittee*.

teleconference: live *closed-circuit* presentation (usually with two-way *audio/video*) *transmitted* simultaneously—generally by *satellite*—to various locations.

Teledata: Danish *videotex* system (1982).

Télédiffusion de France—TDF: government operated all-French-*transmissions* organization.

Telefis Eireann: Eire government *television network*.

telegenic: looking good on *television*.

Telegraphon: 1893 *Poulsen* magnetic *audio recorder* using metal ribbon.

Télématique: experimental French *Télétel* directory data base (1981).

Télé Monte Carlo: Monte Carlo/Italian *television network*.

telephone coincidental interview: audience survey technique: "Are you *viewing*/listening?" (Poor at early/late hours; misses homes without phones.)

telephone filter: device passing *audio frequencies* between 200–2,700 *Hz* only.

telephone recall interview: audience technique researching recent *viewing*/listening. (Misses homes without phones.)

telephoto: narrow-angle, long *focal length lens* used for distant objects. Compare: *bugeye, diopter lens, fisheye*.

teleport: *video*-voice-data business *satellite transmission/reception* center with terrestrial network *interconnections*. See: *ATA*.

TelePrompTer: proprietary *cueing* device rolling up or electronically projecting *script* material; if desired, readable via 45° half-silvered mirror directly "through" *camera lens*. See: *prompter*.

telerecording—kinescoping: low-quality direct *reversal motion picture film* of *television tube picture*. Also called *kine ("kinny"), TVR*.

Telesat: Canadian *communications satellite* system, established with *Anik 1* (1972) at 104° W; *Anik 2* now at 109° W; *Anik 3* at 114° W. First to use lightweight, semiportable *earth station* pickups.

Télétel: French *videotex* system (1975). See: *Bildschirmtext, Captain, Minitel, Prestel, Telidon*.

teletext: over-the-air (or wired) graphic information distribution system reaching suitably equipped *receivers*.

Teletext: British *BBC/IBA* (1972) *alphanumeric* data *transmission* system utilizing *television signal blanking interval*. See: *Antiope, Viewdata*. Compare: *Ceefax, Oracle, Slice, Videotex*.

telethon: lengthy (usually fund-raising) star entertainment *program*.

teletype: receive-only news typewriter.

Televisa: Mexican *broadcasting* conglomerate.

television—TV: technique for electronic *transmission* of *pictures*, first proposed by Carey (1875), Senlecq (1877), demonstrated by Nipkow (1884); now, with accompanying *sound*, most effective means of modern mass communication. 1,000+ *commercial*, 300+ *non-commercial VHF/UHF television stations* (1988) reach 89 million U.S. *households* (98%).

Television Bureau of Advertising: see: *TVB*.

Television Bureau of Canada: see: *TVBC*.

television day part: generally—daytime, 10 am–4:30 pm; early evening, 4:30–7:30 pm; *prime* access, 7:30–8 pm; *prime*, 8–11 pm; late night, 11 pm–1 am. Also: weekend children's, 8 am–2 pm; weekend afternoon, 2–5 pm.

television game: see: *video game*.

television home: see: *household*.

Television Information Office—TIO: industry promotional organization; dissolved 1988.

Television/Radio Age: bimonthly industry periodical.

Tele-X: high-power cooperative Scandinavian *satellite* (1986). See: *Nord-Sat*.

Telidon: complex *videotex* system of Canadian Department of Communications (1981) on *vertical blanking lines* 15 and 16. See: *Bildschirmtext, Captain, Prestel, Teletel*.

"tell" story: *television* news report with no available pictures.

telly: (chiefly British) abbreviation for the *television* system.

telop(ticon): obsolete *television camera chain* device *transmitting* small (4″ × 5″) opaque art cards. See: *balop*.

Tel-Sat: high-power Swiss *satellite* (1986).

Telset: Finnish *videotex* system (1982).

TelShop: *satellite/cable network* home shopping service (1986).

Telstar: initial overseas *television communications satellite* with onboard *transponder*, launched in 15,000 mph low elliptical 157-minute orbit by *Comsat*, January 10, 1962. Compare: *Early Bird*.

Telstar 301: *AT&T-Comsat 24-transponder C-band communications satellite* at 96° W (1983). See: *Telstar 401*.

Telstar 302: *AT&T-Comsat 24-transponder C-band communications satellite* at 86° W (1984). See: *Telstar 402*.

Telstar 303: *AT&T-Comsat* 24-*transponder C-band communications satellite* at 125° W (1985).

Telstar 401: planned *AT&T-Comsat* 24 *Ku-band*/24 *C-band transponder communications satellite* at 101° W (to replace *Telstar 301, 1992*).

Telstar 402: planned *AT&T-Comsat* 24 *Ku-band*/24 *C-band transponder communications satellite* at 93° W (to replace *Telstar 302, 1993*).

Telstar 403: planned *AT&T-Comsat* 24 *Ku-band*/24 *C-band transponder communications satellite* (1994).

temperature: *Kelvin (°K)* scale based at absolute zero; triple point of water (interface of solid, liquid, vapor) at 273.6 °K = 0.01 °C, 32.02 °F.

tempex—carnet: European customs form covering temporary equipment importation.

tempo: musical performance speed.

Tempo Television: NBC/TCI *satellite/cable* business/sports programming service; planned-*DBS satellite* operator (1995).

10: 10-second *commercial* message. See: *ID*. Compare: *minute, 30, split-30, 15*.

10K: see: *brute*.

10 KHz: existing *separation* standard between Western Hemisphere *AM broadcast frequency allocations*. See: *NRSC*. Compare: *9 KHz*.

tenner: heavy-duty *fresnel-lensed spotlight* with 10,000-*watt bulb*.

terahertz—THz: one trillion *hertz*.

terawatt—TW: one trillion *watts*.

terminal: equipment *power* or *signal connection* point. See: *electrode*. Also: Computer *input* location.

termination: *resistance* at end of any *video signal* conductor (always 75 *ohms*).

terrain modelling: fractal *CGI* program creating natural-looking screen surfaces.

terrestrial: over-the-air *broadcasting* from land-based *antenna*. Compare: *cable, satellite*.

Tesla, Nikola: rotating *recording head* theorist, 1887.

test bars—steps: *bar-shaped* pattern in *videotape recording* for *playback alignment*. See: *bar test pattern, color bars*.

test (market) commercial: *on-air broadcast advertising* message produced for use in limited markets, for audience research. Often prepared within curtailed *production* budget.

test pattern: optical chart checking *television camera, monitor* or *receiver contrast, linearity* and *picture resolution*. See: *limiting resolution*.

tetrode: *amplifying vacuum tube* with two variably-charged wire mesh *grids* controlling electron flow between *negative filament (cathode)* and *positive plate.* Compare: *diode, klystrode, pentode, triode.*

TF—till forbid: *broadcast schedule* with termination date left to *advertiser's* discretion.

TFC—The Fashion Channel: Video Marketing Network *satellite/cable* home shopping service (1987).

TF-1—Télévision Française 1: oldest French government *television network;* privatized 1987. Compare: *A2, FR3.*

TF-2—Télévision Française 2: French government *television network.*

Thaumatrope: 1825 French *persistence-of-vision* toy. Compare: *Phenakistoscope, Praxinoscope, Zöetrope.*

THD—total harmonic distortion: standard *distortion* measurement (as a percentage).

The Movie Channel: see: *TMC.*

thermal imaging: *vidicon camera tube* system responding to subject's radiated heat, not light.

thermal noise: random motion of electrons in a *conductor.* See: *S/N.*

thermal rating: equipment temperature operating limit.

thermoplastic: *image-recording* technique utilizing electron beam to deform surface of special plastic *film.* Compare: *photoplastic.*

thimble: impact-printing (single-character) element. Compare: *ball, daisy wheel, dot matrix, ink jet.*

thin: insufficiently *exposed negative.* Compare: *dense.*

30: 30-second *commercial* message. Compare: *minute, split-30, 15, 10.*

35mm: *film stock 35mm* wide, adopted 1907 as international standard (reputedly based on distance between Edison's outstretched thumb and forefinger): 16 *frames* to *foot,* 1½ *feet per second* at *sound speed* (24 *fps*). Compare: *16mm, Super 8, 8mm.*

30 frames: *sound film* shot at 30 *fps;* requires no *frame conversion* to match 30 *fps television* systems. See: *3/2 pulldown.*

Thirty Rock: *Variety's* epithet for New York corporate headquarters of *NBC* (located at 30 Rockefeller Plaza); matches *Black Rock (CBS), Hard Rock (ABC).*

33⅓ rpm—long playing—LP: (1948) popular *phonograph disk* rotation speed. Compare: *compact disk, 45 rpm.*

Thomson-CSF: major French electronics manufacturer.

thread—thread up: *set up film* (or *tape*) in *projection* (or *record/playback*) *path.*

3-D: three-dimensional *computer*-generated imagery. Also: Novelty three-dimensional viewing system.

threefold: three self-supporting hinged *flats*.

3/2 pulldown: *film* (24 *fps*)-to-tv (30 *fps*) *frame conversion scanning* system.

3-Sat: Mainz-based European *satellite/cable programming* service.

¾": see: *D-1, D-2, U-Matic*.

3-year period: *FCC* minimum period for *license*-holding; *antitrafficking* regulation abandoned 1986.

throw: distance from *projector lens* to *screen;* distance from *luminaire* to subject.

throw away: underplay performance.

thruster: *satellite* motive power source (catalytic reactor or electrothermal hydrazine).

THS—Thames: one of British *IBA*'s *"Big Five"* (the *Central Companies*).

ticket: loosely, engineer's required *FCC* license.

tied-off: locked *camera* position (without *pan* or *tilt*).

tie-down (chain, cable): anchor connecting *tripod* to *stage screw*.

tie mike: see: *lapel mike*.

tiering: additional *cable* services for additional fees.

tight: *camera* subject *framing* with no top and side room. Compare: *loose*. Also: *Program* material running very close to allotted time. Compare: *long, short*. Also: Tight (miking): see: *presence*.

tightwinder: *rewind (take-up)* attachment centering *film* on *core*.

tilt: *camera* movement along vertical *arc,* from fixed position. Compare: *pan*. Also: Deficient *low-frequency* response.

tilt wedge: accessory increasing normal *camera mount tilt*.

time: loosely, *scheduled* program or *commercial*.

time—day part: *broadcast* period, usually for *commercial* advertising sale. See: *daytime, drive time, fringe evening time, prime time*.

time base corrector: *videotape recorder playback circuitry* generating perfect *picture sweep synchronization* (1972).

time base error: *videotape recording/playback* tracking artifact, created by mechanical imperfection.

timebase stability: degree of regularity of *videotape head* drive *servo signal* (*quadruplex*, every $\frac{1}{2,000}$ second; *helical scan*, every $\frac{1}{30}$ second).

time buyer: *advertising agency* or service executive executing *client broadcast media plan*. See: *schedule*.

time check: clock synchronization.

time code—edit code: *SMPTE* standard *videotape retrieval* system (similar to *motion picture edge number* identification) usually recording eight-digit *address* (hours, minutes, seconds, *frames*) on *control track*. See: *address code*. Compare: *talking clock*.

time compression: *video editing* system sampling and shortening *filmed/recorded* material without *audio pitch* alteration. Compare: *time expansion*.

time division multiple access: *computerized millisecond transmitted-signal* analysis, permitting optimum *channel* sharing.

time expansion: *video editing* system sampling and lengthening *filmed/recorded* material without *audio pitch* alteration. Compare: *time compression*.

time lapse: single-*frame* photography at precise periodic intervals. Also: plot discontinuity, usually indicated by *optical dissolve*.

timer: *VCR* preset *record* function.

time shift: *record (VCR) television* programming for subsequent viewing.

time slot: *broadcast* period. See: *slot*.

timing: subjective alteration of *printing light intensities* and *color filters* to achieve *balanced film positive* from *unbalanced negative* material.

tinny: lacking in *low frequencies*.

tint: degree of white mixed into pure *hue*.

TIO—Television Information Office: industry promotional organization, dissolved 1988.

tip penetration: pressure of *record/playback head* against *videotape surface*.

Tiros: ten U.S. (1960-on) research low-orbit weather *satellites*. See: *LEO*. Compare: *Essa, Itos*.

Tiros-N: U.S. (1978-on) low-orbit weather *satellites*. See: *LEO*. Compare: *Essa, Itos*.

TIS—Travelers' Information Service: local motorist radio information, *transmitted* at 530 and 1650 *HKz*.

tit: in Britain, start button.

Titan: Martin-Marietta *satellite*-launching rocket.

title: line(s) of descriptive information on *screen* or *television tube*. See: *drop shadow, subtitle*. Compare: *caption*.

title card: *titling* artwork for *film* or *television camera* photography. See: *hot press*.

titler: see: *character generator*.

tivicon: low-light *camera pickup tube* with silicon diode coated *target*.

TLC—The Learning Channel: *satellite/cable* adult education programming service (1980).

TMC—The Movie Channel: 24-hour *Viacom satellite/pay cable* feature *motion picture* programming.

TNT—Turner Network Television: *satellite/cable* programming service (1988).

Todd-AO: 70mm *film print* system with 2.2:1 *aspect ratio*.

to length: matching predetermined *time slot*.

tolerance: acceptance limit.

tombstone: final (immobile) full product layout formerly required in *NAB Code* toy *commercials*.

tone: pure *hue* with added black or white; degree of gray mixed into pure *hue*. Also: *1,000 Hz audio lineup signal*.

tone control: electronic *circuit filter* varying *high/low frequency response*.

tongue: *dolly boom*.

top 40: popular music *radio station* contemporary hit *format*.

top hat—high hat: *tripod* extension for high *camera* angles; also used separately for low *camera* angles.

topless: sexually oriented "conversation" *radio programming*, banned 1973 by FCC.

top loading: *VCR* equipment with *cassette/disk* insertion from above. Compare: *front loading*.

top 100: the major U.S. markets. See: *MNA*.

torus: *earth station antenna* design (horizontally spherical; vertically parabolic) simultaneously *receiving* several *satellite signals*. Compare: *spherical*.

Toshiba: major Japanese electronics manufacturer.

total audience plan: *spot* announcement combination package designed to deliver maximum weekly *broadcast* audience.

total audience rating: number of *television homes* viewing at least six minutes of a *program*.

total survey area: see: *TSA*.

touch screen—touch terminal: terminal with functions responding to finger or *stylus screen* commands.

touch-tone: *keypad* telephone pulse/tone input. Compare: *rotary*.

tower: loosely, *broadcast station antenna*.

tpi: (screw) threads per inch.

TPO: *transmitter power output*.

t/r: *transmitting/receiving earth station.*

trace: *cathode-ray tube* display created by moving *beam.*

track: (helical, longitudinal, or spiral) *recorded signal path* on *tape, film, or disk.* Also: *Videotape* or *film audio (soundtrack).* Also: Camera *dolly* planks or rails. Also: Follow performer's movement with moving *camera.* See: *follow shot, truck.* Compare: *pan, zoom.* Also: Follow *satellite* path with *earth station antenna.*

tracking: *videotape playback-to-recording head path* match. Also: Following *prerecorded path.*

trade out: see: *barter.*

Trades Union Congress—TUC: British labor union parent body. Compare: *AFL/CIO.*

traffic: control *commercial production* requirements for *broadcast advertising.*

trafficking: short term *station/license* turnover.

tranny: in Britain, pocket *radio receiver* (from *transistor*). Also: In Britain, *transparency.*

transceiver: equipment *transmitting* and *receiving broadcast signals.*

transcoding: translating *PAL* color *signals* to *SECAM, NTSC* standards, or vice versa; loosely, converting any formatted *signal* to a different format.

transcription: under the *AFTRA* Code, any form of *audio* reproduction for *broadcast.* Compare: *ET.*

transducer: any device converting electrical into magnetic or mechanical energy (or vice versa).

transfer: *film* copy of *television picture tube image.* Also: *Re-record tape signal* onto another *tape,* or onto *negative film soundtrack.* See: *optical transfer.*

transfer fee: proposed government *trafficking* surcharge. See: spectrum fee.

transformer: *voltage*-changing device.

transient: momentary *aberrant signal* response to *input* change.

transistor: tiny *semiconductor* performing identical control and *amplification* functions of larger (obsoleted) *vacuum tube;* capable of 1,000x *amplification.* Invented by Bardeen, Brattain, Schockley (1947). See: *chip, integrated circuit, microprocessor.*

transistor radio: pocket *radio* containing *transistorized circuits.*

transition: *optical* or *audio effect* between *scenes* or program sections. Compare: *straight cut.*

translator: *FCC*-authorized (1970) low-power *transmitters amplifying* inadequate *station signal* on different *channel.* 789 *FM,* 2,869 *VHF,* 1,921 *UHF* on air, 1988. Compare: *booster.*

translucent: material transmitting light but breaking up ray structure. Compare: *transparent.*

transmission controller (coordinator): in Britain, *CCR (central control room)* "in charge" technician.

transmission print: see: *show print.*

transmit: *broadcast* an electronic *signal.*

transmitter: specialized equipment to accomplish above.

transparency: transparent *positive still film,* usually in color.

transparent: material transmitting light without breaking up ray structure. Compare: *translucent.*

transponder: *communications satellite circuitry receiving/retransmitting audio/video earth signals; 36 MHz bandwidth* (1,200 *channels*).

transport: mechanical equipment—motor, *capstan, reel spindles* and controls—to move *tape* past *recording/playback heads.*

transverse: *quad VTR scanning.*

trap: device blocking *cable feeder signals* from non-subscribing household *dropline.*

trapeze: device suspending *set luminaire* from overhead rope/chain.

trash tv: loud, vulgar, interview/*panel show.*

traveler: stage curtain, opening horizontally.

traveling matte: action *matte* utilizing special *film filters* and lighting. Compare: *chromakey, rotoscope.*

TRDS: *geosynchronous* tracking and data relay *communications satellite.*

treads: in Britain, *set* stairs.

treatment: rough *script* outline.

treble: standard *audio frequency range* (3,500–10,000 *Hz*). Compare: *bass, mid-bass, mid-range, mid-treble.*

tree: high *spotlight* support with horizontal arm *mountings.* Also: **tree:** *cable network* disseminating *headend* (root) *signals* via *trunk*(s), branches *(feeders),* stems *(droplines),* and leaves *(terminals).*

triad: *television picture tube's RGB* three-color *phosphor* dot cluster.

triangle: theoretical principle of *key, back,* and *fill* lighting.

triaxial: short lightweight *television cable,* carrying *power* as well as *sound, video,* and *control signals.* Compare: *coaxial.*

trickle charger: *(AC) converter* dribbling *(DC)* electrons into *storage battery,* usually over 12–14 hours.

triggyback: *time* period for three *20-second commercials* sold for (only) the price of a *one-minute spot.*

trim: removed (unused) *head/tail* portions of *selected film take*. Compare: *out-take*. Also: Change *projector arc carbons*.

Trinicon: improved *television camera pickup tube*. Compare: *image orthicon, Leddicon, Newvicon, Plumbicon, Saticon, vidicon*.

Trinity Broadcasting Network: 24-hour non-commercial religious *satellite/cable* programming service.

Trintex: *IBM*/Sears (formerly *IBM*/Sears/*CBS*) home *PC* access information service; now called *Prodigy Computer Services*. See: *interactive, videotex*.

triode: *amplifying vacuum tube* (invented as *"audion"* by *De Forest*, 1906) containing single variably charged wire mesh *grid* controlling electron flow between *negative filament (cathode)* and *positive plate*. May be used as *oscillator* to generate *high frequency AC*. Now often replaced by N-P-N or P-N-P *transistors*. Compare: *diode, pentode, tetrode*.

tripack: color *film* with three layers of *emulsion*. Compare: *bipack*.

tripod: three-legged *camera* support. Compare: *monopod*.

trombone: *set luminaire* support.

troposphere: atmospheric band 7 to 10 miles high, "bouncing" *UHF radio waves* (300–3,000 *MHz*) for several hundred miles. Compare: *heaviside layer, ionosphere*.

truck: extensive lateral *camera dolly* movement. Compare: *arc*.

true DBS: see: *BSS band*. Compare: *quasi-DBS*.

trunk: *cable* system *head end-to-feeder connection;* can carry 80 *channels*.

TSA—total survey area: area containing 98% of weekly audience. Largest *ARB (radio)* audience research market classification. Compare: *ADI, metro*.

T(ransmission)-stop: *aperture setting* indicating amount of light actually transmitted by *lens* after *absorption* and reflection; replaces theoretical *f-stop* system. Adjacent *T-stop* numbers double (or halve) amount of transmitted light.

TTL: through-the-*lens video camera reflex viewfinder*.

tube—vacuum tube: glass-enveloped electron control-and-*amplification* device, obsoleted by *transistor*. Called *valve* in Britain. Also: **tube:** loosely, *picture tube*, or *television* itself.

tubesville: (from "down the tube [drain]") disasterville.

tune: adjust *radio receiver* or *transmitter* to specific *frequency*.

tuner: *AM/FM receiver signal detector*. Compare: *amplifier*.

tungsten: artificial light *filament* (3,200 °K).

tungsten-halogen: small, highly efficient lamp; *tungsten filament* in *halogen* (see: *halide*) gas-filled quartz envelope.

turkey: flop show.

Turner Broadcasting System: see: *TBS*.

turn fast: in Britain, operate *motion picture* camera at faster-than-normal *frame speed,* producing "slow-motion" effect in normal *projection.*

turnkey: completely installed system, ready for operation.

turn over: in Britain, camera *action cue.*

turnover: index of *reach* versus *frequency;* ratio of net unduplicated *cumulative audience* over several periods to average audience size per period. Also: Audience *tune-in/tune-out* during program. Compare: *churn.*

turn slow: in Britain, operate *motion picture* camera at slower-than-normal *frame speed,* producing "speed-up" effect in normal *projection.*

turntable: motor- or hand-driven rotating platform; used in varying sizes for *phonograph* records, camera subjects, stagecraft, etc.

turret: old rotatable *television camera mount* holding up to 5 *lenses;* obsoleted by *zoom lens.*

turtle: three-legged floor stand for *spud.* Compare: *century stand.*

TVB—Television Bureau of Advertising: *broadcast* industry markerting organization. Compare: *BBTV, RAB, TVBC.*

TVBC—Television Bureau of Canada: *broadcast* industry marketing organization. Compare: *TVB.*

TVE-I,II: Spanish government *television networks.*

TV-5: Paris-based French-Belgian-Swiss *satellite/cable programming network* (1986).

TV Globo: Brazilian *television network.*

TV Guide: consumer *television* program magazine (1953).

TVHH—television households: research estimate of number of *households* with one or more *television sets.*

TVQ: *television* performer "awareness/preference" rating, based on annual questionnaires to 1,250 U.S. sample families.

TV Marti: (after 1895 Cuban revolutionary Jose Martí). Proposed (1988) U.S. government *television station* for Cuba-oriented *programming.* See: *Radio Marti.*

TVRO—television receive only: *backyard* consumer *earth station* (1.7 million, 1988). See: *downlink.*

TV-SAT-1: initial high power West German *DBS* (1987, failed 1988).

TV-SAT-2: second high power West German *DBS* (1988).

TV stereo: *bi-channel television audio transmission.*

TV-3: Catalan-language Spanish *television network.*

TWD—trouble west of Denver: any unidentified telephone *network transmission* problem.

tweak: exactly *align* electronic equipment.

tweaker: in Britain, tiny screwdriver.

'tweens: see: *in-betweens.*

tweeter: smaller member of pair of *loudspeakers,* emphasizing *high frequencies.* Compare: *woofer.*

Twentieth Century Fox Film: major entertainment conglomerate.

24-track: standard music *recording format* (uses 2″ *audio tape*).

twinkle—edge beat—light bearding: *video* fault during sharp transitions.

twitter: fine horizontal flickering created by *interlaced scanning.*

2-D: two-dimensional *computer*-generated imagery.

twofold: free-standing center-hinged *flat.*

2″—two-inch: see: *quad.*

two-shot, three-shot: two persons in frame, etc.

two-step: *phonograph disk* duplication method, using silverplate of original *acetate recording* to produce hard mold for high-quantity *vinyl pressing.* Compare: *one-step.*

two-track: see: *half track.*

two-way: *cable* system capability to *transmit signal upstream* as well as *down;* basic *FCC* requirement after 1986. See: *interactive.*

TX: *transmit.*

Tyler mount: gyroscopically gimballed vibration-free helicopter *camera mount.*

Type A: proposed *SMPTE 1″* educational/industrial *non-segmented helical videotape format.*

Type B: *SMPTE 1″ segmented helical format.*

Type C: *SMPTE* compromise *1″ non-segmented helical format.*

Type D: proposed *SMPTE 1″ non-segmented helical format; reel* and *cassette.*

Type D-1: *SMPTE ¾″ cassette component digital format.* See: *D-1.*

Type D-2: *SMPTE ¾″ cassette composite digital format.* See: *D-2.*

Type D-3: see: *D-3.*

Type E: *SMPTE ¾″ Sony cassette format.*

Type F: *SMPTE ½″ open reel format* (obsolete).

Type G: *SMPTE ½" Beta cassette format.*

Type H: *SMPTE ½" VHS cassette format.*

Type L: proposed *SMPTE ½" Betacam cassette format.*

Type M: proposed *SMPTE ½" Recam cassette format.*

U

UBC—Universal Bar Code: optically coded product identification system. See: *wand*.

Uher: high-quality portable ¼″ *audio tape recorder* for location *production*.

UHF—"U"—ultra high frequency: supplemental *television broadcast band* with limited *signal range—channels* 14 to 83; 470 to 890 *MHz*. 481 U.S. commercial, 212 educational stations on air, 1988.

UL—Underwriters' Laboratories: insurance-company-sponsored research group testing safety standards.

ulcer: in Britain, a *cookie*.

Ultracam: *35mm motion picture camera*.

ultrasonic: above audible (20–20,000 *Hz*) range. Compare: *infrasonic, sonic*.

ultrasonic cleaner—sonic cleaner: *ultra high-frequency soundwave film* cleaning device.

U-Matic: *SONY*-pioneered ¾″ *video cassette recording/playback* system (1971).

umbrella: umbrella-shaped "bounce" light reflector.

unaffiliated: non-*network broadcasting station*. Compare: *independent*.

unbalanced: *film emulsion* exposed to light of incorrect or varying *color temperature*. Compare: *color balanced*.

under—behind: low-*level background audio*. Compare: *up*.

undercrank: operate *motion picture camera* at slower-than-normal *frame speed*, producing "speed-up" effect in normal *projection*. Called *turn slow* in Britain. Compare: *overcrank*.

underexposure: too-rapid *shutter speed* and/or insufficient *aperture* mismatched to *film emulsion* characteristics, resulting in undesirable "light" *negative* (or *reversal*) and "dark" *print*. Compare: *overexpose*.

underground television: see: *alternative television*.

understudy: substitute performer. See: *standby*. Compare: *stand-in*.

underwriting: acknowledged corporate support for *public broadcasting*. See: *enhanced underwriting*.

unidirectional—cardioid: single direction *microphone pickup*.

Unilux: *motion picture strobe* light photography system.

Unisats: low/high-power U.K. *satellites* (1987).

Unisette: *BASF* ¼" *audio cassette*. See: *Elcaset*. Compare: *Compact*.

United Cable Television Corporation: major *MSO* (with between one and five million *subscribers*, 1988).

United Scenic Artists: scenic designers' union.

unit manager: *network* employee coordinating (among other elements) *program's commercial* advertising material.

universe: total audience population projected from research sample.

Univision: Hallmark Spanish-language *satellite/cable television network*.

unmodulated: medium with no *signal*. Compare: *modulate*.

unwired network: unconnected-*station time* sold *en bloc* by national advertising representative.

up: high-*level background audio*. Compare: *under*.

up-cut: *edit* tightly.

up-front: pre-season (end of June–beginning of July) *television timebuying*. See: *scatter market*.

UPI—United Press International: subscriber news service for *broadcast stations*, newspapers. Compare: *AP, Reuters*.

uplink: ground-to-*satellite transmission*. Compare: *downlink*.

upscale: higher than average income, education, or other major *demographic* consideration.

upstage: stage area farthest from audience (or *camera*). Compare: *downstage*. Also: Unprofessionally overshadow a fellow performer.

upstream: reversed *cable transmission* between *subscriber* and *head end*. See: *interactive, two-way, up the line*. Compare: *downstream*.

up the line: toward *signal's* source. Compare: *down the line*.

urban—rhythm and blues—R & B: black-oriented popular *radio station* program *format*.

US—naff: in Britain, useless, no good. Compare: *NG*.

USAN—USA Network: *MCA*/Paramount *satellite/cable* programming service. See: *Calliope*.

USCI—United Satellite Communications Inc.: U.S. low-power five-*channel DBS* service (1984) over *Anik C-II*. Operated by *Comsat,* financed by *General Instrument*/Prudential Insurance; abandoned 1985.

use: *air* performance.

USIA—United States Information Agency: government news and propaganda arm operating worldwide *broadcast* facilities.

USP—unique selling proposition: putative superiority of advertised product.

USSB—United States Satellite Broadcasting Company: planned *DBS satellite* operator, 1992.

V

V: see: *volt*.

vacuum guide: device holding *videotape* close to *quad VTR record/playback heads*.

vacuum tube—tube: glass-enveloped electronic control and *amplification* device, obsoleted by *transistor*. Designated *"V"* on *schematics*. Called *valve* in Britain.

valley: low point between two *signal peaks*.

value: degree of *color luminosity*.

valve: in Britain, obsolete glass electronic control and *amplification* device. Designated *"V"* on *schematics*.

vamp: improvise, especially music. See: *ad lib*.

van: *remote videotape recording* vehicle.

vanda: (telephone company contraction) *video and audio connection*.

variable area: standard *film optical soundtrack*, utilizing variations in *modulation* width. (See below.)

variable density: alternate type of *film optical soundtrack*, utilizing variations in *modulation density*. (See above.)

variable speed motor—wild motor: *film camera* attachment permitting controlled *over-* or *undercranking*.

variable speed playback: unique *helical-scan videotape recording* system feature (not possible with *quad*).

Variety: weekly entertainment industry newspaper.

"vast wasteland": 1961 characterization of U.S. *television* programming by *FCC* Chairman Newton Minow.

vault: fireproof *film* storage facility.

VBI—vertical blanking interval: see: *blanking interval*.

VCP: *video cassette player*-only.

VCR—video cassette recorder: *videotape recorder/player* (usually ½" or ¾"). Consumer versions *(VHS, Beta)* in 59% (51 million) U.S. homes, 1988.

VC-II—Videocipher II: *General Instrument*'s *satellite signal encryption* system.

VDT—video display terminal: *computer* display *readout*.

vector graphics: *CGI* from numerical *screen* coordinates.

vectorscope: round (green screen) *oscilloscope CRT* for visual angle calibration of *amplitude* and *phase* of *television color signals*.

velocity compensator: *quad videotape playback* accessory eliminating *banding* (horizontal color *distortion*).

velocity error: *time base* variations in rotational speed between *recording* and *playback heads*.

velour: non-reflective *drape* material, usually black.

venetian blind effect: see: *hum bars*.

VERA—Vision Electronic Recording Apparatus: early (1952) *BBC b/w video recording* technique, with *tape speeds* up to 200 *ips*.

vertical blanking interval—VBI: see: *blanking interval*.

vertical hold: *picture* roll control on home *television receiver*.

vertical interval: in Britain, brief moment, measured in *microseconds*, during which electron *scanning beam* returns to top of *television picture tube*. See: *Ceefax, Oracle, Slice, Teletext, Viewdata*.

vertical interval editing: imperceptible *helical VTR editing* during *vertical blanking pulse*.

vertical interval reference—VIR: additional *signal transmitted* during *vertical blanking pulse*.

vertical interval switch: replace one *video signal* with another during *vertical blanking pulse*.

vertical resolution: number of horizontal lines in *television image*. Compare: *horizontal resolution*.

vertical retrace: see: *blanking interval*.

vertical saturation—rotation: heavy *commercial scheduling* throughout *broadcast* day to reach all of *station's* audience. Compare: *roadblocking, horizontal saturation*.

very large scale integration—VLSI: measure of *semiconductor* design complexity; up to 100,000 *circuits* on single *silicon chip*. Compare: *IC, LSI, MSI, SSI*.

VFL—variable focal length: see: *zoom lens*.

VHD—video high density: non-grooved *capacitance* (900 rpm) *video disk*, "read" by stylus. Compare: *CED, LaserVision*.

VHF—"V"—very high frequency: original *television broadcast band—6-MHz bandwidth, channels* 2 to 13; 54 to 216 *MHz*. 538 U.S. *commercial*, 118 *educational stations* on air, 1988. Also: In Britain, *FM radio broadcasting*.

VH-1—Video Hits One: (1985) Viacom *satellite/cable* programming service.

VHS—Video Home System: ½" *JVC*-developed *VCR format*. Compare: *Beta, 8mm*.

VHS-C: small *VHS cassette format* for *JVC camcorder*. Compare: *Betamovie*.

Viacom International: entertainment conglomerate (mainly owned by National Amusements, Inc.) and major *MSO* (with between one and five million *subscribers,* 1988).

vidclip: brief promotional film excerpt for television use. Compare: *sound bite*.

video: (from Latin "see") *picture* portion of *television broadcast*. Compare: *audio*. Also: *Storyboard* or *script* "pictures." Also: see: *music video*.

video analyzer: electro-optical device *scanning* color *negative* to establish proper *printing exposures*. See: *Hazeltine*.

video assist—video tap: *television viewing* system coupled to *film camera*. Compare: *Gemini*.

video cartridge: single-reel *Ampex* and *RCA station playback* device containing short 2" *quad videotape* (usually *commercial*).

video cassette: two-reel container for (usually ½" or ¾") *videotape*. See: *U-Matic, VHS*.

VideoCipher II: see: *VC-II*.

videoconference: see: *teleconference*.

video disk: technique for inexpensive mass production of *television recordings*—utilizing *laser* beams, metal *styli*, etc., invented by *Baird* (1926), developed by Gregg, Johnson, DeMoss (1960). Transparent *disk* helium-*laser* reading system abandoned 1981; replaced with reflective *disk*, accessing 54,000 separate *television frames*. Also: *Slow-motion* or *freeze frame* equipment (1965). See: *slow-mo*.

video engineer—shader: technician controlling *television picture* quality (*black level, color balance, exposure gamma, video gain*) for *switcher*.

video gain: *television picture* black-to-white ratio *(contrast* control on home *receivers).*

video game: *microprocessor* attachment modifying home *television receiver* into controllable *CRT* "playing area".

videogram: *television* reproduction in *cassette* or *disk* form.

videography: monthly industry magazine.

video hum—hum: light/dark bands running horizontally through *television picture.*

video leader: standard *SMPTE* designation: :10 *color bars;* :15 *slate;* :08 *countdown;* :02 black. See: *leader.*

video looping: *video signal feed* to multiple *monitors.*

Videoplayer: obsolete Kodak device projecting *Super 8 film* into home *television receiver.*

video processing amplifier—proc amp: electronic device altering *video signal* (*sync, picture,* color) characteristics.

video signal: electrical *television picture frequencies,* ranging from zero to approximately 4 *MHz.*

video tap: see: *video assist.*

videotape: non-*sprocketed* plastic tape ¼″ to 2″ wide, coated with magnetizable metallic *oxides* to *record* (or *re-record*) *television* presentations. Compare: *audio tape.*

videotex(t): *television* text/graphics information *transmission* system, utilizing full *tv signal* (Fedida, 1971); reaching 1.2 million U.S. homes, 1988. See: *Bildschirmtext, Prestel, Teletel, Telidon.* Compare: *teletext.*

Videotex: Knight-Ridder/Times Mirror *television* information *transmission* system (discontinued 1986).

video track: *videotape picture recording* area. Compare: *audio track, control track.*

Videovoice: *(RCA)* device *transmitting slow-scanned stills* or *freeze-framed television pictures* over ordinary (3 *KHz bandwidth*) telephone *circuits.*

vidicon: moderately sensitive, durable *television camera pickup tube,* often used in *closed circuit/film chain* operations (1950). Compare: *image orthicon, Leddicon, Newvicon, Plumbicon, Saticon, Trinicon.*

vidisk: see: *video disk.*

Viditel: Dutch *videotex* system.

Vidtronics: *Technicolor videotape-to-film transfer* system combining (3) *b/w color-separated kinescope negatives* into final color *print.* Compare: *laser.*

Viewdata: *interactive* British graphic information distribution system, using *Teletext* phone lines with properly equipped home *television receivers*. See: *Antiope*. Compare: *Ceefax, Oracle, Slice*.

viewer: *film editing* device. Also: Person watching *television*.

Viewer's Choice: *Viacom pay-per-view cable programming* service.

viewfinder: see: *finder*.

viewing: *videotape playback*.

Viewtron: experimental Florida *videotex* system (Knight-Ridder, ex-*AT&T*).

vignettes: *camera* shots through various-shaped opaque *masks*. Also: Brief *television commercial* scenes.

v.i. meter—v.u. meter: needle/dial device indicating *recording level* on logarithmic *decibel* scale (standardized color design based on 1938 U.S. government post card).

(poly)vinyl(chloride)—PVC: *phonograph record pressing* material.

virgin: *tape* on which no *signal* has yet been *recorded*. Compare: *erase*.

Visc: rigid *(Panasonic)* home *video disk*, 450 rpm, similar to *phonograph record*.

visible noise—snow: *television picture breakup*, caused by weak *video signal* reception. Called *shash* in Britain.

vision mixer: in Britain, *video switching* technician.

VISN—Vision Interfaith Satellite Network: *satellite/cable* religious programming service.

Visnews: London-based international *television* news agency serving 79 countries (1988); jointly owned by *BBC, Reuters, NBC*.

Vistavision: horizontal-projection *35mm film* system with 1.85:1 *aspect ratio*.

Vitaphone: original *Warner* Bros. "talking picture" *disk recording* system (1926).

VITS—vertical interval test signal: included in *vertical blanking interval;* permits on-air test of *video* system.

vizmo: *rear projection* device inserting visual *backgrounds* into *live television program*. Compare: *front projection*.

VLA—very large array: *radio* astronomy *antenna* facility.

VLBA—Very Long Baseline Array: 10 linked 82-foot diameter radiotelescope *antennas*, extending across U.S. from Hawaii to Virgin Islands.

VLF—very low frequency: *radio waves* below 30 *KHz*.

VLP: see: *LV*.

VLSI—very large scale integration: measure of *semiconductor* design complexity; up to 100,000 *circuits* on single *silicon chip*. Compare: *IC, LSI, MSI, SSI*.

VO—voice over—off camera: *television* performer heard but not seen. Compare: *OC*. Called *commentary over, out-of-vision (OOV)* in Britain.

VOA—Voice of America: *USIA*-operated *shortwave* service *transmitting* State Department *programming* (30 *transmitters* in U.S., 70 overseas).

voice mail: *computerized* business telephone call processing.

volt—v: basic unit of *potential* difference and electromotive force. Compare: *ampere, ohm, watt*.

volume: *audio intensity*. See: *loudness*.

volume control—fader—pot: *rheostat* raising or lowering *audio* or *video* levels.

Vortex—Magnum: *Titan*-launched U.S. military *satellites* electronically monitoring (since 1978) USSR military and diplomatic conversations.

V/O Vneshtorgreklama: USSR state advertising commission.

VPA—Videotape Production Association: U.S. trade group of *videotape production/post production* facilities. See: *ITS*. Compare: *AICP*.

VPS—viewers per set: audience survey count of *viewers* in same *household*.

VRC-12: workhorse U.S. Army short range *transceiver;* also used by France, Switzerland, South Africa, etc.

VTR—videotape recorder: complex electronic/mechanical device (introduced 1956) *recording television sound* and *picture* on *magnetic tape* for instantaneous *monitor playback*. Compare: *ATR, projector, VTR*.

VTR operator: engineer handling *videotape recording*. Compare: *projectionist*.

V-2: Nazi military forerunner of USSR rocket that launched and orbited first *satellite* (*Sputnik*, 1957).

v.u. meter: see: *v.i. meter*.

W

W: see: *watt*. Also: East-of-Mississippi *call letter* prefix.

waiver: approved departure from standard procedure (in *production* requirements, *talent* payments, etc.)

walkie-talkie: portable *battery*-operated *wireless transmitter/receiver*.

walk-on: nonspeaking performer.

walkthrough: rough *rehearsal* without *cameras*.

walla-walla: onomatopoeic crowd sound. See: *omnies*.

wall rack: wall-mounted *editing bin*.

wall-to-wall: 24-hour *broadcast* schedule.

(optical) wand: hand-held *UBC bar code scanning stylus*.

wander: slow *DC* variation in *signal* base line.

WARC—World Administrative Radio Conference: international *frequency-allocation* body.

wardrobe: performers' costumes. Called *frocks* in Britain.

warm: slightly yellowish or reddish *television picture*. Compare: *cool*.

warmup: *live* introduction to *broadcast* audience, prior to *air*.

Warner/Amex (Satellite Entertainment Corporation)—WASEC: *multichannel (MTV, Nickelodeon, The Movie Channel)* Warner Brothers/American Express *satellite/cable* programming service; sold to *Viacom*. Still maintains Warner Cable Communications; major *MSO* (with between one and five million *subscribers*, 1988).

waste circulation: nonpotential customers exposed to *television commercial*.

water bag: water-filled heavy rubber bag to weight *set*-stand legs, etc. Compare: *sandbag.*

watt: (after Scots inventor) unit of electric power equal to one *ampere* of current under one *volt* of pressure. *Wattage* = *voltage* × *amperage.* One *watt* = 673 *lumens.* Compare: *ampere, ohm, volt.*

wave: disturbance transferring energy between adjacent particles in medium or space. Electromagnetic waves travel 3×10^{10} centimeters (186,000 miles) per second.

wave form monitor—WVFM: *oscilloscope* tube for visual analysis (and adjustment) of *television signal* characteristics.

wavefront reconstruction: (invented by Gabor, 1947) precursor of *holography.*

waveguide: straight nitrogen-filled metal pipe *transmitting* many *EHF signals* simultaneously.

wavelength: loosely, *broadcast frequency;* measurable distance between corresponding *wave* points of like *phase.* Longer *wavelength* = lower *frequency.* See: *amplitude.*

wax pencil—wax crayon: see: *china marker.*

wearout: *television* advertising overexposure, creating *viewer* indifference.

Weather Channel: (1982) *satellite/cable* weather reporting service.

weather day: adjusted compensation for rained-out *production.*

weathergraphics: *computer*-generated *television* weather visuals.

weave: undesirable horizontal *film* movement in *projector gate.*

web: *broadcast network.*

wedge—step wedge—step tablet: length of *motion picture negative* for *processing* control; each *frame* progressively darker. Compare: *camera test, cinex.* Also: *Test pattern* design to check *camera resolution.*

weighting: *television* market "points" for *talent re-use* fee calculation.

Westar: *Western Union C-band geosynchronous communications satellite* program.

Westar I: *Western Union communications satellite* at 99° W (1974, retired).

Westar II: *Western Union 12-transponder C-band communications satellite* at 78.5° W (1974, retired).

Westar III: *Western Union 24-transponder C-band communications satellite* at 91° W (1979); drifted 1987.

Westar IV: *Western Union 24-transponder C-band satellite* at 99° W (1982). Carries all *PBS* programming.

Westar V: *Western Union* 24-*transponder C-band satellite* at 122.5° W (1982); mislaunched, retrieved by *shuttle* "Discovery" 1984; planned re-launch 1989.

Westar VI: *Western Union* 24-*transponder C-band satellite* at 91° W (1986).

western: commercial music style with western U.S. folk roots. See: *country*. Compare: *bluegrass, folk.*

Western Union: *communications satellite* operator. See: *Westar.*

"Westinghouse Rule": see: *Prime Time Access Rule* (based on Westinghouse Broadcasting Company's successful petition to *FCC*).

wet cell: *storage battery* requiring water for electricity-producing chemical reaction. See: *lead acid accumulator*. Compare: *dry cell.*

wet gate—liquid gate: *printing* process placing tetrachlorethylene coating solution on *negative film* to minimize surface defects.

WGA—Writers' Guild of America: *script*writers' union; *WGA*-East and *WGA*-West.

WGN-TV: Chicago *superstation.*

whip (wizz) pan: in Britain, image-blurring *pan* shot, usually transitional.

white area: region unserved by *broadcast* facility.

white (peak) clip: automatic reduction of excessively bright *television picture* areas to correct *voltage* (1.0 *v*). See: *reference white.*

white noise: *random noise* in particular *bandwidth.*

wide angle: short *focal length lens* with viewing angle over 45°.

wideband: *rf transmission* on multiple *frequencies*. See: *bandwidth.*

widen: *dolly* or *zoom back* from *tight* camera position.

wide-screen: any *frame aspect ratio* between 1.33:1 and 2.66:1—usually 2:1.

width: horizontal size of *television picture*. Compare: *height.*

wild: related *elements recorded* separately. Compare: *sync.*

wild motor—variable speed motor: *camera* attachment permitting controlled *over-* or *undercranking.*

wild spot: *commercial* prepared for local use by *advertiser* with national or regional product distribution. Compare: *participation.*

wild track: *recording* non-*synchronized sound.*

wind: see: *A-wind, B-wind.*

window: margin for technical error.

windscreen—windshield: *microphone* covering. Compare: *pop filter.*

windup: cue to *talent* to finish.

wing: perform without *rehearsal*. Compare: *block.*

wipe: *optical effect* using line or shape to generate new scene. Also: *Erase magnetically recorded* information.

wire frame: *CGI* 3-D "see-through" object outline.

wireless (telegraphy): originally, *transmission* of (telegraph) *signals* through space by means of *electromagnetic waves.* Now called *radio* in U.S., *wireless* in Britain. See: *Morse code, radiotelegraphy.*

wireless cable: see: *MCTV.*

wireless mike: performer's concealed *microphone, broadcasting voice signal* directly to *receiver/recorder* (1953). Called *radio mike* in Britain. Compare: *lapel mike.*

Wireless Ship Act: initial U.S. federal communication law (1910).

wire recorder: *magnetic recording* device preceding development of more convenient *audio tape recorder.*

wire service: press association *broadcast* news wire. See: *AP, Reuters, UPI.*

Wold Corporation: *satellite* programming service.

"woof": technician's "OK."

woofer: larger member of a pair of *loudspeakers,* emphasizing *low frequencies.* Compare: *tweeter.*

wordies: in Britain, the *script.*

worklight: permanent (relatively dim) stage or *studio set* illumination.

work picture: *picture* sequence (usually with *work track*) assembled by *film editor* for approval. See: *dirty dupe.*

work print: *editor*'s rough combination of *picture* and *track.* Called *cutting copy* in Britain.

work station: *terminal connection* for *mainframe computer.*

work track: *audio* sequence (usually with *work picture*) assembled by *film editor* for approval.

worldize: *play back* and *re-record background sound* (music, *effects,* etc.) *live* on *location.* Compare: *mixing studio.*

wow: slow repetitive variation in *audio tape recording* or *playback speed,* causing unacceptable *distortion.* Compare: *flutter.*

WPIX-TV: New York *superstation.*

wrap: finish—and put away equipment. Also: Contact area between *tape* and *recorder heads.*

write enable: *computer recording mode.*

write protect: *computer* non-*recording mode.*

Writers' Guild of America—WGA: *script*writers' union; *WGA*-East and *WGA*-West.

Writers' Guild of Great Britain: *script*writers' union.

writing speed: *videotape* movement past *recording head(s)*. Compare: *linear speed*.

WTBS-TV: Atlanta *superstation*.

WWOR-TV: New York *superstation*.

X: single-*frame* indication.

xenon: quartz glass *projector lamp* containing xenon gas; offers long life expectancy, constant *color temperature,* and high illumination efficiency.

Xerox: one of several low-cost graphic reproduction processes; now essential for *film animation.*

X1, X2, X3: *Beta television* 1-hour, 2-hour, 3-hour *cassette* speeds.

x-ray—border: overhead *luminaire strip.*

X-sheet: *animation exposure* directions.

X, Y, Z axes: three-dimensional space coordinates—X = horizontal; Y = vertical; Z = *screen picture* depth.

Y

yagi: directional *television receiver antenna.*

Y & R—Young & Rubicam: one of seven major (1987 gross *billings* between $3 and $5 billion) worldwide *advertising agencies.*

Y-axis: see: *X, Y, Z axes.*

yellow: subtractive element of color *negative film.* See: *cyan, magenta.*

yoke: *television scanning* and *picture tube* magnetic neck coil to coordinate *deflection* of electron stream *(beam)* from *tube gun.*

Y signal: *color television luminance signal* (4.5 *MHz*). Compare: *B-Y signal, I signal, Q signal, R-Y signal.*

YTV—Yorkshire: one of British *IBA's* *"Big Five"* (the *Central Companies*).

Z

Z: *impedance* symbol.

zapping: (remote control) *viewer channel*-switching or deletion of *television commercial audio*. Wryly called "the greatest threat to capitalism since Karl Marx." Compare: *zipping, grazing.*

Z-axis: see: *X, Y, Z axes.*

zero cutting: *negative editing* technique utilizing *A*- and *B-rolls* to hide *splice* marks.

ZDF—Zweite Deutsche Fernsehen: West Germany's "second *television* network." Compare: *ARD-I,II.*

zenith: 90°; straight up.

Zenith Corporation: major U.S. electronics manufacturer.

zip pan—swish pan: image-blurring *pan* shot, usually *transitional.* Called *flash pan* or *whip (wizz) pan* in Britain.

zipping: (remote control) *viewer* fast-forwarding of *VCR* programming, bypassing *commercial* material. Compare: *zapping.*

Zöetrope: early slotted-drum *animation* device (Horner, 1834). Compare: *Phenakistoscope, Praxinoscope, Thaumatrope.*

zonal stripe: in Britain, clear *35mm sprocketed* film with continuous ferrous *oxide* strip for *recording soundtrack.*

Zonda: USSR *satellite*-launch rocket system.

Zone I, I-A, II: basic *FCC FM station* operating area classifications.

zoom: alter *lens focal length;* "*dolly*" along *Z-axis* without moving *camera* with no change in *parallax.* Compare: *track.*

zoom lens: variable *focal length lens* (usually 10 to 1) originally designed to eliminate *lens* changing; now used to create effect of rapid (or slow) *camera* movement to or from a subject. Compare: *prime lens.*

zoom ratio: relation between largest/smallest *zoom lens* image.

Zöopraxiscope: early "moving picture" *projector* (Muybridge, 1880).

Zworykin, Vladimir: U.S. *television* pioneer: See: *iconoscope.*

Extended Reference

RADIO AND TELEVISION PROGRAMMING AND PRODUCTION

Focal Encyclopedia of Film and Television Techniques. New York: Hastings House. 1969.

Head, Sidney W. *Broadcasting in America*. 4th ed. Boston: Houghton Mifflin. 1976.

Levitan, Eli L. *An Alphabetical Guide to Motion Picture, Television, and Videotape Production*. New York: McGraw-Hill. 1970.

Millerson, Gerald. *The Technique of Television Production*. 11th ed. Boston: Focal Press. 1985.

———. *The Technique of Lighting for Television and Motion Pictures*. 2nd ed. Boston: Focal Press. 1982.

Terrace, Vincent. *Encyclopedia of Television*. New York: Zoetrope. 1986.

Wurtzel, Alan. *Television Production*. 2nd ed. New York: McGraw-Hill. 1983.

NETWORK AND STATION OPERATIONS

Brown, Les. *Television: The Business Behind the Box*. New York: Harcourt Brace Jovanovich. 1971.

Eastman, Susan Taylor, Sidney W. Head, and Lewis Klein. *Broadcast/Cable Programming*. 2nd ed. Belmont, California: Wadsworth. 1985.

Hilliard, Robert. *Radio Broadcasting*. 3rd ed. White Plains, New York: Longman. 1985.

Keith, Michael C., and Joseph M. Krause. *The Radio Station*. Boston: Focal Press. 1986.

Lichty, Lawrence W., and Malachi C. Topping. *American Broadcasting*. New York: Hastings House. 1975.

Oringel, Robert. *Television Operations Handbook*. Boston: Focal Press. 1984.

Tyrell, Robert W. *The Work of the Television Journalist*. New York: Hastings House. 1972.

BROADCAST EQUIPMENT AND ENGINEERING

Benson, K. Blair. *Television Engineering Handbook*. New York: McGraw-Hill. 1986.

Carlson, A. Bruce. *Communications Systems*. 3rd ed. New York: McGraw-Hill. 1986.

Chetty, P.R.K. *Satellite Technology and Its Applications*. Blue Ridge Summit, Pennsylvania: Tab Books. 1988.

Gibilisco, Stanley. *Encyclopedia of Electronics*. Blue Ridge Summit, Pennsylvania: Tab Books. 1985.

Gibson, Stephen W. *Cellular Mobile Radiotelephones*. Englewood Cliffs, New Jersey: Prentice-Hall. 1987.

Grob, Bernard. *Basic Television and Video Systems*. New York: McGraw-Hill. 1984.

Hennie, Keith. *Radio Engineering Handbook*. 5th ed. New York: McGraw-Hill. 1959.

Johnson, Richard C., and Henry Jasik. *Antenna Engineering Handbook*. 2nd ed. New York: McGraw-Hill. 1984.

Jones, William B. Jr. *Optical Fiber Communications Systems*. New York: Holt Rinehart Winston. 1988.

Jordan, Edward C. *Reference Data for Engineers: Radio, Electronic, Computer and Communications*. 7th ed. Indianapolis, Indiana: Sams. 1986.

McGinty, Gerald P. *Videocassette Recorders*. New York: McGraw-Hill. 1979.

MacLanachan, William. *Television and Radar Encyclopedia*. New York: Pitman. 1954.

Rainger, Robert. *Satellite Broadcasting*. New York: Wiley. 1985.

Stark, Henry, Franz B. Tuteur, and John B. Anderson. *Modern Electrical Communications: Analog, Digital, and Optical Systems*. 2nd ed. Englewood Cliffs, New Jersey: Prentice-Hall. 1988.

Traister, John E., and Robert J. Traister. *Encyclopedic Dictionary of Electronic Terms*. Englewood Cliffs, New Jersey: Prentice-Hall. 1984.

AUDIO AND VIDEOTAPE RECORDING AND OPERATIONS

Ballou, Glen. *Handbook for Sound Engineers: The New Audio Cyclopedia*. Indianapolis, Indiana: Sams. 1987.

Borwick, John. *Sound Recording Practice*. 3rd ed. New York: Oxford. 1987.

Camras, Marvin. *Magnetic Recording Handbook*. Englewood Cliffs, New Jersey: Van Nostrand Reinhold. 1988.

Eargle, John. *Handbook of Recording Engineering*. New York: Van Nostrand Reinhold. 1986.

Mee, C. Denis, and Eric D. Daniel. *Magnetic Recording*. New York: McGraw-Hill. 1987.

Woram, John M. *The Recording Studio Handbook*. Plainview, New York: Elar Books. 1982.

AGENCY AND CLIENT ADVERTISING PROCEDURES

Ulanoff, Stanley M. *Advertising in America*. New York: Hastings House. 1977.

MEDIA USAGE AND RESEARCH

Sandman, Peter M., David M. Rubin, and David B. Sachsman. *Media*. 2nd ed. Englewood Cliffs, New Jersey: Prentice-Hall. 1976.

ALLIED FIELDS

Belzer, Jack. *Computer Science and Technology*. New York: Dekker. 1980.
Encyclopedia of Artificial Intelligence. New York: Wiley. 1987.
Helms, Harry. *Computer Handbook*. New York: McGraw-Hill. 1983.
Milutinovic, Veljko. *Computer Architecture*. New York: Elsevier. 1988.
Ralston, Anthony, and Edwin D. Reilly. *Encyclopedia of Computer Science and Engineering*. Englewood Cliffs, New Jersey: Van Nostrand Reinhold. 1983.

About the Author

LINCOLN DIAMANT is President of Spots Alive, Inc. He has been a writer-producer for CBS and NBC; advertising director of the World Publishing Company; and a television production executive for Ogilvy & Mather, McCann-Erickson and Grey. He has taught U.S. broadcasting history and hands-on television techniques at Hofstra and Pace Universities, and has served around the world as a television festival judge. Mr. Diamant, a Fellow of the Royal Society of the Arts, is a founder and former vice-president of the Broadcast Advertising Producers Society of America and a member of the Broadcast Pioneers, the International Radio & Television Society and the National Academy of Television Arts & Sciences.